Effective Human Resource Management

Effective Human Resource Management

A Global Analysis

Edward E. Lawler III and John W. Boudreau

Stanford Business Books
An Imprint of Stanford University Press
Stanford, California

Stanford University Press
Stanford, California

Special discounts for bulk quantities of Stanford Business
Books are available to corporations, professional associations,
and other organizations. For details and discount information,
contact the special sales department of Stanford University
Press. Tel: (650) 736-1782, Fax: (650) 736-1784

Printed in the United States of America on acid-free,
archival-quality paper

Library of Congress Cataloging-in-Publication Data
Lawler, Edward E., author.
  Effective human resource management : a global analysis /
Edward E. Lawler III and John W. Boudreau.
      pages cm
  "This is a report of the results from the Center for Effective
Organizations' (CEO's) sixth study of the human resources
(HR) function in large corporations"—Preface.
  Includes bibliographical references.
  ISBN 978-0-8047-7687-5 (pbk. : alk. paper)
  1. Personnel management. 2. Organizational effectiveness.
I. Boudreau, John W., author. II. University of Southern
California. Center for Effective Organizations. III. Title.
  HF5549.L2884 2012
  658.3—dc23   2011051606

Typeset by Classic Typography in 10½/14 Palatino

CONTENTS

TABLES AND EXHIBITS

TABLES

EXHIBITS

PREFACE AND ACKNOWLEDGMENTS

This is a report of the results from the Center for Effective Organizations' (CEO's) sixth study of the human resources (HR) function in large corporations. Like the previous studies, it measures whether the HR function is changing and whether it is effective. All of our research studies have focused on whether the HR function is changing to become an effective strategic partner. The present study also analyzes how organizations can more effectively manage their human capital. It gathered data on many of the same topics that we studied in 1995, 1998, 2001, 2004, and 2007. Thus it allowed us to compare data from our earlier studies to data we collected in 2010. For the first time we collected data from multiple countries so that we can determine how corporations in the U.S. and other countries differ.

We are deeply indebted to Walt Cleaver and the Human Resource Planning Society for its support of all six of our studies. Thanks also go to Jay Jamrog, Kevin Oakes, and the Institute for Corporate Productivity (i4cp) for its support of our 2007 and 2010 surveys. A number of individuals and organizations helped us with international data collection. Special thanks go to the following: Sherry Benjamins, Vicki Culpin, Anne-Marie Dolan, Mike Dulworth, Dana Grgas, Sophie Gross, Mike Haffendon, Chunhui Huo, Volker Jacobs, Andrew Lambert, Chaoping Li, Mindy Meisterlin, Russell Morris, Katie O'Brien, Serge Sardo, Eric St-Jean, Anne Tsui, Mark Vickers, Jeff Webb, and Ruth Wright.

We would also like to thank Lois Rosby for her help in preparing the manuscript. Alice Yee Mark, Aaron Griffith, and Beth Neilson helped with the data collection and did terrific work analyzing the data.

The Marshall School of Business of the University of Southern California deserves special thanks and recognition for its continuing support of the activities of CEO. In addition, we would like to thank the corporate sponsors of CEO for their support of the Center and its mission; their support is vital to the overall success of the Center and is directly responsible for enabling us to do the kind of research reported here.

The Center has been and continues to be focused on doing research that improves how organizations are managed. During 2009, the Center celebrated its thirtieth anniversary.

Special thanks go to Susan Mohrman. She has made many contributions to this research effort. She and Ed did the first three surveys, and she worked with us on the fourth.

The SHRM Foundation deserves special thanks for funding this research. Its financial support made it possible for us to gather international data for the first time.

Preface and Acknowledgments

THE AUTHORS

Edward E. Lawler III is Distinguished Professor of Business and Director of the Center for Effective Organizations in the Marshall School of Business at the University of Southern California. He has been honored as a top contributor to the fields of organizational development, human resources management, organizational behavior, and compensation. He is the author of over 400 articles and forty-six books. His most recent books include *Achieving Strategic Excellence: An Assessment of Human Resource Organizations* (2006), *Built to Change* (2006), *The New American Workplace* (2006), *America at Work* (2006), *Talent: Making People Your Competitive Advantage* (2008), *Achieving Excellence in Human Resources Management: An Assessment of Human Resource Functions* (2009), *Useful Research: Advancing Theory and Practice* (2011), and *Management Reset: Organizing for Sustainable Effectiveness* (2011). For more information, visit http://www.edwardlawler.com and http://ceo.usc.edu.

John W. Boudreau is Professor at the Marshall School of Business, University of Southern California, and Research Director at the Center for Effective Organizations. He is recognized for break-through research on human capital, talent, and sustainable competitive advantage. Boudreau advises numerous organizations, including early-stage companies, global corporations, government agencies, and non-profit organizations. His research has been featured in *Harvard Business Review*, the *Wall Street Journal*, *Fortune*, and *Business Week*. He is the author of over sixty books, chapters, and scholarly articles. His most recent books include the second edition of *Investing in People*, with Wayne Cascio, *Retooling HR*, and *Transformative HR*, with Ravin Jesuthusan. His columns and online articles appear in *Talent Management* magazine and *CFO* magazine, among others.

Effective Human Resource Management

CHAPTER 1

What HR Needs to Do

A changing workforce, global competition, advances in information technology, new knowledge, the 2008 global recession, demands for sustainable performance, and a host of other changes are forcing organizations to constantly examine and reevaluate how they operate (Lawler and Worley 2011). They are utilizing new technologies, changing their structures, redesigning work, relocating their workforces, and improving work processes to respond to an increasingly demanding, unpredictable, and global competitive environment. These important changes have significant implications for how their human capital should be managed and their human resources functions should operate. But are organizations changing their human capital management policies, practices, and processes? Are they redesigning their HR functions?

During the last decade it has been difficult to find a management book or business magazine that doesn't point out how many of the changes in the business world have made human capital—people—an organization's most important asset in the United States as well as in the rest of the developed world. Human capital management has been the focus of a great deal of writing focused on finding, motivating, developing, and monitoring the "right talent."

The annual reports of many corporations in North America, Europe, and Australia argue that their human capital and intellectual property are their most important assets. In many organizations, compensation is one of the largest, if not the largest, cost. In service organizations it often represents 70 to 80 percent of the total cost of doing business. Adding the costs of training and other human resources management activities to compensation costs means that the human resources function often has responsibility for a very large portion of an organization's total expenditures, and this portion is growing.

In most organizations the cost of human capital is not the only, or even the most important, determinant of an organization's effectiveness. Even when compensation accounts for very little of the cost of doing business, human capital has a significant impact on the performance of most organizations (Cascio 2000; Cascio and Boudreau 2011). In essence, without effective human capital, organizations are likely to have little or no revenue. Even the most automated production facilities require skilled, motivated employees to operate them. Knowledge-work organizations depend on employees to develop, use, and manage their most important asset, knowledge. Thus, although the human capital of a company does not appear on the balance sheet of corporations, it represents an increasingly large percentage of many organizations' market valuation (Lev 2001; Huselid, Becker, and Beatty 2005).

Not all organizations can or should look upon their human capital as a major source of competitive advantage (Lawler 2008). In some organizations it may be sufficient to simply have talent that can and will adequately do relatively simple jobs. But in an increasing number of organizations, having the best talent and talent management processes can be a source of competitive advantage. It can make it possible for companies to be more innovative and agile, develop superior products and customer knowledge, and offer superior services.

Role of the Human Resources Organization

The HR function typically adds value by performing an administrative role. The human resources function in most organizations plays a key role in determining how their human capital is managed and serviced. How well it does this helps determine how much value it adds. But two other roles that it can take on allow it to add greater value. Lawler (1995) has developed this line of thought by describing three roles HR can take on. The first is the familiar human resources management role (Exhibit 1.1).

The second is the role of business partner (Exhibit 1.2). It emphasizes developing systems and practices to ensure that a company's human resources have the needed competencies and motivation to perform effectively. In this approach, HR has a seat at the table when business issues are discussed and brings an HR perspective to these discussions. When it comes to designing HR systems and practices, this approach focuses on creating systems and practices that support the business strategy. HR focuses on the effectiveness of the human capital management practices and on process improvements in them. HR is expected to help implement changes and to help managers effectively deal with "people issues."

The business partner approach positions the HR function as a value-added part of an organization, so that it can contribute to business performance by effectively managing what is the most important capital of most organizations, their human capital (Ulrich 1997; Ulrich, Losey, and Lake 1997; Ulrich and Brockbank 2005). But this approach may not be the one that enables the HR function to add the greatest value given the increasingly important role that talent plays in determining organization performance. By becoming a strategic partner (see Exhibit 1.3), HR has the potential to add more value in those situations where human capital can be a difference maker.

AIMS	Support business.
	Provide HR services.
PROCESS	Build performance management capabilities.
	Develop managers: link competencies to job requirements and career development.
	Plan succession.
	Enhance organizational change capabilities.
	Build an organization-wide HR network.
PLANNING	HR (and all other functions) inspect business plans; inputs from HR may be inserted in the planning process.

Exhibit 1.1. HR management

AIMS	Line management owns human resources as a part of its role.
	HR is an integral member of management teams.
	Culture of the firm evolves to fit with strategy and vision.
PROCESS	Organize HR flexibly around the work to be done (programs and projects, outsourcing).
	Focus on the development of people and organizations (road maps, teams, organization design).
	Leverage competencies, manage learning linkages; build organizational work redesign capabilities.
PLANNING	An integral component of strategic and business planning by the management team.

Exhibit 1.2. Business partner

AIMS	HR is a major influence on business strategy.
	HR systems drive business performance.
PROCESS	Self-service for transactional work.
	Transactional work outsourced.
	Knowledge management.
	Focus on organization development.
	Change management.
	Human resource processes tied to business strategies.
PLANNING	HR is a key contributor to strategic planning and change management.

Exhibit 1.3. Strategic partner

In acting as a strategic partner, HR plays a role that includes helping the organization develop its strategy. Not only does HR have a seat at the strategy table, HR helps to set the table with information about organizational capabilities, talent analytics, and the labor market. It helps shape and enhance strategies by bringing a human capital decision science to strategy discussion.

In a knowledge business, a firm's strategy must be closely linked to its talent. Thus, the human resources function is well positioned to do both strategy formulation and implementation. Its expertise in attracting, retaining, developing, deploying, motivating, and organizing human capital is critical to both. Ideally, the HR function should be knowledgeable about the business and expert in organizational and work design issues so that it can help develop needed organizational capabilities and facilitate organizational change as new opportunities become available.

To be a strategic partner, HR executives need an expert understanding of business strategy, organization design, and change management, and they need to know how integrated human resources practices and strategies can support organization designs and strategies. This role requires extending HR's focus beyond delivery of those HR services and practices that are associated with being a business partner to a focus on decisions about organization design change, and business strategy.

As a strategic partner, HR can bring to the table a perspective that is often missing in discussions of business strategy and change—a knowledge of the human capital factors and the organizational changes that are critical in determining whether a strategy can be implemented. Many more strategies fail in execution than in their conception (Lawler and Worley 2006). What sounds good often cannot be implemented for a variety of reasons, including talent management and organization design.

Despite compelling arguments supporting human resources management as a key strategic issue in most organizations, our research and that of others finds that human resource executives often are not strategic partners (Lawler 1995; Brockbank 1999; Lawler, Boudreau, and Mohrman 2006; Lawler and Boudreau 2009). All too often, the human resources function is largely an administrative function headed by individuals whose roles are focused on cost control and administrative activities (Ulrich 1997; Lawler and Mohrman 2003a; Boudreau and Ramstad 2005a; Lawler and Boudreau 2009). Missing almost entirely from the list of HR focuses are such key organizational challenges as improving productivity, increasing quality, facilitating mergers and acquisitions, managing knowledge, implementing change, developing business strategies, and improving the ability of the organization to execute strategies. Since these areas are critical determinants of organizational performance, the HR function is missing a great opportunity to add value.

There is some evidence that the situation of HR is changing, and that the human resources function is beginning to redefine its role in order to increase the value it adds. The first five phases of the present study (data collected in 1995, 1998, 2001, 2004, and 2007) found evidence of some change in large U.S. corporations, but there was more discussion of change than actual change (Lawler and Mohrman 2003a; Lawler, Boudreau, and Mohrman 2006; Lawler and Boudreau 2009).

It is quite possible significant change has occurred. A lot has happened since our 2007 study; most notably a major recession occurred. It forced most organizations to make many tough decisions about their costs and structure and as a result about their human capital. In many respects it created a situation in which HR's value as a strategic partner could be demonstrated. "All" HR had to do in many organizations was effectively deal with downsizing the workforce, with its budget, and help the organization change its strategy and structure. If it did this well, there is little doubt that it would be seen as more of a strategic partner and as a more effective function; but did it?

In our previous studies, no data were collected from companies outside the U.S.; as a result no conclusions were reached about HR functions in other countries. The purpose of the present study is to determine whether HR has turned the corner and become a strategic partner and to determine how HR operates in corporations that are based in Europe, China, U.K., Canada, and Australia.

Creating Change

Describing the new role of the human resources is only the first step in transitioning the HR function to becoming a business partner and contributor to organizational effectiveness. For decades, the human resources function has been organized and staffed to carry out administrative activities. Changing that role requires a different mix of activities and people. It necessitates reconfiguring the HR function to support changing business strategies and organization designs. It also requires the employees in the HR function to have very different competencies than they traditionally have had (Ulrich et al. 2008).

It is clear that information technology (IT) will play an increasingly important role in the future of the HR function (Lawler, Ulrich, Fitz-enz, and Madden 2004). With HR information technology, administrative tasks that have been traditionally performed by the HR function can be done by employees and managers on a self-service basis. Today's HR IT systems simplify and speed up HR activities such as salary administration, job posting and placement, address changes, family changes, and benefits administration; they can handle virtually every administrative HR task. What is more, these systems are available around the clock and can be accessed from virtually anywhere by anyone, thus making self-service possible, convenient, and efficient.

Perhaps the greatest value of HR IT systems results from enabling the integration and analysis of the HR activities. They make HR information much more accessible so that it can be used to guide strategy development and implementation. Metrics can be easily tracked and analyses performed that make it possible for organizations to develop and allocate their human capital more effectively (Boudreau and Ramstad 2007; Lawler, Levenson, and Boudreau 2004).

A strong case can be made that HR needs to develop much better metrics and analytics capabilities. Our previous five studies identified metrics as one of four characteristics that lead to HR's being a strategic partner in U.S. corporations. Managers in them want measurement systems that enhance their decisions about human capital. All too often, however, HR focuses on the traditional paradigm of delivering HR services quickly, cheaply, and in ways that satisfy clients (Boudreau and Ramstad 1997, 2003).

HR has become more sophisticated in the measures it uses, yet according to our 2007 data this has not led to HR being strategic partners or to organizations being more effective. Business leaders can now be held accountable for HR measures, such as turnover, employee attitudes, bench strength, or performance distributions; however, this is not the same as creating an effective organization. The issue is how to use HR measures to make a true strategic difference in an organization's performance.

Boudreau and Ramstad (2007) have identified four critical components of measurement systems that drive strategic change and organizational effectiveness: logic, analysis, measures, and process. Measures represent only one component of this system. Though measures are essential, without the other three components they are destined to remain isolated from the true purpose of the HR measurement systems.

Boudreau and Ramstad have also proposed that HR can make great strides by learning how more mature and powerful decision sciences have evolved their measurement systems (Boudreau and Ramstad

1997). They identify three anchor points—efficiency, effectiveness, and impact—that connect decisions about resources such as money and customers to organizational effectiveness and that can similarly be used to understand HR measurement.

1. *Efficiency* asks, "What resources are used to produce our HR policies and practices?" Typical indicators of efficiency would be cost-per-hire and time-to-fill vacancies.

2. *Effectiveness* asks, "How do our HR policies and practices affect the talent pools and organization structures to which they are directed?" Effectiveness refers to the effects of HR policies and practices on human capacity (a combination of capability, opportunity, and motivation), and the resulting "aligned actions" of the target talent pools. Effectiveness includes trainees' increased knowledge, better selected applicants' enhanced qualifications, or performance ratings of those receiving incentives.

3. *Impact* is the hardest question of the three. Impact asks, "How do differences in the quality or availability of different talent pools affect strategic success?" This question is a component of talent segmentation, just as for marketers a component of market segmentation concerns "How do differences in the buying behavior of different customer groups affect strategic success?"

Most HR measurement systems largely reflect the question of efficiency, though there is some attention to effectiveness as well, through focusing on such things as turnover, attitudes, and bench strength (Gates 2004). Rarely do organizations consider impact (such as the relative effect of different talent pools on organizational effectiveness). More important, it is rare that HR measurement is specifically directed toward where it is most likely to have the greatest effect—on key talent. Attention to non-financial outcomes and sustainability also needs to be increased, and strategic HR can affect these as well (Boudreau and Ramstad 2005a).

The Emerging HR Decision Science

The majority of today's HR practices, benchmarks, and measures still reflect the traditional paradigm of excellence defined as delivering high-quality HR services in response to client needs. Even as the field advocates more "strategic" HR, it is often defined as delivering the HR services that are important to executive clients (leadership development, competency systems, board governance, etc.). This traditional service-delivery paradigm is fundamentally limited, because it assumes that clients know what they need. Market-based HR and accountability for business results are now recognized as important (Gubman 2004). However, these often amount merely to using marketing techniques or business results to assess the popularity of traditional HR services, or their association with financial outcomes.

Fields such as finance have a different approach. They have augmented their service delivery paradigm with a "decision science" paradigm which teaches clients the frameworks to make good choices. This is not to suggest simply by applying finance and accounting formulas to HR programs and processes, but to learn how these fields evolved into the powerful, decision-supporting functions they are today. Their evolution provides a blueprint for what should be next for HR. The answer lies not just in benchmarking HR in other organizations, but in evolving to be similar to more strategic functions such as finance and marketing.

In marketing, decision science enhances decisions about customers. In finance, decision science enhances decisions about money. In human capital, a decision science should enhance decisions about organization talent that are made both within and outside the HR function. Boudreau and Ramstad have labeled this emerging decision science "Talentship," because it focuses on decisions that improve the stewardship of the hidden and apparent talents of current and potential employees (Boudreau and Ramstad 2005a, 2007).

Organization Design

Organization design is a key factor in enabling organizations to develop capabilities and, therefore, to perform in ways that produce a competitive advantage (Galbraith 2002). Organization design is more than structure; it includes elements such as management processes, rewards, people systems, information systems, and work processes. These elements must fit with the strategy and with each other for an organization to perform effectively.

Organization designs involve complex tradeoffs and contingencies. Clearly, one design approach does not fit all organizations. As new business models emerge, new approaches and organizational forms spring up to deal with the complex requirements that organizations must address. These new models include complex partnerships, globally integrated firms, customer-focused designs, and network organizations. Furthermore, multi-business corporations are recognizing that different businesses exist in different markets and face varying requirements. Consequently, variation in organization design is increasing both within multi-business corporations and between businesses (Galbraith 2002). Thus, for the company and the HR function, one size does not fit all situations. Different organizational forms require different kinds of HR contribution, and thus different HR functional designs and systems.

Contributing to effective organization design is a major domain in which the HR function has the opportunity to add strategic value (Lawler 2008). Increasingly, the only sustainable competitive advantage is the ability to organize effectively, respond to change, and manage well (Mohrman, Galbraith, and Lawler 1998; Lawler and Worley 2006; Lawler and Worley 2011). Confirmation of this statement is provided by Lawler, Mohrman, and Benson's (2001) study of the Fortune 1000, which shows a significant relationship between firm financial performance and the adoption of new management practices designed to increase the capabilities of the firm.

Recently, Lawler (2008) has argued that three different approaches to managing talent have encouraged companies to look to human capital for competitive advantage. They represent different approaches to organizing and managing talent, and need to be supported by different organization designs and HR practices. For example, the low-cost operator approach calls for an organization design that has high-structure jobs and excellent control systems. On the other hand, the high-involvement approach and the global competitor approach require interesting, challenging jobs as well as flat structures that put people in contact with the external environment. Both picking the right approach to management and then implementing it effectively represent a chance for the HR function to add significant value.

Design of the HR Function

All parts of organizations—operating units and staff functions alike—need to be designed to deliver high value. For staff groups, doing so requires the development of a business model—a value proposition defining what kind of value they will deliver that the company is willing to pay for because it enhances company performance. It also requires them to determine how their services can best be delivered.

The HR function must think about whether the elements of its design indeed do create a high performance organization—that is, one capable of delivering maximum value while consuming the fewest possible resources. Doing so means concentrating on the way HR organizes to deliver routine transactions services, traditional HR systems development and administration, and strategic business support.

HR must develop structures, competencies, customer linkages, programs, management processes, reward systems, and information systems that ensure scarce resources are optimally deployed to deliver value. In addition to making sure the HR function is optimally designed, HR can add value by helping design the key features of the rest of the organization.

In many respects it is useful to think of HR functions as multiple product businesses. They have customers, products and services, revenue, and competitors (self-service vendors and consulting firms). In order to exist they need to perform in a way that makes them the "best buy" in one or more areas.

Organization design decisions for HR as well as for companies as a whole are made in four key areas:

1. Which activities should be centralized and leveraged, and which should be decentralized in order to provide focus on the unique needs of different parts of the organization? Some organizations are combining centralization and decentralization, trying to be big (coordinated) in functions such as purchasing, when there is an advantage to being big; and small (decentralized and flexible) in functions such as new product development, when there are advantages to being small and agile.

2. Which functions should be performed in-house and which should be outsourced? Companies should outsource when they can purchase high-quality services and products more inexpensively or reliably than they can generate internally.

3. Which functions should be hierarchically controlled, and which should be integrated and controlled laterally? In some areas, organizations function in a lateral manner, integrating and creating synergies across various parts of the organization, creating cross-functional units to carry out entire processes, and collaborating with suppliers and customers. Organizations are searching for ways to leverage across business units while setting up organizational and management approaches that give the optimal levels of flexibility and control to various business units.

4. Which processes should be IT-based? Today, most organizations are wired and have ERP systems that can do a great deal of the administrative work of HR, but is it advantageous to have them do it?

Traditionally HR (and many other staff groups such as IT) has been organized in a hierarchical manner, and HR has seen its mission as designing, administering, and enforcing adherence to HR policies and systems. As a result, all too often HR has been seen as expensive and rigid, a necessary evil consuming resources disproportionate to the value that it adds to the company. Among the changes in structure and process that are being advocated and used by some for HR are:

1. Decentralizing business support to operating units in order to increase responsiveness.

2. Contracting with business units for the services that are to be delivered, and perhaps even requiring services to be self-funding as a way of ensuring that businesses get only the services that they are willing to pay for and that they see as contributing to business performance.

3. Creating efficient central services units and/or outsourcing, transnational series.

4. Creating centers of excellence that provide expert services, often in a consulting capacity.

5. Increasing the rotation of people within various staff functions and between staff and line, and having fewer lifelong careers within a narrow staff function, in order to broaden the perspectives of HR staff professionals and increase their awareness of business issues, as well as increasing depth of understanding of HR issues among line management.

6. Expanding the scope of the HR function to include communications and sustainabilities, to mention just two areas.

Conclusion

The future of the HR function in organizations is uncertain. On the one hand, if it doesn't change, it could end up being largely an administrative function that manages an information technology-based HR system and vendors who do most of the HR administrative work. On the other hand, it could become a driver of organizational effectiveness and business strategy. In many organizations one of the key determinants of competitive advantage is effective human capital management. More than ever before, the effectiveness of an organization depends on its ability to address issues such as knowledge management, change management, and capability building, which could fall into the domain of the HR function. The unanswered question at this point is whether HR will rise to the occasion and address these issues.

In order to increase HR's contribution to organizational effectiveness, HR must rethink its basic value proposition, structure, services, and programs in order to address how it can add value in today's economy with its new organizational forms and business strategies. HR faces a formidable challenge just in helping organizations deal with the human issues that are raised by large-scale, strategic change. To face these challenges effectively, human resources has to focus on how it can add value and how it is organized; it must improve its competencies and develop new ones.

CHAPTER 2

Research Design

Our study focuses on how human resources organizations are designed and operate and how they are changing in response to the strategic and organizational initiatives that businesses are undertaking. It examines the extent to which the design and activities of the HR function are *actually* changing by analyzing survey data from 1995, 1998, 2001, 2004, 2007, and 2010. We examine the use of practices that are expected to represent the new directions that human resources organizations must take in order to fit with the changes that are occurring in the organizations they serve. We also examine how these changes are related to the strategic role of HR, its effectiveness, and the effectiveness of organizations. Finally, we examine the impact of how the HR function is designed and operates on its effectiveness. The study focuses in depth on eleven areas:

1. *HR Activities.* In order to assess how HR has changed, questions were asked about how the activities of HR have changed. Of particular interest is whether HR is doing less administration and more strategic work.

2. *HR Role and Activities.* Because of changes in the business environment, it is reasonable to expect that the HR function may have changed. A major focus of the study is to learn to what extent the HR function is changing, particularly with respect to becoming a strategic partner. It also looks at which organization designs and HR practices are associated with HR being a strategic partner. Of particular concern is whether attention to strategic services, such as organization design and development, is related to the effectiveness of the HR function and organizational effectiveness. We also focus on finding out how much increase or decrease there has been in the emphasis on traditional HR activities such as HR planning, compensation, recruitment, selection, and HR information systems. Of particular interest is whether HR is doing less administrative and more strategic work.

3. *Decision Science for Talent Resources.* Numerous books and articles that discuss talent have highlighted the fact that organizations are increasingly competing for human capital and that their ability to successfully compete can be a source of competitive advantage. They also, of course, need to effectively manage the talent. Our study therefore focuses on whether organizations have developed a decision science for their important talent decisions and whether this is related to how effectively they manage it and to organizational effectiveness.

4. *Design of the HR Function.* We examine whether changes have occurred in the way the HR function is organized in order to increase the value that it delivers. Because of their role in determining the balance between efficiency and customer-focused support, we look at the adoption of shared services and centers of excellence. We also look at the use of self-service and HR generalists.

5. *Outsourcing.* Outsourcing is becoming an increasingly popular way to deliver HR services and gain HR expertise. Potentially it is a way to deal with changes in the demand for HR services as well as a way to control costs. Thus, we focus both on how common different approaches to outsourcing are, and how effective they are.

6. *Information Technology.* HR information systems (HRISs) can potentially radically change the way HR services are delivered and managed. Thus, the present study examines how companies are using information technology in their HR functions. It also focuses on how effective organizations consider their HRISs to be in influencing employee satisfaction and providing strategic information.

7. *Metrics and Analytics.* It is important to know both what measures HR organizations collect and how they analyze them. Thus, our study looks at what metrics are being collected and utilized. It also looks at how effectively metrics and analytics are being used.

8. *HR Skills.* Critical to the effectiveness of any HR function are the skills of the HR professionals and staff. Thus, the present study examines how satisfied organizations are with their HR professionals' skills in a variety of areas. It also looks at the importance of the skills needed in order for HR professionals to serve as true business and strategic partners.

9. *HR Effectiveness.* The effectiveness of the HR function is a critical issue. Particular emphasis in our study is placed on the effectiveness of the HR function in doing many of the new activities that are required in order for HR to be a business and strategic partner. These include managing change, contributing to strategy, managing the outsourcing of HR, and operating shared service units. Perhaps the crucial issue with respect to effectiveness concerns what practices lead to an effective HR organization. Thus, the present study focuses on what HR structures, approaches, and practices are associated with effectiveness in an HR organization.

10. *Organizational Performance.* The effectiveness and structure of the HR function is just one of many influences on an organization's overall performance, but it can be a significant influence. Human capital is an important driver of organizational performance in most

organizations. Thus, the relationship between organizational performance and how the HR function is designed and operates is an important focus of the present study.

11. *International.* In our previous surveys we gathered data only from U.S. corporations. The economy has become increasingly global since we began this research in 1995; thus it is particularly important to consider how HR functions in different countries. For the first time, in our 2010 survey we collected data from corporations in five countries in addition to collecting data from U.S. corporations.

Sample

This is the sixth study in a series examining whether there is change in the human resources organizations of large and medium-sized U.S. corporations. In the first study in 1995, surveys were mailed to HR executives at the director level or above in 417 large and medium-sized service and industrial firms (Mohrman, Lawler, and McMahan 1996). The executives chosen had broad visibility to the human resource function across the corporation. Responses were received from 130 companies (19.6 percent response rate). The second study was done in 1998. Surveys were mailed to similar executives at 663 similar firms, with 199 usable surveys returned (17.9 percent response rate) (Lawler and Mohrman 2000). In the third survey, done in 2001, 966 surveys were mailed and 150 usable surveys were received (15.5 percent response rate) (Lawler and Mohrman 2003a). For the 2004 study, surveys were again mailed to HR executives with corporate visibility of the HR function in large and medium-sized companies (Lawler, Boudreau, and Mohrman 2006).

For the 2007 survey, questionnaires were once again mailed to HR executives in medium and large companies. For the first time, data were also gathered by using the Internet. The Institute for Corporate Productivity (i4cp) created a web-based version of our survey and used it to collect data from 43 companies, giving us a total sample of 106 companies.

All the 2010 survey data were collected using the Internet. Data were collected from companies with 1,000 or more employees. HR executives were given a link and asked to respond. For the first time, data were collected from multiple countries. In addition to the U.S., data were collected from HR executives in Australia, Canada, Europe, U.K., and China. Access to them was provided by the organizations listed in Exhibit 2.1. Appendix A lists the individuals who worked with us in each country.

Country	Sample Size	Research Partners
USA	190	HRPS (Human Resource Planning Society)
		i4cp
		Conference Board—USA
Australia	36	AHRI (Australian Human Resources Institute)
Canada	45	Conference Board of Canada
China	215	Institute of Organization and HR, University of China
Europe	66	Ashridge Business School
		Baumgartner Executive Networks
UK	45	Ashridge Business School

Exhibit 2.1. Sample

A complete copy of the 2010 survey with frequencies and means for each item in the U.S. sample can be found in Appendix B.

For the first time in 2004, data were collected from non-HR senior managers. In 2007 and in 2010 data were again collected from non-HR senior managers in U.S. corporations. A cover letter to the U.S. HR executives asked that the survey be distributed to individuals who were not in HR, but were in a position to evaluate the function. In 2010 the manager's questionnaire was made available by a link and the questions were answered online. At least one manager questionnaire was received from 35 U.S. organizations in 2010. A complete copy of the 2010 manager survey with frequencies, means, and variances for the U.S. can be found in Appendix B. When multiple responses were received from a company, a mean response for the company was computed and used in all the data analyses.

Measures

The 2010 HR survey is a slightly altered version of the previous surveys. It covers thirteen general areas:

1. General descriptive information about the demographics of the firm and the human resources function.

2. The organizational context that the human resources function serves, including its broad organizational form, management approach, and the amount and kinds of strategic change and organizational initiatives being carried out by the company (expanded in 2007; some items changed in 2010).

3. The changing focus of the human resources function measured in terms of how much time it is spending in different kinds of roles compared with five to seven years ago.

4. The degree of emphasis that a number of human resources activities are receiving and the involvement of HR in business strategy.

5. The human resource function's use of various organizational practices to increase efficiency and business responsiveness and the extent to which human resources is investing in a number of initiatives to support change.

6. The use of outsourcing and its effectiveness (altered in 2007 and 2010).

7. The use of information technology and its effectiveness (new in 1998; expanded in 2001; reduced in 2007).

8. The use of HR metrics and analytics as well as their effectiveness (new in 2004; expanded in 2007).

9. How the effectiveness of HR programs and activities is measured (new in 2004; expanded in 2007).

10. How HR leaders and business leaders make decisions that involve human capital (new in 2004).

11. The skill requirements for employees in the HR function and satisfaction with current skills.

12. The perceived effectiveness of the human resource function and the importance of a variety of HR activities.

13. Overall organizational performance in comparison to competitors (new in 2010).

The findings will be reported in roughly this order in the chapters that follow.

Staffing of Human Resources Function

In the U.S. firms studied, the average number of employees in the human resources function was 406. The ratio of total employees to HR employees was 80 to 1. This ratio is slightly lower than the ratio found in 2001, 2004, and 2007.

The ratio of HR staffing in this study is somewhat lower than those found in other studies. For example, the 2000–2001 BNA survey reports a ratio of 100 to 1 (Bureau of National Affairs 2001). Thus, despite the introduction of information technology and the downsizing of corporate staff groups, there is no dramatic decrease in the size of the HR function relative to the rest of the organization. Why this is true is unclear at this point. It may reflect the increased importance of the function and an increase in its work load or simply that it is a well-institutionalized part of most organizations that is difficult to reduce in size.

The respondents were asked to state the background of their current heads of human resources. In 77.1 percent of U.S. companies, the top human resources executive came up through the human resources function. In the other 22.9 percent of cases, these executives came from functions including operations, sales and marketing, and legal. This result is similar to findings of the 2001, 2004, and 2007 surveys. The percentage from HR varied slightly in the other countries with a low of 69.2 percent in Europe and a high of 77.8 percent in the U.K.

Why do some firms continue to place executives in charge of the human resources function who are not "traditional" human resources executives? There are three likely reasons. First, senior executives without an HR background are being put in charge of HR in order to develop them because they are candidates for the CEO job. Second, they are being put in charge of HR in order to make it run more like a business and be more of a business partner. Third, failed line managers are being put into HR because it is a "safe" pre-retirement job. The survey did not ask why this is being done, so we can only speculate that in the majority of cases it is done in order to change the HR function or to develop an executive. In today's business world it is too important a position to use as a "dumping ground."

The Strategic and Organizational Context

Human resource organizations exist in organizational environments that are as turbulent as the competitive environments in which companies find themselves. As companies take measures to survive and prosper, they make changes and introduce initiatives that change the organization, the competencies it has, the way it manages its human resources, and its expectations of and relationships to its employees (Boudreau and Jesuthasan 2011; Lawler and Worley 2011). Thus, in order to understand the HR function it is important to examine how its characteristics are related to its strategic focuses.

Table 2.1 shows the prevalence of five strategic focuses that are often part of a company's business strategy. It also shows that in the U.S. sample, the items measuring strategic focus factor into five types of focus: growth, information, knowledge, sustainability, and innovation. The focus concerned with information is rated the highest while the item on customer focus is the most highly rated single item. There are a few significant differences among the data from the different surveys. However, there is no overall trend which shows some focuses

Table 2.1. Strategic focuses, USA only						
	Means					
Strategic Focus	1995[1]	1998[2]	2001[3]	2004[4]	2007[5]	2010[6]
Growth	**3.1**	**3.4[4]**	**3.0**	**2.9[2]**	**3.1**	**3.0**
Building a global presence	3.4	3.2	3.0	2.9	3.1	3.1
Acquisitions	2.8[2]	3.5[1,4,6]	3.1	2.9[2]	3.2	3.0[2]
Information-Based Strategies	—	**4.0**	**4.0**	**3.9**	**3.8**	**3.8**
Customer focus	—	4.4	4.4	4.4	4.4	4.3
Technology leadership	—	3.6[5]	3.5	3.4	3.2[2]	3.3
Knowledge-Based Strategies	—	—	**3.3**	**3.4**	**3.3**	**3.3**
Talent management	—	—	3.7[6]	3.7	3.6	3.4[3]
Knowledge / intellectual capital management	—	2.9	2.9	3.1	3.1	3.2
Sustainability	—	—	—	—	**3.6**	**3.6**
Innovation	—	—	—	—	**3.6**	**3.4**

NOTE: Items with (—) were not asked.

Response scale: 1 = Little or no extent; 2 = Some extent; 3 = Moderate extent; 4 = Great extent; 5 = Very great extent

[1,2,3,4,5,6] Significant differences between years ($p \leq .05$).

Table 2.2. Strategic focuses, by country						
	Means					
Strategic Focus	USA[1]	Canada[2]	Australia[3]	Europe[4]	UK[5]	China[6]
Growth	**3.0[6]**	**2.8**	**2.6[4]**	**3.4[3,6]**	**3.2[6]**	**2.6[1,4,5]**
Building a global presence	3.1[4]	2.6[4]	2.6[4]	3.6[1,2,3,6]	3.4	2.7[4]
Acquisitions	3.0[6]	3.0[6]	2.6	3.1[6]	3.0[6]	2.4[1,2,4,5]
Information-Based Strategies	**3.8[6]**	**3.6**	**3.4**	**3.7**	**3.8**	**3.5[1]**
Customer focus	4.3[6]	4.1	4.1	4.1	4.2[6]	3.7[1,5]
Technology leadership	3.3	3.1	2.8	3.2	3.3	3.3
Knowledge-Based Strategies	**3.3[6]**	**3.2**	**3.3**	**3.2**	**3.0**	**2.9[1]**
Talent management	3.4[6]	3.4	3.5	3.4	3.1	3.0[1]
Knowledge / intellectual capital management	3.2[6]	3.0	3.2	3.0	3.0	2.8[1]
Sustainability	**3.6[6]**	**3.6**	**3.7**	**3.7[6]**	**3.4**	**3.2[1,4]**
Innovation	**3.4**	**3.3**	**3.6**	**3.4**	**3.6**	**3.2**

Response scale: 1 = Little or no extent; 2 = Some extent; 3 = Moderate extent; 4 = Great extent; 5 = Very great extent

[1,2,3,4,5,6] Significant differences between countries ($p \leq .05$).

consistently increasing and others decreasing; instead, the results suggest that the focuses vary in importance based on what is happening during a particular time period.

Table 2.2 presents the strategic focus data for each country. Building a global presence is the one focus which shows some significant differences. The European companies have the strongest focus on it.

China is the country that differs the most; it has low ratings of growth (acquisitions and global presence) and the lowest ratings of sustainability and knowledge management.

On balance, these data support the point that organizations exist in dynamic environments and need to have in place a variety of strategic and organizational initiatives to position themselves to perform successfully. The human resource function, if it is to add value and act as a strategic partner, needs to help ensure that the organizational capabilities and competencies exist to cope with a dynamic environment and changing organizational focuses. In order to determine how it is coping, we will look not only at how the human resource function is performing and changing, but also at how it is being driven by companies' strategies.

The management approaches that organizations can take vary widely and should influence what the HR function can and should do. Thus in the 2010 survey we asked the respondents how much their company uses five different management approaches:

- Bureaucratic (hierarchical structure, tight job description, top-down decision making)

- Low-cost operator (low wages, minimum benefits, focus on cost reduction and controls)

- High involvement (flat structure, participative decisions, commitment to employee development and careers)

- Global competitor (complex, interesting work; best talent hired; low commitment to employee development and careers)

- Sustainable (agile design, focus on financial performance and sustainability)

Four of these approaches are described in more detail in a book by O'Toole and Lawler (2006). In our 2010 survey we added an additional management approach, sustainable management, which is fully described in a recent book by Lawler and Worley (2011). As can be seen in Table 2.3, high involvement is the most frequently used approach in the U.S. companies studied, as it was in 2007.

The results from the international sample shown in Table 2.4 are similar to the U.S. results. The largest difference is a slightly higher use rate of the sustainable approach in other countries. It shows that the high-involvement approach is used the most by the companies in our international sample, while the low-cost operator approach is used the least.

The very noticeable outlier is China. It uses the low-cost operator approach the most and the high-involvement approach the least in comparison to the other countries. It also is a relatively low user of the

Table 2.3. Management approaches, USA only

To what extent do the following approaches describe how your organization is managed?	Percentages					Means	
	Little or No Extent	Some Extent	Moderate Extent	Great Extent	Very Great Extent	2007	2010
Bureaucratic (hierarchical structure, tight job descriptions, top-down decision making)	12.8	29.9	24.6	27.8	4.8	**2.66**	**2.82**
Low-cost operator (low wages, minimum benefits, focus on cost reduction and controls)	40.0	29.2	21.6	7.6	1.6	**2.07**	**2.02**
High involvement (flat structure, participative decisions, commitment to employee development and careers)	9.1	25.7	26.2	29.4	9.6	**3.04**	**3.05**
Global competitor (complex, interesting work; best talent hired; low commitment to employee development and careers)	20.4	28.5	23.1	21.0	7.0	**2.55**	**2.66**
Sustainable (agile design, focus on financial performance and sustainability)	4.8	18.2	27.8	38.0	11.2	**N/A**	**3.33**

No significant differences between years ($p \leq .05$).

Table 2.4. Management approaches, by country

To what extent do the following approaches describe how your organization is managed?	Means					
	USA[1]	Canada[2]	Australia[3]	Europe[4]	UK[5]	China[6]
Bureaucratic (hierarchical structure, tight job descriptions, top-down decision making)	2.8	2.5	2.8	2.6	2.7	2.8
Low-cost operator (low wages, minimum benefits, focus on cost reduction and controls)	2.0[6]	1.8[6]	1.9[6]	2.1[6]	2.2[6]	2.8[1,2,3,4,5]
High involvement (flat structure, participative decisions, commitment to employee development and careers)	3.0[6]	3.1	3.2[6]	3.2[6]	2.9	2.7[1,3,4]
Global competitor (complex, interesting work; best talent hired; low commitment to employee development and careers)	2.7[6]	2.3[4]	2.6	3.1[2,6]	3.0[6]	2.3[1,4,5]
Sustainable (agile design, focus on financial performance and sustainability)	3.3	3.6[6]	3.5	3.4	3.4	3.0[2]

Response scale: 1 = Little or no extent; 2 = Some extent; 3 = Moderate extent; 4 = Great extent; 5 = Very great extent
[1,2,3,4,5,6] Significant differences between countries ($p \leq .05$).

global competitor approach. The most obvious explanation for the tendency of China to use different management approaches is its level of economic and management development.

Throughout the report, we will relate the way the HR function operates to these five approaches. They are not meant to include all possible management approaches, nor is it expected that any companies will be totally managed in one way. They are included because they provide a useful way to identify the overall management approach that a large corporation is taking and how HR practices are related to the way a company is managed.

CHAPTER 3

Role of Human Resources

A key issue for HR functions is how they divide their time between doing administrative activities and services, and higher value-added business partner and strategic work. A major criticism of HR functions for decades has been that they are too bogged down in administration and policing, and the results of our previous surveys support this conclusion.

Time Allocation

As with our previous surveys, respondents were asked to estimate the percentage of time that their human resources function currently spends in carrying out five roles and how much time was spent on them five to seven years ago. Table 3.1 shows that the U.S. respondents report the function currently spends the most time on service provision (30.4 percent). When this is combined with the time they spend on records and auditing/controlling, they report that 57 percent of their time is currently spent on administration and services.

The responses from Canada, Australia, Europe, and the U.K. are very similar to the U.S. responses. The data from them (Table 3.2) show only small differences among these four countries and in comparison to the U.S. The results for China do show a much smaller amount of time spent being a strategic business partner. What most likely accounts for this is the different level of economic development that exists in China.

Table 3.1. Percentage of time spent on various human resources roles, USA only			
	Means		
HR Roles	**5 to 7 Years Ago**	**Current**	**Difference**
Maintaining records Collect, track, and maintain data on employees	23.2	13.6	Significant decrease
Auditing/Controlling Ensure compliance to internal operations, regulations, and legal and union requirements	15.7	12.5	Significant decrease
Human resources service provider Assist with implementation and administration of HR practices	32.8	30.4	Significant decrease
Development of human resources systems and practices Develop new HR systems and practices	14.4	16.7	Significant increase
Strategic business partner Member of the management team. Involved with strategic HR planning, organizational design, and strategic change	13.9	26.8	Significant increase

Table 3.2. Percentage of current time spent on various human resources roles, by country

HR Roles	Means					
	USA	Canada	Australia	Europe	UK	China
Maintaining records Collect, track, and maintain data on employees	13.6	17.4	16.1	22.3	20.2	19.4
Auditing/Controlling Ensure compliance to internal operations, regulations, and legal and union requirements	12.5	12.4	14.2	12.4	13.5	20.1
Human resources service provider Assist with implementation and administration of HR practices	30.4	30.4	27.3	28.4	26.2	29.5
Development of human resources systems and practices Develop new HR systems and practices	16.7	17.2	15.6	16.9	16.5	16.0
Strategic business partner Member of the management team. Involved with strategic HR planning, organizational design, and strategic change	26.8	22.7	26.8	20.0	23.6	15.0

Table 3.3. Percentage of time spent 5–7 years ago on various human resources roles, by country

HR Roles	Means					
	USA	Canada	Australia	Europe	UK	China
Maintaining records Collect, track, and maintain data on employees	23.2	26.2	26.0	35.6	31.1	31.5
Auditing/Controlling Ensure compliance to internal operations, regulations, and legal and union requirements	15.7	16.4	18.0	14.1	16.5	21.2
Human resources service provider Assist with implementation and administration of HR practices	32.8	31.4	29.3	27.2	31.4	27.1
Development of human resources systems and practices Develop new HR systems and practices	14.4	15.0	11.7	12.2	10.5	11.0
Strategic business partner Member of the management team. Involved with strategic HR planning, organizational design, and strategic change	13.9	11.0	14.9	10.9	10.6	9.2

When asked about what their HR's time allocation was five to seven years ago, U.S. HR executives report that there has been significant change in how their function's time is spent, when they look back. According to them, currently less time (57 percent vs. 72 percent) is being spent on record-keeping, auditing, and service provision, and more time (28 percent vs. 44 percent) is spent on the development of new HR systems and practices and being a strategic business partner.

Our results from other countries are very similar to those from the U.S. with respect to how they spent their time five to seven years ago. As shown by a comparison between Tables 3.2 and 3.3, the time-spent estimates suggest that in all countries the time spent on strategy has increased over the last five to seven years. The movement toward spending more time on strategic business partnering appears to be the right way for HR to change; it means that HR is adding more value.

Overall, our respondents are reporting a significant and encouraging movement toward HR becoming a strategic partner and doing higher value-added activities. However, before we conclude that this has actually occurred, it is important to compare the results for the U.S. from 1995, 1998, 2001, 2004, 2007, and 2010.

The U.S. data from 1995, 1998, 2001, 2004, and 2007 are almost identical to the data collected in 2010 when the same questions were asked (see Tables 3.4 and 3.5). There is no significant change in the current time responses or in the five-to-seven-years-ago responses from 1995 to 2010. In other words, there has been no change in any of the responses about how time is spent from 1995 to 2010. This raises serious questions about the validity of the reports by our respondents about how things were five to seven years ago.

It might be expected that the 2010 estimates of how things were five to seven years earlier would be somewhat in line with how things were said to be in our 2001 study, in our 2007 study, and especially in our 2004 study (six years ago), but they are not. Instead, rather than showing a change in time spent, the 1995, 1998, 2001, 2004, and 2007 results for how time is spent are the same as the results for 2010! This finding suggests that the HR executives who responded in 2010, as well as those who responded in 1995, 1998, 2001, 2004, and 2007, may have perceived more change in their role than has actually taken place. In short, they may be guilty of wishful thinking and a selective memory.

What should we believe: retrospective reports of the way things were, or data from the past about the way things were at the time the data were collected? The answer is obvious: individuals are much better at reporting how things are now than what they were like years ago. Reports concerning how things were in the past often include changes that reflect favorably on the individual. In this case, it is possible that HR executives want to see themselves as more of a strategic partner now than they were in the past. This is quite likely, given the many books and articles which have called for this to happen and the advantages it offers those in the HR profession.

The complete lack of change in the reports of how time is spent is very surprising and concerning: the results from 1995 are almost identical to those from 2010. It is almost an understatement to say that the world of business has changed dramatically since 1995. Thus it is surprising, indeed shocking, that how HR spends its time has not.

Table 3.4. Percentage of current time spent on various human resources roles, by years

HR Roles	Means					
	1995	1998	2001	2004	2007	2010
Maintaining records Collect, track, and maintain data on employees	15.4	16.1	14.9	13.2	15.8	13.6
Auditing/Controlling Ensure compliance to internal operations, regulations, and legal and union requirements	12.2	11.2	11.4	13.3	11.6	12.5
Human resources service provider Assist with implementation and administration of HR practices	31.3	35.0	31.3	32.0	27.8	30.4
Development of human resources systems and practices Develop new HR systems and practices	18.6	19.2	19.3	18.1	19.2	16.7
Strategic business partner Member of the management team. Involved with strategic HR planning, organizational design, and strategic change	22.0	20.3	23.2	23.5	25.6	26.8

Table 3.5. Percentage of time spent 5–7 years ago on various human resources roles, by years

HR Roles	Means					
	1995	1998	2001	2004	2007	2010
Maintaining records Collect, track, and maintain data on employees	23.0	25.6	26.7	25.9	26.3	23.2
Auditing/Controlling Ensure compliance to internal operations, regulations, and legal and union requirements	19.5	16.4	17.1	14.8	15.2	15.7
Human resources service provider Assist with implementation and administration of HR practices	34.3	36.4	33.1	36.4	33.0	32.8
Development of human resources systems and practices Develop new HR systems and practices	14.3	14.2	13.9	12.6	13.5	14.4
Strategic business partner Member of the management team. Involved with strategic HR planning, organizational design, and strategic change	10.3	9.4	9.1	9.6	12.1	13.9

Each time we have done our survey we have expected to see some change in how HR spends its time, but it has not appeared. This time we thought the chance of significant change was high because of the recession and the many changes that have occurred in the global business environment. The reality that HR has not changed makes us wonder what if anything can cause HR to spend more time on being a strategic business partner. It is less surprising that HR continues to believe it has changed, even though it has not! We have seen this pattern in each of our previous surveys. This may be a major problem if it leads to HR executives believing they have made progress toward an objective they feel is important when in fact they haven't.

Strategic Focuses

The relationships between the strategic focuses and how HR spends its time are shown in Table 3.6. The correlations in the table show a clear pattern: maintaining records, auditing/controlling, and providing services are negatively related or not significantly related to all the strategic focuses. Most of the negative relationships are statistically significant. A similar result was found in our 2004 and 2007 studies. Apparently, the weaker an organization's strategic focus in these areas, the more the HR function spends its time maintaining records, auditing/controlling, and providing HR services.

As was true in 2004 and 2007, time spent on strategic business partnering by the HR function is positively related to all the strategic focuses. Time spent on developing HR systems is also positively related to all the strategic focuses. Although the relationships are not strong, this finding suggests that HR is much more involved in strategic business partnering when an organization has a clear strategic focus, regardless of what that focus is. One implication of this finding is that in

Table 3.6. Relationship of HR roles to strategic focuses

HR Roles	Strategic Focuses				
	Growth	Information-Based Strategies	Knowledge-Based Strategies	Sustainability	Innovation
Maintaining records	−.07	−.14^t	−.25***	−.17*	−.26***
Auditing/ Controlling	−.07	−.18*	−.23**	−.18*	−.07
Providing HR services	−.07	−.02	−.06	−.05	−.12
Developing HR systems	.14^t	.16*	.18*	.09	.19*
Strategic business partnering	.06	.09	.21**	.17*	.20**

Significance level: $^t p \leq .10$; $^* p \leq .05$; $^{**} p \leq .01$; $^{***} p \leq .001$

Table 3.7. Relationship of HR roles to management approach

HR Roles	Management Approach				
	Bureaucratic	Low-Cost Operator	High Involvement	Global Competitor	Sustainable
Maintaining records	.19*	.30***	−.23**	−.12	−.11
Auditing/ Controlling	.12	.09	−.18*	−.06	−.17*
Providing HR services	.14^t	.10	−.04	−.06	−.02
Developing HR systems	−.11	−.20**	.16*	.23**	.09
Strategic business partnering	−.24**	−.20**	.16*	.03	.11

Significance level: $^t p \leq .10$; $^* p \leq .05$; $^{**} p \leq .01$; $^{***} p \leq .001$

order for HR to become more strategic, organizations themselves may need to become more strategic. Of course, one way for this to happen is for HR to provide leadership and help the rest of an organization become more strategic. If it can accomplish this, we believe there is a good chance HR will spend more time on strategy and the development of HR systems that support their organization's strategy.

Management Approach

The management approach organizations take has a low, but in several cases a significant, relationship to how HR spends its time. As is shown in Table 3.7, taking a low-cost operator approach is associated with spending significantly more time maintaining records, while taking a high-involvement approach and taking a bureaucratic approach is associated with spending less. As might be expected, strategic business partnering and developing HR systems are higher in high-involvement organizations, while they are lower in bureaucratic and low-cost operator organizations. This finding reinforces the point that what HR does is at least partially determined by the way an organization is managed. Simply stated, bureaucratic organizations have bureaucratic HR functions.

Conclusion

Once again the obvious conclusion is that HR has not changed how it allocates its time. It remains a function that spends the majority of its time on services, controlling, and record-keeping. This is true in the U.S. and in the other countries studied. Once again HR executives report that they are spending more time providing strategic services, but our longitudinal data do not show any change.

CHAPTER 4

Human Resources Role with Boards

There are a number of issues boards deal with that require HR expertise and information. This raises the important question of whether when they face these issues they call on HR. If they do, it is a clear indication that HR at least has a part-time seat at the most important decision-making table in the organization. If it does not, it is hard to see how HR can play a significant role with respect to most key strategic decisions.

Table 4.1 shows the responses to a question which asks about the type of help HR gives to boards. The question was first asked in 2004, so there are only data from 2004, 2007, and 2010 in the table.

Two issues, executive compensation and succession, have been and continue to be the ones on which HR is most likely to be asked for help in U.S. corporations. This finding is not surprising, given that these are areas where most HR functions can and should be able to provide help. Nevertheless, it is disappointing that such organizational issues as change consulting and strategic readiness receive such low ratings. They and three others have average ratings below the response "asking for help to a moderate extent." Particularly low is help with board effectiveness.

The fact that workforce condition is the third most requested area is a positive. This is an area where HR should have good information, and it is a critical organizational performance determinant. If

Table 4.1. Corporate boards, USA only								
	Percentages					Means		
HR Help	Little or No Extent	Some Extent	Moderate Extent	Great Extent	Very Great Extent	2004[1]	2007[2]	2010[3]
Executive compensation	8.6	8.6	9.2	30.5	43.1	4.2	4.1	3.9
Addressing strategic readiness	16.3	19.8	34.3	24.4	5.2	2.8	2.8	2.8
Executive succession	6.9	10.3	19.5	35.6	27.6	3.8	3.8	3.7
Change consulting	23.3	24.4	24.4	20.3	7.6	2.6	2.7	2.6
Developing board effectiveness/ corporate governance	38.8	19.4	23.5	16.5	1.8	2.5	2.5	2.2
Risk assessment	19.7	32.9	20.2	23.1	4.0	2.4	2.6	2.6
Information about the condition/ capability of the workforce	9.9	16.9	29.7	32.0	11.6	3.3	3.3	3.2
Board compensation	31.4	13.6	16.6	24.3	14.2	3.4[3]	3.0	2.8[1]
[1,2,3,] Significant differences between years ($p \leq .05$).								

Table 4.2. Corporate boards, by country

HR Help	Means					
	USA[1]	Canada[2]	Australia[3]	Europe[4]	UK[5]	China[6]
Executive compensation	3.9[6]	3.6[6]	3.7	4.1[6]	3.6	3.0[1,2,4]
Addressing strategic readiness	2.8	2.3[5]	2.9	2.9	3.0[2]	2.8
Executive succession	3.7[6]	3.5[6]	3.4	3.8[6]	3.4[6]	2.8[1,2,4,5]
Change consulting	2.6	2.6	2.9	3.1	3.1	2.7
Developing board effectiveness/ corporate governance	2.2[4]	2.1[4]	2.6	2.8[1,2]	2.8	2.5
Risk assessment	2.6	2.3	2.9	2.8	2.7	2.5
Information about the condition/ capability of the workforce	3.2	3.0	3.4	3.5	3.5	3.3
Board compensation	2.8[6]	2.3[4]	2.6	3.1[2,6]	3.0[6]	2.3[1,4,5]

Response scale: 1= Little or no extent; 2 – Some extent; 3 – Moderate extent; 4 – Great extent; 5 – Very great extent

[1,2,3,4,5,6] Significant differences between countries ($p \leq .05$).

HR performs well in areas like succession planning, it may well be asked for help in executing change and strategic readiness. So far, however, this doesn't seem to be happening. A comparison of 2004, 2007, and 2010 results reveals no significant change. Overall, it is clear that in most companies HR at least has its "foot in the boardroom door," but that is all.

International

The data from other developed countries (Table 4.2) are similar to the U.S. data, but there are some interesting differences. This is not surprising since all of the countries have different board structures and are subject to different regulations and membership rules. If anything is a surprise, it is that the differences among the developed countries are not greater. As it is, the U.S. and Canada boards seem to ask for the least organization development help. Across all of the areas, Canadian boards stand out among the developed countries by asking for the least help.

Not surprisingly, the results from China are different given the ownership structures that include government-owned firms. It is somewhat surprising the differences are not larger. As it is, three differences stand out. Corporate boards in China ask for less help with executive compensation, succession, and board compensation. These are the three areas where U.S. boards ask for the most help. It almost goes without saying that the different labor markets U.S. and Chinese firms face, as well as the history of board governance in the two countries, most likely account for this difference.

Strategic Focuses

The relationship between the help provided to the board and strategic focuses is shown in Table 4.3. As might be expected because of the direct relationship to human capital, boards ask for the most help when organizations have knowledge-based strategies. Those organizations that have an organizational performance strategy also have boards who are high users of HR. Somewhat surprisingly, the lowest relationship is with growth, although it is still significant. Overall, it is clear that the more organizations have strong strategic focuses, the more likely they are to call on HR for help.

Table 4.3. Relationship of strategic focuses with corporate boards

HR Help	Strategic Focuses				
	Growth	Information-Based Strategies	Knowledge-Based Strategies	Sustainability	Innovation
Executive compensation	.18*	.28***	.30***	.13^t	.30***
Addressing strategic readiness	.25***	.20**	.43***	.29***	.35***
Executive succession	.26***	.34***	.36***	.31***	.33***
Change consulting	.24***	.23**	.34***	.29***	.27***
Developing board effectiveness/ corporate governance	.28***	.25***	.29***	.18*	.24**
Risk assessment	.21**	.29***	.32***	.27***	.30***
Information about the condition/ capability of the workforce	.21**	.25***	.40***	.33***	.30***
Board compensation	.27***	.25***	.24**	.11	.19*

Significance level: $^t p \leq .10$; $^* p \leq .05$; $^{**} p \leq .01$; $^{***} p \leq .001$

Table 4.4. Relationship of management with corporate boards

HR Help	Management Approach				
	Bureaucratic	Low-Cost Operator	High Involvement	Global Competitor	Sustainable
Executive compensation	−.31***	−.20**	.32***	.10	.17*
Addressing strategic readiness	−.29***	−.13^t	.40***	.14^t	.23**
Executive succession	−.37***	−.20**	.36***	.18*	.26***
Change consulting	−.16*	−.13^t	.22**	.16*	.31***
Developing board effectiveness/ corporate governance	−.19*	−.15^t	.22**	.09	.25***
Risk assessment	−.22**	−.06	.26***	.08	.26***
Information about the condition/ capability of the workforce	−.26***	−.06	.27***	.18*	.31***
Board compensation	−.15*	−.16*	.23**	.16*	.06

Significance level: $^t p \leq .10$; $^* p \leq .05$; $^{**} p \leq .01$; $^{***} p \leq .001$

The use of HR for board compensation help shows the weakest relationship to most of the strategic focuses. This is not surprising since support with compensation is needed regardless of the strategy. On the other hand, addressing strategic readiness is related to most of the focuses. This result likely reflects the close connection between most strategies and the strategy formulation and implementation process. One without the other is unlikely to be effective. Overall, the more an organization has one of the five strategies focuses, the more likely it is to use HR.

Management Approach

Table 4.4 shows the relationship between the management approaches and board help. The strongest relationships are with the high-involvement approach and the bureaucratic approach. The more the high-involvement approach to management is utilized, the more active HR is with the board. This finding makes good sense and reinforces the point that when organizations take talent seriously as a source of competitive advantage, HR organizations can and do play a more important role (Lawler 2008). Also, supporting this conclusion is the negative relationship between the bureaucratic approach and how active HR is with the board. This finding is not surprising given the reality that the bureaucratic approach does not place great importance on human capital.

The sustainable approach shows the second strongest positive relationship to boards getting help from HR. This is not surprising given the emphasis this approach puts on human capital (Lawler and Worley 2011).

Conclusion

HR has a limited role when it comes to supporting boards. Its major support areas are executive compensation and succession. Overall, its level of support is not high and has declined with respect to executive and board compensation. The management approach of an organization has a strong relation to its overall level of support. It is high in high-involvement and sustainable management organizations and low in bureaucratic organizations. Providing support to boards is clearly an area where HR could do more.

CHAPTER 5

Business and HR Strategy

The involvement that the HR function has in the strategy development and implementation process—how much and what kind—is a critical determinant of the influence it has and the value it adds. Strategy is an area where there is a growing consensus among executives and researchers that human capital needs to be given more consideration because it is such an important determinant of what strategies an organization can and should pursue (Boudreau 2010; Lawler 2008; Lawler and Worley 2011). It also may be a key determinant of how a strategy should be pursued.

Type of Involvement

The involvement of the HR function in business strategy can take a variety of forms. Table 5.1 shows that in 2010, virtually all HR functions report that they are involved in business strategy. However, in almost 70 percent of the companies studied, HR is less than a full partner in the eyes of their HR executives and managers. When the 2010 data are compared to those of 1998, 2001, 2004, and 2007, there is no statistically significant change in the extent to which HR reports being involved in business strategy. Still it is important to note that the 2007 and 2010 data look like the 1998 data, which found the lowest level of involvement of the previous studies. Thus, the data do not suggest that the HR function is becoming more of a strategic partner in most organizations; instead, at best, it shows a stagnant situation.

The surprising data in Table 5.1 are from managers. In 2010 they tend to see HR as having a larger role in strategy than do HR executives, and

Table 5.1. HR's role in business strategy, USA only								
	1998	2001	2004		2007		2010[1]	
Role in Strategy	**HR Executives**	**HR Executives**	**HR Executives**	**Managers**	**HR Executives**	**Managers**	**HR Executives**	**Managers**
No role	4.2	3.4	2.0	5.3	5.7	4.9	4.3	2.9
Implementation role	16.8	11.6	12.2	18.4	17.0	19.5	17.4	2.9
Input role	49.6	43.8	45.9	52.6	45.3	48.8	47.3	64.7
Full partner	29.4	41.1	39.8	23.7	32.1	26.8	31.0	29.4
Mean	3.04	3.23	3.23	2.87[1]	3.04	2.89	3.05	3.13

Response scale: 1 = No role to 4 = Full partner
[1] Significant difference ($p \leq .05$) between HR executives and managers.

more than they have seen in the past. It is not clear why this change has occurred, since our HR executives data do not show a larger role for HR. It may have occurred and be unrecognized by them since they are "raising the bar" when it comes to what their strategy role is, or it may simply be a function of some changes in our pool of respondents.

In 2004 managers not in the HR function (from here on we will refer to them as "managers") reported lower levels of strategic involvement on the part of the HR function than did their counterparts in HR. As can be seen in Table 5.1, in 2007 only 26.8 percent of managers saw HR as a full partner in developing and implementing the business strategy, compared to 32.1 percent of HR executives who self-reported that they are. This actually is a smaller difference than we found in 2004 (23.7 percent vs 39.8 percent).

The finding of a difference between HR executives and managers in our 2004 and 2007 surveys is not surprising, in the light of an earlier study that asked HR executives and line managers about the role of HR (Society for Human Resource Management 1998); it too found a significant difference between HR executives and managers in their estimates of the role HR plays in business. Not surprisingly, in this study HR executives saw themselves as more of a business partner than did managers: 79 percent of HR executives said they were business partners, whereas only 53 percent of the line managers shared this view.

International

The international data in Table 5.2 are very similar to the U.S. data with the exception of China. In all the countries, except for China, HR may not be a full partner but at least has an input role with respect to business strategy. In the case of China, HR rarely has a full partner role and most of the time does not have either an input or a full partner role.

Table 5.2. HR's role in business strategy, by country						
	Means					
Role in Strategy	USA[1]	Canada[2]	Australia[3]	Europe[4]	UK[5]	China[6]
No role	4.3	2.2	9.4	4.6	2.2	15.5
Implementation role	17.4	24.4	12.5	15.4	17.8	41.3
Input role	47.3	42.2	40.6	56.9	42.2	37.6
Full partner	31.0	31.1	37.5	23.1	37.8	5.6
Mean	3.05[6]	3.02[6]	3.06[6]	2.98[6]	3.16[6]	2.33[1,2,3,4,5]

[1,2,3,4,5,6] Significant difference between countries ($p \le .05$).

Table 5.3. Strategic focuses and HR's role in business strategy					
	Strategic Focuses				
Role in Strategy	**Growth**	**Information-Based Strategies**	**Knowledge-Based Strategies**	**Sustainability**	**Innovation**
No role	3.0	3.3	2.7[1]	3.5	2.6[1]
Implementation role	2.8	3.4[1]	2.8[1]	3.0[1]	2.9[1]
Input role	3.1	3.8[1]	3.3[1]	3.7[1]	3.4
Full partner	3.0	4.1[1]	3.7[1]	3.9[1]	3.8[1]

Response scale: 1 = Little or no extent; 2 = Some extent; 3 = Moderate extent; 4 = Great extent; 5 = Very great extent
[1] Significant difference ($p \le .05$) from one other role in strategy.

Table 5.4. Management approach and HR's role in business strategy					
	Management Approach				
Role in Strategy	**Bureaucratic**	**Low-Cost Operator**	**High Involvement**	**Global Competitor**	**Sustainable**
No role	4.0[1]	2.6	1.9[1]	2.9	2.8
Implementation role	3.3[1]	2.3	2.4[1]	2.7	3.1
Input role	2.7[1]	1.8	3.1[1]	2.6	3.4
Full partner	2.6[1]	2.0	3.5[1]	2.7	3.5

Response scale: 1 = Little or no extent; 2 = Some extent; 3 = Moderate extent; 4 = Great extent; 5 = Very great extent
[1] Significant difference ($p \le .05$) from one other role in strategy.

Strategic Focuses

The role that HR plays in the strategy process is related to the strategic focus of the organization. As can be seen in Table 5.3, when HR has an important role in strategy, four of the five strategic orientations are higher; growth is the exception. The strongest relationship is with innovation; the second strongest is with knowledge. This result was also found in the 2004 and 2007 surveys. It makes the point that HR is most likely to play a major role in strategy when a clear strategy exists and it is related to the organization's human capital.

Management Approach

Table 5.4 shows the relationship between HR's role in strategy and the management approach of an organization. It shows that when HR has a major role in strategy, high-involvement management and sustainable management are the most common management approaches. On the other hand, in a low-cost operator company or a bureaucratic company it is very unlikely that HR plays a major role in strategy. These findings are not surprising; they fit well with how these approaches think about the role of people. In high-involvement and sustainable management, people are front and center, while in the others, they are "something to be dealt with." They do raise an interesting question about causation. Does this relationship exist because HR's strategy role leads to high-involvement and sustainable management being practiced, or the reverse? It is a question that the data cannot answer, but our view is that the major direction of causation is from the management style to role of HR. That said, there most likely are companies where the reverse is true.

Strategy Activities

HR can make a number of contributions to the strategy process in a business; some involve implementation, while others involve strategy development. Table 5.5 presents the data from a question that identifies some key specific activities that HR may engage in with respect to business strategy (asked for the first time in 2004).

HR executives report that they are particularly likely to be involved in designing an organization's structure and in planning for the implementation of strategy. Implementation is a logical area of involvement for HR, so it is not surprising that this is rated as a major involvement area for HR. A comparison among the 2004, 2007, and 2010 data for HR executives

Table 5.5. Business strategy activities, USA only								
	HR Executives				Managers			
	Means			Correlation with HR Role in Strategy	Means			Correlation with HR Role in Strategy
Activities	2004[1]	2007[2]	2010[3]		2004[1]	2007[2]	2010[3]	
Help identify or design strategy options	2.9	3.0	2.8	.65***	2.7	2.5[a]	2.8	.62***
Help decide among the best strategy options	3.0	3.1	2.9	.70***	2.9	2.6[a]	2.8	.69***
Help plan the implementation of strategy	3.6	3.8	3.6	.58***	3.4	3.2[a]	3.6	.62***
Help identify new business opportunities	2.0	2.2	2.0	.52***	2.0	1.7[a]	2.2	.67***
Assess the organization's readiness to implement strategies	3.5	3.5	3.2	.54***	3.4	3.2	3.6[a]	.69***
Help design the organization structure to implement strategy	3.8	3.9	3.6	.58***	3.5	3.5	3.7	.68***
Assess possible merger, acquisition, or divestiture strategies	2.9	3.0	2.7	.38***	2.3[a]	2.3[a]	2.7	.52**
Work with the corporate board on business strategy	2.6	2.9	2.6	.58***	2.5	2.3[a]	2.9	.61***

Response scale: 1 = Little or no extent; 2 = Some extent; 3 = Moderate extent; 4 = Great extent; 5 = Very great extent

[a] Significant difference ($p \leq .05$) between HR executives and managers in year.

[1,2,3] No significant difference ($p \leq .05$) between years.

Significance level: [1] $p \leq .10$; * $p \leq .05$; ** $p \leq .01$; *** $p \leq .001$

shows no significant changes in HR's involvement in strategy activities. This is consistent with the finding reported in Chapter 3 that HR has not changed its time allocation.

Perhaps the best summary of the results for HR executives is that HR is more likely to play a role in the implementation of business strategy than in the development of it or making key decisions concerning what it will be. Finally, it is worth noting that, as was pointed out in Chapter 4, HR is not likely to be involved with the corporate board in discussions of business strategy, nor in identifying new business opportunities.

Table 5.5 also shows how managers rate the involvement of HR in strategy. Their ratings are very similar to those of the HR executives. The 2010 ratings are higher than the managers' ratings in 2004 and 2007. The 2010 results are not consistent with the 2004 and 2007 finding that managers in general tend to see less involvement of HR in strategy than HR executives do. All but one of the items is rated lower in 2004 by managers than by HR executives. However, only one of the differences reaches statistical significance. In 2007 the same pattern exists with six of the differences reaching statistical significance. In 2010 the pattern is very different; only one item reaches statistical significance and it is because managers gave HR a higher score than did HR executives. Overall, our 2004 and 2007 data show that managers simply don't see HR as involved in business strategy as do HR executives, even when it comes to such specifics as recruiting and developing talent; but our 2010 data suggest these differences no longer exist.

It is interesting that the relative degree of involvement in different activities as seen by managers and HR executives is very similar. Managers agree with HR executives that the major involvement of HR executives is in recruiting and developing talent and other implementation issues that are involved in strategy. They also agree that HR has little involvement in identifying new business opportunities.

Table 5.5 also shows the relationship between the business strategy activities and HR's role in strategy. Not surprisingly, as seen by managers and HR executives, the relationship is strong, which indicates that these activities are associated with the degree of involvement HR has in the strategy process. The weakest relationship in 2010 for both HR executives and managers is with assessing mergers and divestitures, although even here the relationship is quite strong.

International

The international data in Table 5.6 show some significant differences. Australia and the U.K. stand out as the countries where HR is most active in business strategy activities, particularly identifying and deciding among strategy options. China stands out as the country where HR is the least active. This finding is consistent with the earlier finding that in China it is rarely a full partner in strategy development and implementation.

Strategic Focuses

As can be seen in Table 5.7, there are numerous, significant relationships between the company strategic focus areas and the role that HR plays in the strategy process. Four of the strategic focuses—information, knowledge, sustainability, and innovation—are associated with HR's active involvement in almost all of the business strategy activities listed

Table 5.6. Business strategy activities, by country						
	Means					
Activities	**USA[1]**	**Canada[2]**	**Australia[3]**	**Europe[4]**	**UK[5]**	**China[6]**
Help identify or design strategy options	2.8[6]	2.8[6]	3.4[4,6]	2.5[3]	3.1[6]	2.2[1,2,3,5]
Help decide among the best strategy options	2.9[6]	2.8	3.4[4,6]	2.6[3]	3.1[6]	2.3[1,3,5]
Help plan the implementation of strategy	3.6[6]	3.4[6]	3.8[6]	3.6[6]	3.5[6]	2.5[1,2,3,4,5]
Help identify new business opportunities	2.0	2.0	2.3	2.1	2.2	2.1
Assess the organization's readiness to implement strategies	3.2[6]	3.2[6]	3.4[6]	3.4[6]	3.3[6]	2.6[1,2,3,4,5]
Help design the organization structure to implement strategy	3.6[6]	3.6[6]	3.8[6]	3.4	3.7[6]	3.0[1,2,3,5]
Assess possible merger, acquisition, or divestiture strategies	2.7[6]	2.6[6]	2.6[6]	2.6[6]	2.8[6]	1.9[1,2,3,4,5]
Work with the corporate board on business strategy	2.6[3,5,6]	2.4[3,5]	3.2[1,2,6]	2.7[6]	3.2[1,2,6]	2.1[1,3,4,5]

Response scale: 1 = Little or no extent; 2 = Some extent; 3 = Moderate extent; 4 = Great extent; 5 = Very great extent
[1,2,3,4,5,6] Significant difference between countries ($p \leq .05$).

Table 5.7. Relationship of business strategy activities to strategic focuses					
	Strategic Focuses				
Activities	**Growth**	**Information-Based Strategies**	**Knowledge-Based Strategies**	**Sustainability**	**Innovation**
Help identify or design strategy options	.02	.31***	.42***	.35***	.30***
Help decide among the best strategy options	.11	.35***	.46***	.36***	.39***
Help plan the implementation of strategy	.14[t]	.40***	.44***	.35***	.39***
Help identify new business opportunities	.17*	.27***	.38***	.21**	.31***
Assess the organization's readiness to implement strategies	.14[t]	.30***	.48***	.25***	.35***
Help design the organization structure to implement strategy	.22**	.33***	.38***	.27***	.37***
Assess possible merger, acquisition, or divestiture strategies	.31***	.21**	.25***	.28***	.24***
Work with the corporate board on business strategy	.12	.27***	.43***	.27***	.32***

Significance level: [t] $p \leq .10$; * $p \leq .05$; ** $p \leq .01$; *** $p \leq .001$

in Table 5.7. Knowledge-based strategies are related to all activities. Growth is related to the fewest.

It is a bit surprising that a strategic focus on growth has only weak relationships to the strategy activities of the HR function while the other four have strong, positive relationships. The strength of these relationships strongly indicates that the more corporations have a strategic focus, the more the HR function engages in these strategy activities. This is not surprising, since in order to effectively perform most of the strategy activities studied, HR needs the guidance of a well-articulated strategy. In total, the results on strategic focuses suggest that almost regardless of the strategic focus in an organization, there are HR strategy activities that are relevant and important.

Management Approach

The relationships between business strategy activities and the management approach used are shown in Table 5.8. Most of the relationships are statistically significant and paint a clear picture. Bureaucratic and low-cost operator companies tend to have HR functions that are relatively inactive with respect to strategy. The opposite is true of high-involvement organizations: their HR functions are very active in both strategy creation and implementation. Sustainable management organizations also tend to have active HR organizations, but the relationship is not as strong as it is for high involvement. Overall, how an organization is managed clearly makes a difference in the strategy activities of HR, but it is not certain why. Is it because the management approach shapes the HR function, or vice versa? Our view is that in most cases it is the former.

Table 5.8. Relationship of business strategy activities to management approach					
	Management Approach				
Activities	Bureaucratic	Low-Cost Operator	High Involvement	Global Competitor	Sustainable
Help identify or design strategy options	–.21**	–.11	.27***	.00	.26***
Help decide among the best strategy options	–.22**	–.07	.30***	.06	.32***
Help plan the implementation of strategy	–.26***	–.17*	.39***	.11	.32***
Help identify new business opportunities	–.12	–.10	.27***	.13^t	.19*
Assess the organization's readiness to implement strategies	–.25***	–.16*	.42***	.14^t	.22**
Help design the organization structure to implement strategy	–.27***	–.21**	.44***	.21**	.20**
Assess possible merger, acquisition, or divestiture strategies	–.28***	–.20**	.27***	.17*	.19*
Work with the corporate board on business strategy	–.19*	–.14^t	.38***	.07	.22**

Response scale: 1 = Little or no extent; 2 = Some extent; 3 = Moderate extent; 4 = Great extent; 5 = Very great extent

Significance level: ^{t} $p \le .10$; * $p \le .05$; ** $p \le .01$; *** $p \le .001$

Table 5.9. HR Strategy, USA only				
	Means			**Correlation with HR Role in Strategy (2010)**
HR Strategy	**2004[1]**	**2007[2]**	**2010[3]**	
Data-based talent strategy	2.7	2.6	2.7	**.31***
There is a human capital strategy that is integrated with business strategy	3.2	3.3	3.0	**.46***
Provides analytic support for business decision making	2.9	2.8	2.8	**.43***
Provides HR data to support change management	3.2	3.0	3.0	**.45***
Drives change management	3.4	3.2	3.1	**.49***
Makes rigorous data-based decisions about human capital management	2.7	2.6	2.7	**.44***

Response scale: 1 = Little or no extent; 2 = Some extent; 3 = Moderate extent; 4 = Great extent; 5 = Very great extent

[1,2,3] No significant differences between years (p ≤ .05).

Significance level: [1] $p \le .10$; * $p \le .05$; ** $p \le .01$; *** $p \le .001$

HR Strategy

Data on the HR strategy of organizations are presented in Table 5.9. The results from 2004, 2007, and 2010 are essentially identical. With respect to the current level of activity, none of the mean scores are particularly high. The highest in 2010 is 3.1 on a 5-point scale. It appears that to a moderate extent, HR drives change management, develops a human capital strategy that is integrated with business strategy, and provides HR data to support change management.

However, HR is not particularly active in the use of data and analytics. Data-based decision making about human capital and data-based talent strategies are the lowest-rated HR strategy activities. A comparison of 2010 data with the 2004 and 2007 data shows no major changes in what HR does (questions were asked only in 2004, 2007, and 2010). This finding is consistent with the point that HR is not changing. It is interesting to look back at the results of our 2007 survey. HR executives responding to it said that all of the items in Table 5.9 were activities they would increase (question not asked in 2010).

In 2007, all of the strategy items were rated near the top of the scale (2.6 or greater on a 3-point scale) on the future focus of the HR organization. Apparently, all these items represent the way that HR plans to be involved in the strategy process, but there are no data to suggest this is happening. Thus, there is a major question concerning when and if these strategies will be put in place. HR executives said they planned to do these things in both our 2004 and 2007 surveys, but as noted, the comparison between 2007 and 2010 shows no change.

Table 5.10. HR strategy, by country	Means					
HR Strategy	USA[1]	Canada[2]	Australia[3]	Europe[4]	UK[5]	China[6]
Data-based talent strategy	2.7[6]	2.5	2.8	2.8[6]	2.5	2.4[1,4]
A human capital strategy that is integrated with business strategy	3.0[6]	2.8	3.0[6]	3.0[6]	2.8	2.3[1,3,4]
Provides analytic support for business decision making	2.8	2.8	3.0	2.9	2.8	2.5
Provides HR data to support change management	3.0[6]	2.9	3.2	3.2[6]	3.0	2.6[1,4]
Drives change management	3.1[6]	2.9[6]	3.2[6]	3.0[6]	3.2[6]	2.2[1,2,3,4,5]
Makes rigorous data-based decisions about human capital management	2.7	2.5	2.7	2.6	2.7	2.5

Response scale: 1 = Little or no extent; 2 = Some extent; 3 = Moderate extent; 4 = Great extent; 5 = Very great extent

[1,2,3,4,5,6] Significant difference between countries ($p \leq .05$).

The correlations between the current activity levels and HR's overall role in strategy are also presented in Table 5.9. They are all high. Data-based talent strategies is the lowest in 2007, but it is still high significantly. It is not entirely clear why this relationship is relatively weak, given that it is potentially an important part of the strategy process. One possibility is because effective measurement systems require not just data but sound analytics, good logic, and attention to change management processes (Boudreau and Ramstad 2006). It may be that today's HR data focus primarily on the quality of measures and do not sufficiently reflect the other elements of a complete data-based decision strategy.

What the results in Table 5.9 do show is a clear pattern of the types of HR activities that are related to it having a role in strategy. They provide a useful set of practices that HR organizations should consider adopting in order to play an important role in strategy formulation. However, as already noted, the fact that there is no change in their adoption from 2004 to 2010 raises the question of whether or not they are practices that will actually be put in place by HR functions.

International

The international data on HR strategy are presented in Table 5.10. They show significant differences only with respect to China. It clearly shows the lowest ratings of any country. Canada shows a tendency to have the lowest ratings among the other countries, but the differences are small.

Strategic Focuses

Table 5.11 shows the relationship between the current HR strategy activities and the strategic focuses of the organization. There are a number of strong significant relationships, reinforcing the point that if an organization has a clear strategic focus, HR is likely to be actively engaged in these activities. All of the HR strategy items show significant correlations with all of the strategic focuses. This finding suggests that all are potentially useful activities in most organizations. The lowest correlations are with growth, but even four out of six of these are highly significant.

Perhaps the most interesting finding in the table is the pattern of strong correlations between knowledge-based strategies and the HR strategy items. It is clear that when an organization has a knowledge-based strategy, it particularly emphasizes the role of HR processes and measures as it should, since talent is a particularly critical asset in organizations that have knowledge-based strategies. This finding is further confirmation of the future importance of HR strategic activities, since more and more organizations are developing knowledge-based strategies.

Management Approach

The human capital strategy activities in Table 5.12 show significant correlations with three of the five management approaches. It is interesting that all the activities are negatively correlated with the low-cost operator approach. On the other hand, they are all positively correlated with the high-involvement approach and the sustainable management approach. This once again highlights the large difference in how these approaches treat talent and the HR function.

Conclusion

Overall, the data suggest that HR still has a considerable way to go when it comes to adding value as a strategic player. In most organizations, HR is still not a full partner in the business strategy process. This is

Table 5.11. Relationship of current HR strategy to strategic focuses					
	Strategic Focuses				
HR Strategy	Growth	Information-Based Strategies	Knowledge-Based Strategies	Sustainability	Innovation
Data-based talent strategy	.28***	.34***	.48***	.24***	.33***
There is a human capital strategy that is integrated with business strategy	.25***	.40***	.58***	.33***	.50***
Provides analytic support for business decision making	.13^t	.42***	.55***	.35***	.46***
Provides HR data to support change management	.16*	.35***	.52***	.35***	.41***
Drives change management	.24***	.34***	.46***	.37***	.40***
Makes rigorous data-based decisions about human capital management	.24***	.37***	.51***	.31***	.37***

Response scale: 1 = Little or no extent; 2 = Some extent; 3 = Moderate extent; 4 = Great extent; 5 = Very great extent

Significance level: $^t p \leq .10$; $^* p \leq .05$; $^{**} p \leq .01$; $^{***} p \leq .001$

Table 5.12. Relationship of current HR strategy to management approach

HR Strategy	Management Approach				
	Bureaucratic	Low-Cost Operator	High Involvement	Global Competitor	Sustainable
Data-based talent strategy	−.09	−.03	.29***	.21**	.28***
There is a human capital strategy that is integrated with business strategy	−.23**	−.15*	.39***	.26***	.31***
Provides analytic support for business decision making	−.22**	−.07	.36***	.15*	.33***
Provides HR data to support change management	−.23**	−.10	.37***	.13ᵗ	.34***
Drives change management	−.35***	−.19*	.42***	.19**	.30***
Makes rigorous data-based decisions about human capital management	−.18*	−.02	.29***	.24***	.40***

Significance level: ᵗ $p \leq .10$; * $p \leq .05$ ** $p \leq .01$; *** $p \leq .001$

particularly true in the case of China. The low level of strategy involvement in China is not surprising given its level of economic development. It is surprising and disappointing in the case of the other countries.

The data suggest that HR is making little progress in the U.S. Overall, the 2010 results are very similar to the 1998 results. A lot has changed in the world of business since 1998, but our data suggest that HR hasn't become a full strategic business partner nor has it made a major commitment to developing an HR strategy. This is true even though a number of business changes have occurred that would seem to be ones that would lead to HR being more of a strategic partner (Lawler and Mohrman 2003b).

On the encouraging side, HR executives do report being active in a number of areas that are directly tied to the strategic direction of the business. These range all the way from human capital recruitment and development through organization design and strategy development. The challenge for HR is to increase the degree to which it is involved in strategy-related activities, so that it can become a full partner in the high-value-added area of business strategy (Lawler 2003). One finding that suggests this might happen is the higher level of strategy activities in knowledge-based organizations. As more and more organizations in developed countries focus on knowledge, it may lead to HR engaging in more strategy activities.

CHAPTER 6

HR Decision Science

The growing recognition that human capital decisions must become more sophisticated and strategically relevant represents a challenge for both HR professionals and managers throughout organizations. Consistent with the tenets of decision science in other fields, the key issues involve not only the overall sophistication and quality of human capital decisions, but also the quality of the principles underlying those decisions.

High-quality decisions can occur only if HR professionals and other managers understand how human capital affects sustainable organizational effectiveness and if they use that understanding to identify and make key human capital decisions. To date, there has been little research on the decision frameworks used by HR and other business leaders. In this chapter, we present results on the quality of human capital decisions and the relationship between decision quality and the strategic role of HR.

Quality of Decisions about Talent and Human Capital

Table 6.1 shows the responses of HR executives and those of managers to questions designed to tap the state of the decision science for human capital management. The first item poses the fundamental question of whether their organization excels in the competition for critical talent. Both groups rate their organization as moderately effective in competing for key talent, with managers rating this item significantly higher but still near the midpoint of the scale, a somewhat different pattern from 2007, when there was no difference.

Managers report significantly greater business leader talent decision quality than do HR executives. Table 6.1 shows this is true for the question that taps the definition of Talentship: "decisions that depend upon or impact human capital are as rigorous, logical, and strategically relevant as decisions about more tangible resources." It is also true for business leaders' use of sound principles when making decisions in the four areas of behavioral science (numbered 1 through 4 in Table 6.1).

For HR executives, all the ratings are at the midpoint or slightly below, suggesting only moderate decision quality where human capital is involved; while for managers the ratings are closer to 4 on a 5-point scale, suggesting they perceive their understanding and use of sound principles to be relatively good.

The 2010 results for HR executives are similar to those in the 2007 survey, but for managers, the perceived quality of talent decisions and principles is higher in 2010 than in 2007. The correlation results for these items are also notable. While there are significant correlations between HR's role in strategy and perceptions of the quality of business leader decisions and principles, the correlations are higher for the manager

Table 6.1. HR decision making, USA only	HR Executives			Managers		
Decision Making	2007 Mean	2010 Mean	2010 Correlation with HR Role in Strategy	2007 Mean	2010 Mean	2010 Correlation with HR Role in Strategy
We excel at competing for and with talent where it matters most to our strategic success	3.2	3.1	.34***	3.0	3.5[2]	.23
Business leaders' decisions that depend upon or affect human capital (e.g. layoffs, rewards, etc.) are as rigorous, logical, and strategically relevant as their decisions about resources such as money, technology, and customers	2.9	3.0	.43***	3.2	3.8[2]	.58***
Business leaders understand and use sound principles when making decisions about:						
1. Motivation	2.7	2.8	.32***	3.0	3.6[2]	.71***
2. Development and learning	2.8	2.9	.39***	3.0	3.8[2]	.68***
3. Culture	2.9	3.1	.30***	3.1	3.8[2]	.84***
4. Organization design	2.8	2.8	.31***	3.1	3.7[2]	.74***
5. Business strategy	3.6	3.8	.28***	3.7	3.9	.67***
6. Finance	4.0	4.0	.19*	4.1	3.7	.67***
7. Marketing	3.5	3.5	.17*	3.2	3.6	.57**
HR leaders have a good understanding about where and why human capital makes the biggest difference in their business	3.2	3.3	.51***	3.4	3.9[2]	.47**
Business leaders have a good understanding about where and why human capital makes the biggest difference in their business	3.2	3.1	.41***	3.4	3.8[2]	.50***
HR systems educate business leaders about their talent decisions	2.5	2.4	.39***	2.6	3.1[2]	.37*
HR adds value by insuring compliance with rules, laws, and guidelines	3.5	3.4	.15*	3.8[1]	4.0[2]	.65***
HR adds value by delivering high-quality professional practices and services	3.6	3.6	.46***	3.6	3.7	.61***
HR adds value by improving talent decisions inside and outside the HR function	3.6	3.5	.44***	3.4	3.8	.67***

Response scale: 1 = Little or no extent; 2 = Some extent; 3 = Moderate extent; 4 = Great extent; 5 = Very great extent

[1] Significant differences ($p \leq 0.05$) between HR executives and managers in 2007.

[2] Significant differences ($p \leq 0.05$) between HR executives and managers in 2010.

Significance level: [1] $p \leq .10$; * $p \leq .05$; ** $p \leq .01$; *** $p \leq .001$

sample than for the HR executive sample. This is especially true when it comes to the four talent principles. In particular, for the "culture" item, the correlation of .84 between managers' perceptions of business leader understanding and HR's role in strategy suggests that HR's strategic role is strongly associated with manager perceptions that they and their colleagues understand and use principles of culture well. This may reflect the growing attention to "high performance culture" and the emergence of culture as a popular explanation for the demise or survival of many iconic organizations during the 2008 economic downturn.

Items 5, 6, and 7 provide a useful comparison to talent decisions, because they describe decision areas that are more traditionally the domain of business leaders. Here, the average decision quality ratings by HR executives are considerably higher than they are for the talent-related areas, just as they were in the 2007 survey, suggesting that HR executives regard business leaders as more adept at the decision science of traditional business than they are for talent. In contrast, managers rated the non-talent items about the same as the talent-related items, different from the 2007 survey. This speaks again to a pattern of managers regarding their talent-related prowess as somewhat higher in 2010 than the 2007 sample.

The correlations with HR's role in strategy show a divergence between HR executives and managers. HR executives show a lower (though still statistically significant) correlation between items 5, 6, and 7 and HR's role in strategy. The results suggest that HR's strategic role is more strongly related to managers' prowess in talent-related areas than in non-talent-related areas, but the distinction is far less apparent in 2010, particularly among managers. It may be that managers who strive to use sound principles in all areas of management increasingly demand that HR executives play a stronger strategic role, and that is not confined to decision areas that are talent related.

The two items in Table 6.1 that refer to talent segmentation, that is, whether HR leaders or business leaders understand where and why human capital makes the biggest difference in their business, receive moderate ratings from both HR leaders and managers. In the 2010 data, managers again rated both HR and business leaders significantly higher than did HR executives. Again, the ratings by both HR executives and managers displayed strong positive correlations between these items and HR's strategic role.

The question concerning HR systems educating business leaders poses a fundamental issue. If business leaders are to learn to make sound talent decisions, then the HR systems they use should educate them about the quality of those decisions, in the same way that management systems in finance, marketing, and operations management provide clear feedback regarding managers' decision quality (Boudreau and Ramstad 2007; Boudreau 2010). The 2010 results mirror the results in 2007; this question had the lowest ratings by both HR executives and managers of any of the decision science questions. Yet, the correlation between this question and HR's strategic role is positive and significant for both HR executives and managers. As in past surveys, these findings suggest that there is a significant opportunity to improve how well HR systems actually educate leaders about talent decisions, and that the quality of this education is associated with a stronger strategic role for HR.

Finally, the last three items in Table 6.1 ask about how HR adds value. Boudreau and Ramstad (2007) suggest that mature professions evolve to a balance of adding value through compliance, services, and decision support. Table 6.1 shows that both HR executives and managers believe that HR adds value to a moderate or great extent in all three areas. Managers rate compliance value highest, and also tend to give higher ratings than the HR managers.

The overall level of value added by HR leaves room for improvement in all three areas. The correlation pattern is also notable. Both HR executives and managers show a strong association between their perceptions of HR's strategic role and the value added by HR through services and decision support. When it comes to value added through compliance, however, the correlation with HR's strategic role is much smaller among HR managers.

Overall, high-quality HR decisions and sound decision principles are perceived as moderately likely to exist. Across all the items, managers generally perceive them to exist to a greater extent than HR executives, particularly when they are rating their own capabilities. Either HR executives underestimate the sophistication of their counterparts, or managers overestimate their sophistication. While we cannot resolve this question, our experience suggests that it is a bit of both.

On the one hand, managers most likely have undoubtedly increased their awareness of the importance of human capital, and of their role in nurturing and deploying it. HR data and scorecards are more available, providing a basis for improved decisions. On the other hand, there is a great deal that managers still do not know about talent segmentation, motivation, culture, and learning. HR executives likely can see this gap, and it is reflected in their ratings. HR executives often say "our business leaders don't know what they don't know" when it comes to sound principles of human capital decisions. It is easy for managers to regard their performance as sufficient, while HR executives who are more familiar with human resource management see that much more could be accomplished.

HR leaders, who see room for improvement that their counterparts may not see, may need to provide tangible examples of more sophisticated human capital decision principles. As with the development of the decision sciences of marketing and finance, we would expect that as the HR decision science develops, it will become clear that competing effectively with and through human capital requires that leaders *both* inside and outside of HR not be satisfied with the traditional HR service-delivery paradigm. They will realize that it must be extended to include making better decisions about human capital where it matters most to strategic success (Boudreau and Ramstad 1997, 2005a, 2005b, 2005c, 2007).

In summary, the results described in Table 6.1 are remarkably similar to those from HR executives and managers surveyed in 2007. The average ratings of decision science processes and knowledge do not appear to have advanced significantly in the three years between the surveys. The one exception may be that the manager ratings of these items are somewhat higher in 2010, and also more likely to be significantly higher than the corresponding ratings by HR executives. Managers may be becoming more satisfied with HR's contribution, even as HR executives can still see that there is a long way to go.

International

Table 6.2 presents the international results. Overall, most of the frequent differences arise when comparing the sample of Chinese data to those from other countries. The ratings in the Chinese sample are generally lower than the ratings in one or more of the other countries, with many of the differences being statistically significant. The results for the U.K. sample are most similar to those of China; they show the fewest significant differences between them.

The relative pattern of ratings for each country is very similar to the results for the U.S. sample reported in Table 6.1. Most ratings fall near the midpoint of the scale, with the exception of the degree to which HR systems educate business leaders about their talent decisions, which is rated lower. In all the countries, business leaders' use of sound principles is rated higher in traditional management arenas (items 5, 6, and 7) than in talent management and human capital (items 1 through 4). Thus, the conclusions we reached for the U.S. seem to hold for the different national samples in the survey. There appears to be a "solid" but

Table 6.2. HR decision making, by country

Decision Making	Means					
	USA[1]	Canada[2]	Australia[3]	Europe[4]	UK[5]	China[6]
We excel at competing for and with talent where it matters most to our strategic success	3.1[6]	3.2[6]	3.1	3.2[6]	2.9	2.6[1,2,4]
Business leaders' decisions that depend upon or affect human capital (e.g. layoffs, rewards, etc.) are as rigorous, logical, and strategically relevant as their decisions about resources such as money, technology, and customers	3.0	3.3[6]	3.1	3.1	2.9	2.8[2]
Business leaders understand and use sound principles when making decisions about:						
1. Motivation	2.8	2.8	3.1	3.1	3.1	3.0
2. Development and learning	2.9[4]	3.1	3.3	3.3[1]	2.9	3.0
3. Culture	3.1	3.1	3.4	3.2	2.9	3.0
4. Organization design	2.8	2.8	2.9	3.1	2.9	2.9
5. Business strategy	3.8[6]	3.9[6]	3.7	3.8[6]	3.7[6]	3.2[1,2,4,5]
6. Finance	4.0[6]	4.0[6]	3.9[6]	3.9[6]	3.6	3.3[1,2,3,4]
7. Marketing	3.5	3.5	3.4	3.3	3.0	3.3
HR leaders have a good understanding about where and why human capital makes the biggest difference in their business	3.3[6]	3.4[6]	3.6[6]	3.6[6]	3.3	2.9[1,2,3,4]
Business leaders have a good understanding about where and why human capital makes the biggest difference in their business	3.1	3.0	3.1	3.4[6]	2.9	2.8[4]
HR systems educate business leaders about their talent decisions	2.4	2.4	2.8	2.7	2.2	2.5
HR adds value by insuring compliance with rules, laws, and guidelines	3.4[6]	3.4	3.4	3.5[6]	3.2	3.0[1,4]
HR adds value by delivering high-quality professional practices and services	3.6[6]	3.8[6]	3.9[6]	3.6[6]	3.4[6]	2.9[1,2,3,4,5]
HR adds value by improving talent decisions inside and outside the HR function	3.5[6]	3.7[6]	3.6[6]	3.7[6]	3.2	2.9[1,2,3,4]

Response scale: 1 = Little or no extent; 2 = Some extent; 3 = Moderate extent; 4 = Great extent; 5 = Very great extent

[1,2,3,4,5,6] Significant differences between countries ($p \leq .05$).

not exemplary level of talent decision science in all these countries, with particular opportunities for improvement in how well HR systems educate business leaders about their decisions.

HR Decision Science Sophistication and HR's Role in Strategy

The correlation of the competition item with HR's role in strategy is significant among HR executives, but is non-significant for managers outside of HR (first row of Table 6.1). This is the opposite pattern that was revealed in the 2007 survey. It is wise not to over-interpret the results of this one-item finding, but the higher rating and lower correlation for managers may suggest that the 2010 sample saw the talent competition as the job of managers and not particularly related to a strategic HR role. In contrast, it appears that among HR executives, those responding in 2010 demonstrated a much stronger relationship between their perceptions of success in critical talent competitions and their perceptions of their strategic role.

The correlations between the HR decision science questions and the perception of HR's role in strategy in Table 6.1 show a somewhat similar pattern for HR executives and managers. Both samples show many significant and positive correlations between the ratings of the decision science items and HR's role in strategy. Generally, where decision science principles are rated highly, so is HR's role in strategy.

A few correlations fall below .30 in the HR sample, between ratings of business leader decision capability in non-HR areas (strategy, finance, and marketing), and between HR's value added through compliance. Yet, even these correlations are statistically significant, suggesting that in the present sample there is a general association between the perceived decision capability of HR and non-HR leaders, and HR's role in strategy.

These items also show some interesting differences from the pattern in the 2007 survey, particularly for non-HR leaders. In the 2007 sample and in 2004, the items measuring business leaders' prowess at decisions regarding business strategy, finance, and marketing were not significantly correlated with HR's role in strategy. As Table 6.1 shows, in 2010 all of these items revealed very strong correlations with HR's role in strategy, among the sample of managers, which suggests that managers who rate business leaders highly in any decision area (even those not associated with human capital) now also perceive a strong HR strategic role.

In general, most of the correlations for the manager sample were much higher than in 2007, suggesting a general increase in the degree to which managers outside of HR associate excellence in the HR decision science with HR's strategic role. Two exceptions stand out. The first exception has to do with the item in the top row of Table 6.1, the item that rated whether the organization excels in the talent competition. Here the correlation for HR executives was strong and significant, while it was non-significant in 2007. For the manager sample, the opposite pattern emerged. In the 2007 sample, the correlation between this item and HR's role in strategy was strong and significant among managers, while in 2010 it was non-significant. Have managers become less appreciative of HR's role in strategy as key to the organization's ability to compete in talent markets?

The second exception may provide some insight. It has to do with the item reflecting HR's value added through compliance with rules, laws, and guidelines. Though the HR executives results in Table 6.1 are similar to those in 2007 (no relationship), for managers this item was not significantly associated with HR's role in strategy in 2007 (Lawler and Boudreau 2009), while in 2010 it was quite strongly associated. These findings may reflect a renewed appreciation for the value of compliance-related contributions in the wake of new regulations and increased regulatory and investor scrutiny that resulted from the financial crisis of 2008–2009, as well as perhaps a less intensive focus on competing in talent markets due to the return of high levels of unemployment and a perception of fewer labor shortages.

As we noted in the previous analysis of the 2007 sample compared to the 2004 sample, it appears that managers outside of HR may be developing a stronger appreciation of the relationship between their sophistication and capability when it comes to HR decision science principles, and the strength of HR's role in strategy (Lawler and Boudreau 2009). Like the 2007 results, managers outside of HR may actually perceive this relationship more strongly than their HR counterparts, though both clearly see it. This is an important result because it suggests that managers may be starting to see that a strong strategic role for HR enhances their sophistication when it comes to decisions about HR and talent, and/or that when their sophistication is higher it is possible for HR to play a stronger strategic role. It is also notable that in the 2010 sample, HR's strategic role is much more strongly associated with adding value through compliance than in either 2004 or 2007.

We do not know the causal direction of the relationships with strategy involvement. These results might suggest that when organizations achieve high HR strategy involvement, HR executives and managers perceive themselves and their business leaders as better on all elements of the HR decision science. Further they perceive HR leaders to be better at talent segmentation and providing unique strategic insights.

This interpretation is consistent with the typical situation that we see in organizations, where a handful of HR leaders are highly skilled at talent segmentation and strategic insights. Often they developed this ability through fortuitous career opportunities to observe and participate in business strategy. This interpretation would support efforts to get HR leaders more involved in strategy, as a way to enhance the HR decision science.

The causal direction may also be that enhancing the decision science capability of managers outside of HR leads to HR strategic involvement. Our results suggest that some HR leaders are already "at the table" and have opportunities for full partnership in strategy development and implementation, but that both HR executives and other managers are not satisfied with HR's capability (average ratings in Table 6.1 are only at the moderate point on the scale). Improving the decision science capability of managers may make them more capable of effectively working with strategically involved HR leaders.

Strategic Focuses

The relationship between the extent to which organizations are pursuing different strategic focuses and the extent to which they perceive the different elements of a sophisticated HR decision science is shown in Table 6.3. Clearly, the pattern of significant associations varies greatly with different strategic focuses.

Table 6.3. Relationship of HR decision making to strategic focuses					
	Strategic Focuses				
Decision Making	**Growth**	**Information-Based Strategies**	**Knowledge-Based Strategies**	**Sustainability**	**Innovation**
We excel at competing for and with talent where it matters most to our strategic success	.19*	.38***	.51***	.24***	.44***
Business leaders' decisions that depend upon or affect human capital (e.g. layoffs, rewards, etc.) are as rigorous, logical, and strategically relevant as their decisions about resources such as money, technology, and customers	.16*	.47***	.49***	.34***	.44***
Business leaders understand and use sound principles when making decisions about:					
1. Motivation	.20**	.32***	.43***	.29***	.35***
2. Development and learning	.11	.47***	.54***	.34***	.45***
3. Culture	.11	.36***	.40***	.32***	.43***
4. Organization design	.13^t	.35***	.44***	.23**	.42***
5. Business strategy	.24***	.33***	.38***	.29***	.48***
6. Finance	.08	.13^t	.23**	.12	.21**
7. Marketing	.17*	.19*	.34***	.21**	.35***
HR leaders have a good understanding about where and why human capital makes the biggest difference in their business	.16*	.41***	.48***	.38***	.46***
Business leaders have a good understanding about where and why human capital makes the biggest difference in their business	.14^t	.35***	.48***	.31***	.41***
HR systems educate business leaders about their talent decisions	.19**	.39***	.48***	.29***	.36***
HR adds value by insuring compliance with rules, laws, and guidelines	.06	.29***	.20**	.16*	.21**
HR adds value by delivering high-quality professional practices and services	.18*	.44***	.47***	.30***	.44***
HR adds value by improving talent decisions inside and outside the HR function	.20**	.35***	.49***	.26***	.43***
Significance level: $^t p \le .10$; $^* p \le .05$; $^{**} p \le .01$; $^{***} p \le .001$					

Excellence in competing for talent and the extent to which HR decisions by business leaders are made with the same rigor as decisions about other key resources are correlated with all strategic focuses in the 2010 sample. This is somewhat different from 2007, when the item about excellence in competing for talent was correlated only with knowledge-based strategies. The broader array of significant correlations suggests that there may be a wider appreciation of the importance of talent competition and talent decision sophistication among business leaders now than there was in 2007. This is reinforced by the results suggesting that managers associate their talent sophistication with HR's strategic role, more than in 2007.

The correlations are consistently lowest between the HR decision-making items and the pursuit of a growth strategy. The relatively lower correlations for the growth strategy are consistent with the results from 2007, though in the 2010 sample the correlations with the growth strategy were higher and more often significant than they were in 2007. Also, the correlations for the innovation strategy have generally increased compared to 2007, and are more generally statistically significant. In 2007 it appeared that pursuing innovation was not strongly associated with excellence in the human capital decision science, but in 2010 this has changed. It may be that the significance of high-quality human capital decisions for innovation has become more apparent.

The results for items reflecting HR leaders' and business leaders' understanding of talent segmentation (where and why human capital makes the biggest difference), as well as the three items reflecting how HR adds value, showed a significant pattern change in the 2010 sample compared to the 2007 sample. In 2007, these items were generally uncorrelated with the different strategic focuses, though a few correlations with the knowledge-based strategic emphasis were significant. In contrast, the 2010 data showed strong correlations with these items across all strategies except growth. Such a generalized shift suggests that the 2010 data show a stronger association between strategy and a basic understanding about how human capital contributes as well as the nature of HR's contributions.

It is interesting that pursuit of a growth strategy is not highly correlated with talent items. This suggests that organizations pursuing growth strategies have not internalized the connection between high-quality talent decisions and their growth strategies success. It is also notable that across all strategies, HR's ability to add value through compliance is not highly correlated with the strategic emphases, while delivering high-quality services and improving talent decisions on the other hand is. It may be that compliance is seen as "table stakes" rather than as a differentiating factor.

Management Approaches

Table 6.4 shows the relationship between the HR decision-making items and the five management approaches. In general, the results suggest that the level of HR decision science is much more strongly associated with the high-involvement management and sustainable approaches than with the other three approaches. This is consistent with the idea that in the high-involvement approach there is a major reliance on alignment, commitment, and trust at all levels of the organization, and that it demands business leaders attend to talent and human capital issues. It is also consistent with the idea that in sustainability-focused approaches there is a higher level of attention to outcomes that go beyond the traditional financial or competitive growth outcomes. This approach gives attention to the organization's reputation among current and potential employees, labor practices, etc. It may be possible in other approaches to rely on a more traditional approach in which HR has the primary

Table 6.4. Relationship of HR decision making to management approach					
	Management Approach				
Decision Making	**Bureaucratic**	**Low-Cost Operator**	**High Involvement**	**Global Competitor**	**Sustainable**
We excel at competing for and with talent where it matters most to our strategic success	–.30***	–.25***	.50***	.25***	.34***
Business leaders' decisions that depend upon or affect human capital (e.g. layoffs, rewards, etc.) are as rigorous, logical, and strategically relevant as their decisions about resources such as money, technology, and customers	–.19*	–.19*	.40***	.09	.38***
Business leaders understand and use sound principles when making decisions about:					
1. Motivation	–.18*	–.18*	.40***	.20**	.35***
2. Development and learning	–.13ᵗ	–.14ᵗ	.43***	.06	.35***
3. Culture	–.24**	–.23**	.45***	.12	.36***
4. Organization design	–.13ᵗ	–.19*	.30***	.14ᵗ	.36***
5. Business strategy	–.24**	–.14ᵗ	.37***	.26***	.37***
6. Finance	–.17*	–.09	.22**	.08	.15*
7. Marketing	–.21**	–.03	.23**	.14ᵗ	.21**
HR leaders have a good understanding about where and why human capital makes the biggest difference in their business	–.29***	–.19*	.40***	.16*	.40***
Business leaders have a good understanding about where and why human capital makes the biggest difference in their business	–.24***	–.16*	.38***	.19**	.36***
HR systems educate business leaders about their talent decisions	–.08	–.10	.25***	.17*	.31***
HR adds value by insuring compliance with rules, laws, and guidelines	–.15ᵗ	–.04	.17*	.07	.21**
HR adds value by delivering high-quality professional practices and services	–.29***	–.17*	.46***	.06	.31***
HR adds value by improving talent decisions inside and outside the HR function	–.30***	–.18*	.45***	.13ᵗ	.27***
Significance level: ᵗ $p \leq .10$; * $p \leq .05$; ** $p \leq .01$; *** $p \leq .001$					

responsibility for talent management, and is the repository of the decision-making principles, with business leaders outside of HR generally delegating talent issues to HR.

In the 2007 sample, the results showed a general pattern of negative correlations between most of the HR decision science items with the bureaucratic and the low-cost operator approaches. However, those negative correlations were not statistically significant. In Table 6.4, we see that in the 2010 data those relationships are stronger. Table 6.4 clearly shows that an emphasis on bureaucratic or low-cost operator strategies is generally negatively associated with all the HR decision science elements, while those elements are generally significantly and positively associated with the high-involvement, global competitor, and sustainable strategies.

Low-cost operator strategies place a premium on efficiency and low overhead, which often means very lean budgets for HR investments, particularly those seen as overhead. It also means little focus on talent except when considering labor costs. Thus, for HR executives in such organizations, the consequences of a least-cost possible approach to talent may mean being a poor competitor for talent.

For organizations that approach management with a bureaucratic model, we surmise that issues of human capital and workforce management are delegated to a formal human resources function, and are managed largely through formal systems. This is not to say that such systems are unsophisticated or inattentive to human capital issues, but they are generally not as much designed to enhance talent decisions as they are to assure that proper processes are followed. This is somewhat supported by the fact that the item assessing whether HR adds value through compliance is less negatively correlated than other items with the low-cost operator and bureaucratic management approaches.

It is interesting to note that the items reflecting business leader facility with the traditional business disciplines of finance and marketing (6 and 7) show roughly the same correlation pattern as the items that reflect talent disciplines (1 to 4), for the low-cost operator, bureaucratic, and global competitor management approaches. Yet, for the high-involvement and sustainable approaches, the traditional business items have much lower correlations than the talent items. This suggests that the high-involvement and sustainable approaches make demands on business leaders for deeper capability in talent decisions overall, and in the specific talent disciplines. If there was simply a general pattern of perceptions that business leaders in high-involvement and sustainable organizations must be good at everything, we would see the same pattern we see in the more traditional business disciplines; but we do not. Facility with traditional disciplines seems to be a ticket to the game in all approaches, but talent-related facility seems more important in high-involvement and sustainable approaches.

The item regarding whether HR systems educate business leaders on the quality of their decisions shows an interesting pattern. It has non-significant correlations with the bureaucratic and low-cost operator approaches, but strong positive correlations with the high-involvement and sustainable approaches, and low but significant correlations with the global competitor approach. This reinforces the premise that in high-involvement and sustainable approaches the importance and emphasis on human capital as a key to success creates a greater need for leaders both within and outside of HR to be educated about the quality of their human capital decisions. This item also showed significant changes between 2007 and 2010. It was largely uncorrelated with any of the management approaches in the 2007 sample. Thus, it appears that the 2010 sample distinguishes more clearly where educating business leaders contributes to particular management approaches.

The correlations for how HR adds value generally follow the patterns of the other items with strong positive correlations for the high-involvement and sustainable approaches, moderate for the global competitor approach, and negative for the bureaucratic and low-cost operator approaches. The pattern suggests that bureaucratic and low-cost operator approaches actually engender a decreasing emphasis on HR value through services and decisions, while the other three approaches increase the emphasis on this sort of value.

Finally, it is notable that the global competitor approach seems to consistently fall between the strong positive human capital decision emphasis of the high-involvement and sustainable approaches, and the strong negative human capital decision emphasis of the bureaucratic and low-cost operator approaches. This is consistent with the 2007 survey. We surmise that the global competitor approach may require a combination of bureaucracy and cost-control to manage far-flung and diverse operations, and remain cost-competitive in some markets, with the need to use more high-involvement and sustainable approaches in other markets. This broad focus may contribute to the midlevel correlations that we see in Table 6.4.

Conclusion

HR executives and managers rate the human capital decision making both inside and outside of HR as moderately effective. Thus, there is significant room for improvement. That said, business leaders rate the quality of talent decision making significantly more positively than do their HR counterparts. We suspect this rating is the result of a combination of HR managers' tendency to be self-critical about their strategic contribution, and a very real lack of understanding among non-HR managers of the richness and analytical knowledge that exist concerning labor markets, human capital, organization design, and organizational behavior. In other words, they do not know how good the decisions could be.

A significant finding is the strong association between business leader talent decision sophistication and HR's role in strategy, both among HR executives and managers. It would appear that leaders outside of HR are increasingly recognizing the synergy between HR's strategic role and their own ability to make strong decisions about talent and HR.

The decision science facility of organizations appears to vary with the strategy they pursue. It is higher when pursuing information-based, knowledge-based, innovation, and sustainability strategies than growth strategies. Unlike the 2007 sample, where only the high-involvement approach to management was consistently correlated with talent decision sophistication, the 2010 sample revealed a much stronger correlation with high-involvement approaches. It also showed an equally strong correlation with the sustainable approach and a negative relationship with the use of the bureaucratic and low-cost approaches. This suggests that business leader sophistication and HR contribution is higher in strategies where there is a strong line-of-sight between human capital and business outcomes and where managers' talent decisions are clearly tied to business and strategic results. High-involvement and sustainable organizations may create a culture and values that emphasize not just the capability of HR to manage the workforce well, but that it is the responsibility of all leaders to do so.

Generally, our findings continue to argue strongly for the strategic value of organizations having a strong human capital decision support capacity both within and outside their HR functions. There is much room for improvement, as the average ratings of decision quality in 2010 were still close to the midpoint of the scale, as they were in earlier surveys. The 2010 results provide strong evidence of the value of improving the decision science capacity in organizations, particularly those pursuing management approaches and strategies that are workforce-intensive and/or focused on sustainability.

CHAPTER 7

Design of the HR Organization

The organizational and operational approaches employed by an HR function have a major impact on what it is able to do and how well it can perform. For the purpose of this research study, practices and structures were studied that have been suggested as potential facilitators of HR becoming more of a business partner and, in some cases, a strategic partner (Ulrich and Brockbank 2005). The approaches studied were grouped into four scales based on a statistical analysis. The items and the U.S. mean responses to the items are shown in Table 7.1.

Organization Design

The organization design practices used the most by HR are those concerned with decentralization and HR service units. A comparison of the 1995 and 2010 results shows there has been a significant increase in the

Table 7.1. HR organization, USA only							
	Means						**Correlation with HR Role in Strategy**
HR Organization	**1995[1]**	**1998[2]**	**2001[3]**	**2004[4]**	**2007[5]**	**2010[6]**	
HR Service Units	**3.0[4,5,6]**	**3.2**	**3.3**	**3.5[1]**	**3.5[1]**	**3.4[1]**	**.15***
Centers of excellence provide specialized expertise	2.5[2,3,4,5,6]	3.1[1]	3.1[1]	3.3[1]	3.4[1]	3.3[1]	.19*
Administrative processing is centralized in shared services units	3.5	3.4	3.4	3.7	3.5	3.5	.07
Decentralization	**3.3[6]**	**3.3[6]**	**3.3[6]**	**3.1**	**3.1**	**2.9[1,2,3]**	**.02**
Decentralized HR generalists support business units	3.6	3.9	4.0[6]	3.9	3.7	3.6[3]	.12[t]
HR practices vary across business units	2.9[3,4,5,6]	2.6	2.6[1]	2.3[1]	2.5[1]	2.3[1]	−.13[t]
Information Technology	**—**	**—**	**—**	**2.7**	**2.7**	**2.6**	**.15***
Transactional HR work is outsourced	—	2.3	2.3	2.5	2.4	2.3	.14[t]
Some transactional activities that used to be done by HR are done by employees on a self-service basis	—	2.3[4,5,6]	2.5[4,5,6]	2.9[2,3]	3.0[2,3]	2.9[2,3]	.17*
HR "advice" is available online for managers and employees	—	—	—	2.5	2.7	2.6	.07
HR Talent Development	**2.1**	**2.2**	**2.1**	**2.2**	**2.1**	**2.0**	**.32***
People rotate within HR	2.6	2.8	2.8	2.8	2.7	2.5	.33***
People rotate into HR	1.8	1.8	1.8	1.8	1.7	1.8	.26***
People rotate out of HR to other functions	1.8	1.9	1.9	1.9	1.8	1.8	.22**

Response scale: 1 = Little or no extent; 2 = Some extent; 3 = Moderate extent; 4 = Great extent; 5 = Very great extent
[1,2,3,4,5,6] Significant differences ($p \leq .05$) between years.
Significance level: [t] $p \leq .10$; * $p \leq .05$; ** $p \leq .01$; *** $p \leq .001$

use of specialized centers of excellence. Most of this change appears to have occurred between 1995 and 2004—there is little evidence of recent change.

A particularly popular practice from 1995 to 2010 is to have decentralized generalists who support the business units of a company. This configuration is a possible way to position HR as a business partner by getting it "close" to the customers. It, too, has not increased in popularity since 1995.

The use of corporate centers of excellence complements the use of decentralized generalists by giving them a source of expert help. Growth in the use of centers of excellence is consistent with the idea of HR being a business partner since it can provide a higher level of business-relevant HR expertise. Having a processing center can help HR be a business partner as well since it can free HR professionals from doing administrative work.

There is a relatively low rating of the degree to which HR practices vary across business units. It is lower in 2010 than it was in 1995. This finding suggests that while there may be dedicated HR leaders supporting businesses, their role is not to tailor HR practices to those businesses, but rather to work with centers of excellence and HR service units in order to deliver common services to their parts of the organization.

The use of common practices most likely reflects efforts to simplify and to achieve scale leverage in some HR activities, and the tendency for companies to be in fewer unrelated businesses. There are economies of scale to be gained when corporations use the same HR practices in all their units. This is particularly true in the case of transactions and the creation of IT-based self-service HR activities.

The information technology practices show moderate to low use rates and little change in their use rates. One change is worth noting. There is an increase in the degree to which HR transactional activities are done on a self-service basis. This most likely is because the greater availability of HRISs allows for web-based self-service and it can deliver cost savings.

The HR talent management practices are the least used practices shown in Table 7.1. Employee rotation into and out of HR in particular is used infrequently. The lack of rotation is potentially a major problem for the HR function because it means that its members are likely to remain a separate group with a unique perspective, and not be involved in or deeply knowledgeable about the business. There also appears to be relatively little rotation within HR, a practice that creates silo careers and does little to help HR employees develop an understanding of the total HR function.

There are a number of significant relationships between the way that HR is organized and the role it plays in strategy. HR talent development, information technology, and HR service units are all significantly related to HR's role in strategy. This result confirms the point that HR needs to use information technology, have good talent, perform its own operations effectively, and have expertise and services that meet the needs of the business.

Having decentralized HR generalists has a low, but positive relationship to HR's role in strategy. This finding provides support for the view that this is a way to make HR more of a strategic partner by putting it close to the business. On the other hand, the negative correlation for having HR practices that vary across business units suggests that it works against HR playing a role in strategy. This most likely is because it typically exists when there is not a strong corporate HR function.

International

The international data on HR organizations are in Table 7.2. The results for China are different from those of the other countries, especially the U.S. It is a low user of almost all of the organization structures and practices.

Table 7.2. HR organization, by country						
	Means					
HR Organization	USA[1]	Canada[2]	Australia[3]	Europe[4]	UK[5]	China[6]
HR Service Units	**3.4[4,6]**	**3.5[4,6]**	**3.3[6]**	**2.9[1,2,6]**	**2.9[6]**	**2.5[1,2,3,4,5]**
Centers of excellence provide specialized expertise	3.3[6]	3.5[6]	3.0[6]	2.9[6]	2.8	2.2[1,2,3,4]
Administrative processing is centralized in shared services units	3.5[4,6]	3.5[6]	3.6[6]	3.0[1]	3.1	2.7[1,2,3]
Decentralization	**2.9**	**2.8**	**2.8**	**3.1[6]**	**2.8**	**2.7[4]**
Decentralized HR generalists support business units	3.6[6]	3.6	3.5	3.6[6]	3.2	3.1[1,4]
HR practices vary across business units	2.3	2.0[4]	2.2	2.6[2]	2.5	2.4
Information Technology	**2.6[2,5,6]**	**2.0[1]**	**2.4**	**2.3[6]**	**2.0[1]**	**2.0[1,4]**
Transactional HR work is outsourced	2.3[2,4,5,6]	1.7[1]	1.7	1.9[1]	1.8[1]	1.6[1]
Some transactional activities that used to be done by HR are done by employees on a self-service basis	2.9[2,5,6]	2.4[1]	2.7	2.6[6]	2.2[1]	2.2[1,4]
HR "advice" is available online for managers and employees	2.6[6]	2.0	2.8	2.5	2.2	2.2[1]
HR Talent Development	**2.0**	**1.9**	**2.0**	**2.1**	**1.7**	**2.1**
People rotate within HR	2.5	2.2	2.5	2.5	2.2	2.4
People rotate into HR	1.8	1.8	1.7	2.0	1.5	1.8
People rotate out of HR to other functions	1.8	1.6	1.7	1.8	1.5[6]	2.0[5]

Response scale: 1 = Little or no extent; 2 = Some extent; 3 = Moderate extent; 4 = Great extent; 5 = Very great extent

[1,2,3,4,5,6] Significant differences between countries ($p \leq .05$).

The results are similar for the rest of the countries with a few interesting exceptions. Outsourcing transactional work is more common in the U.S. than in other countries. This may reflect the push that it has received from U.S.-based HR consulting firms (e.g. Aon Hewitt) and the large size of many U.S. firms (Lawler, Ulrich, Fitz-enz, and Madden 2004). The U.K. reports very low use of self-service HR transactional programs. This may be because organizations have not invested in the technology that is needed to make this happen. The U.K. also tends to be low on HR talent development, although most of the difference does not quite reach statistical significance.

The largest difference between China and the other countries is in HR service units. Centers of excellence are used much less frequently in China than in any other country. Administrative processing service units are used more frequently than in the other countries, but this difference is statistically significant only with respect to three countries. Information technology is used less by China than the U.S., but other countries share China's low use rate. This is one place where China is among the leaders: HR talent development. Chinese companies are particularly likely to rotate people out of HR.

Strategic Focuses

Table 7.3 shows the relationships between the strategic focuses and HR organization approaches. The use of service units is significantly associated with most of the strategic focuses, indicating the importance of bringing multiple sources of knowledge to bear on strategy implementation. HR talent development and information technology are even more strongly associated with multiple strategic focuses. Only decentralization is not related to multiple strategic focuses; thus it seems safe to conclude that the HR organization designs in Table 7.3 fit most organizations.

All of the strategic focuses are significantly associated with multiple HR organization practices. Knowledge-based and sustainability strategies

Table 7.3. Relationship of HR organization to strategic focuses					
	Strategic Focuses				
HR Organization	**Growth**	**Information-Based Strategies**	**Knowledge-Based Strategies**	**Sustainability**	**Innovation**
HR service units	.03	.20**	.32***	.21**	.25***
Decentralization	.21**	−.02	.02	.02	.11
Information technology	.17*	.34***	.26***	.15*	.40***
HR talent development	.14ᵗ	.35***	.48***	.24***	.42***
Significance level: ᵗ$p \leq .10$; *$p \leq .05$; **$p \leq .01$; ***$p \leq .001$					

Table 7.4. Relationship of HR organization to management approach					
	Management Approach				
HR Organization	**Bureaucratic**	**Low-Cost Operator**	**High Involvement**	**Global Competitor**	**Sustainable**
HR service units	–.00	–.09	.14^t	.18*	.11
Decentralization	–.16*	.04	.07	.24***	–.01
Information technology	.09	–.05	.18*	.19*	.16*
HR talent development	–.13^t	–.11	.34***	.21**	.27***
Significance level: $^t p \leq .10$; $* p \leq .05$; $** p \leq .01$; $*** p \leq .001$					

show the strongest relationships to the HR organization practices. Given their reliance on talent, this is hardly surprising, since these practices are supportive of good talent management.

Management Approach

There are significant relationships between an organization's management approach and the structure of its HR organization (Table 7.4). Not surprisingly, the high-involvement approach is related to the development of HR talent and the use of information technology. Also related to them are the global competitor and sustainable approaches, with the strongest relationships involving the global competitor approach. This is not surprising, since these approaches rely heavily on talent as a source of competitive advantage. The global competitor approach is significantly related to all of the HR organization designs and practices. This suggests that its talent management approach creates a clear mandate for how HR organization should be designed.

Future Organization Design

In 2004 and again in 2007, HR executives were asked to indicate how they see the HR function operating in the future (not asked for in 2010). The data suggest that some important shifts will occur in the way HR operates in the future (see Table 7.5). In both 2004 and 2007, teams and information technology received the highest ratings, indicating that these are viewed as likely and important practices for the future.

The highest rating for individual items went to self-service transactional activities, while a second information technology item (online advice) was tied with other items for the next highest rating. It is clear that organizations intend to use information technology to enable employees to serve themselves both when it comes to transactional activities and when it comes to advice. The results also suggest that organizations expected to make greater use of centers of excellence, service teams, shared service units, and decentralized generalists to support the business units.

Table 7.5. HR organization--future (questions on this table were not asked in 2010)			
	2004 Mean	2007 Mean	Correlation with HR Role in Strategy 2007
HR Teams	**2.5**	**2.5**	**.29****
Centers of excellence provide specialized expertise	2.6	2.5	.28**
HR teams provide service and support the business	2.6	2.5	.04
HR systems and policies are developed through joint line/HR task teams	2.4	2.5	.32***
Decentralization	**2.1**	**2.0**	**.08**
Decentralized HR generalists support business units	2.5	2.4	.07
HR practices vary across business units	1.7	1.6	−.09
Very small corporate staff—most HR managers and professionals are out in businesses	2.1	2.0	.16
Resource Efficiency	**2.4**	**2.4**	**.01**
Administrative processing is centralized in shared services units	2.6	2.4	.08
Low HR/employee ratio	2.2	2.3	−.00
Low cost of HR services	2.4	2.4	−.02
Information Technology	**2.5**	**2.5**	**.18ᵗ**
Transactional HR work Is outsourced	2.2	2.1	.12
Some transactional activities that used to be done by HR are done by employees on a self-service basis	2.8	2.7	.24*
HR "advice" is available online for managers and employees	2.4	2.5	.07
HR Talent Development	**2.0**	**2.1**	**.05**
People rotate within HR	2.3	2.5	.19*
People rotate into HR	1.9	2.0	.02
People rotate out of HR to other functions	1.9	2.0	.05
Hire from the outside for senior HR positions	1.9	2.0	−.10

Response scale: 1 = Not in our plans; 2 = Possible focus; 3 = An important future focus

Significance level: $^t p \leq .10$; $^* p \leq .05$; $^{**} p \leq .01$; $^{***} p \leq .001$

Plans to shift toward the greater use of centers of excellence, teams, and information technology and a greater emphasis on talent development in 2004 and 2007 were all associated with HR's having a more strategic role. A significant relationship with HR talent rotation probably indicates that when HR is involved in strategy, it recognizes the importance of developing people with a broad understanding of HR. The expected growth in the use of centers of excellence fits with the importance of having corporate expertise that can support the strategy development process. Growth in the use of joint task teams is one way to be sure that in the future HR systems will support the business strategy.

Given their correlation with strategic involvement, it is particularly disappointing that HR has not moved ahead with changes it said it would make in 2004 and 2007. They seem to be the right moves but not the ones that HR has made.

Conclusion

Overall, the results show relatively little change in the utilization of the HR organization design approaches studied. There has been a significant growth in teams and centers of excellence, changes that are related to HR's being more of a strategic partner. There also is a trend toward less utilization of HR practices that vary across business units and a greater emphasis on self-service HR practices. But we do not see greater adoption of such things as the career movement of individuals into and out of HR or joint line/HR task teams.

There are a number of important relationships between the characteristics of the HR organization and HR's role in strategy. These relationships are particularly important because they suggest what HR needs to do to become more of a strategic partner; namely, use information technology, establish centers of excellence, use joint task forces, and develop HR talent. Looking to the future, HR organizations have said they plan to use more teams and information technology and improve their efficiency, but so far they do not appear to have done it.

CHAPTER 8

Activities of the HR Organization

To get an in-depth look at the changes that are occurring in the role of HR, we asked whether the focus on and attention to a number of human resources activities has increased, stayed the same, or decreased over the past five to seven years. Our expectation when we began this research in 1995 was that there would be an increase in the focus on a number of HR activities, particularly those related to HR being more of a strategic partner.

HR Activity Levels

Data analyses show four clusters of human resources activities, with four activity items (executive compensation, HR metrics, HRISs, and unions relations) that do not cluster with any others. Table 8.1 shows these activities and how HR executives responded in 1995, 1998, 2001, 2004, 2007, and 2010. Just as they have in our previous surveys, in 2010 our respondents reported increasing their focus on all the items but one (scores higher than 3.0). As was true in 1998, 2001, 2004, and 2007, HR executives report not increasing their organization's focus on union relations. All the areas show a relatively similar amount of increase in 2010 (3.4 is the low and 3.8 is the high). It is hard to see how they can continuously increase the focus in all these areas. Perhaps our respondents are feeling a bit overwhelmed by the multiple demands they face and are reporting that they are facing more demands for performance in all these areas.

A comparison between the 2007 and 2010 data does show some differences in the amount of increase reported. Recruitment and selection shows a significantly lower rating in 2010 in comparison to 2007. This decrease undoubtedly was driven by the recession that began in 2008 and the end of the war for talent. The war received a great deal of attention during the previous ten years. A number of other decreases from 2004 and 2007 to 2010 were also most likely caused by the recession. Compensation and organization development are other areas that show a decrease from 2007 to 2010.

Table 8.1 also shows the correlations between the changes in focus on human resource activities and HR's role in strategy. Not surprisingly, the highest single correlation is between human capital forecasting and planning and HR's role in strategy. The relationship is strong, positive, and very interesting. It suggests that the two very much go together, although it doesn't tell us what the causal direction is. It could be that

HR Activities	Means						Correlation with HR Role in Strategy
	1995[1]	1998[2]	2001[3]	2004[4]	2007[5]	2010[6]	
Design & Organizational Development	—	3.8	3.9	3.9	3.9[6]	3.7[5]	**.38*****
Human capital forecasting and planning[a]	4.1[6]	3.9	4.0	4.1[6]	4.1[6]	3.8[145]	**.41*****
Organization development	4.0[6]	3.8	3.9	3.8	4.0	3.7[1]	**.24*****
Organization design	—	3.6	3.7	3.6	3.7	3.6	**.27*****
Compensation & Benefits	3.9[6]	3.7[4]	3.8	4.0[2,6]	3.8[6]	3.5[1,4,5]	**.18***
Compensation	3.9[6]	3.8	3.9[6]	3.9[6]	3.9	3.6[1,3,4]	**.20****
Benefits	3.9[2,3,6]	3.6[1,4]	3.6[1,4]	4.0[2,3,6]	3.7	3.5[1,4]	**.10**
Executive Compensation	—	—	—	—	—	3.8	**.28*****
Employee Development	—	—	3.6	3.8	3.8	3.6	**.36*****
Training/education	3.8[6]	3.5	3.7	3.7	3.7	3.5[1]	**.27*****
Management development	3.9	3.8	3.8	4.0	3.9	3.7	**.35*****
Performance appraisal	3.8	3.5[4]	3.7	3.9[2]	3.8	3.7	**.10**
Career planning	3.3	3.4	3.3	3.3	3.4	3.4	**.22****
Competency/Talent assessment	—	—	3.7	3.8	4.0	3.8	**.29*****
Recruitment & Selection	3.4[2,3,4,5]	3.9[1]	3.8[1,5]	3.8[1]	4.1[1,3,6]	3.6[5]	**.22****
Recruitment	3.3[2,3,4,5,6]	3.9[1]	3.8[1,5]	3.8[1,5]	4.2[1,3,4,6]	3.6[1,5]	**.18***
Selection	3.5[5]	3.8	3.7	3.8	4.0[1,6]	3.6[5]	**.22****
HR Metrics & Analytics	—	—	—	3.8	3.9	3.8	**.33*****
HR Information Systems	4.1	4.1[6]	4.0	4.0	3.9	3.8[2]	**.13[t]**
Union Relations	3.1[3]	2.9	2.7[1]	3.0	2.8	2.9	**−.06**

Response scale: 1 = Greatly decreased; 3 = Stayed the same; 5 = Greatly increased

[a] "HR planning" prior to 2007

[1,2,3,4,5,6] Significant differences ($p \leq .05$) between years.

Significance level: [t] $p \leq .10$; * $p \leq .05$; ** $p \leq .01$; *** $p \leq .001$

when HR is involved in strategy formulation, it is because it is involved in human capital planning, or the reverse. One possibility is that in some organizations the direction goes one way and in others it goes the reverse. Our guess is that the most prevalent is involvement in strategy leading to more emphasis on human capital. Regardless of which causal direction exists in most companies, if HR wants to be an effective strategic partner, the existence of this correlation makes a strong case for HR developing a high level of competency in organization design, organization development, forecasting, and strategic planning.

Four of the employee development items show significant correlations. Again, it is impossible to tell what is the causal relationship, but our guess is that it is from being involved in strategy to increasing the focus on employee development. New strategies often require new competencies, and HR is in a position to make this point when they are part of the strategy development process.

The question on HR metrics and analytics, which was new in 2004, provides interesting data. It shows a relatively high level of increased focus and a relatively strong correlation with HR's role in strategy. The finding of a positive relationship supports the point that metrics and analytics can be key inputs to both the development of strategy and the successful assessment of strategy implementation. They also often provide a signal of rigor to leaders outside of HR, one that may result in more HR involvement in strategy and business processes.

International

The international data are in Table 8.2. They are very similar to the U.S. data for 2010. In this case nationality does not seem to make a great deal of difference, with two exceptions. Union relations does get a higher rating in Canada, Europe, and China undoubtedly because of the strength of the union movement in these countries. China also shows a few other significant differences. It has seen much less increase in the focus on HR metrics and analytics, and on assessment.

Strategic Focuses

Table 8.3 shows the relationships between HR activities and the five strategic focuses. There are some important relationships here. Strategies that focus on knowledge are significantly related to an increased focus on all the HR activities except for union relations. This is not surprising since knowledge-based strategies depend on having the right talent and effectively developing and managing it.

The results for information-based strategies are generally similar to those for knowledge-based ones; both are strongly related to employee development activities. The most logical explanation for this relationship is that it exists because human capital is a particularly key aspect of an organization's performance capability. In order to execute either of these types of strategic focuses, an organization needs to build its human capital. Thus, successful efforts that focus on these strategies require increased attention to human capital.

Sustainability and innovation are both related to employee development and organization design and development. This follows logically from the need these strategies create for talent and performance. Both require HR organizations that develop talent and focus on organization development (Lawler and Worley 2011).

Table 8.2. Change in focus on human resource activities, by country

HR Activities	Means					
	USA[1]	Canada[2]	Australia[3]	Europe[4]	UK[5]	China[6]
Design & Organizational Development	**3.7**	**3.9**	**3.8**	**3.7**	**3.8**	**3.6**
Human capital forecasting and planning[a]	3.8[6]	4.0[6]	3.6	3.8	3.5	3.5[12]
Organization development	3.7	4.0	4.0	3.7	3.9	3.7
Organization design	3.6	3.7	3.8	3.6	3.9	3.6
Compensation & Benefits	**3.5**	**3.8**	**3.8**	**3.7**	**3.6**	**3.8**
Compensation	3.6[6]	3.9	3.7	3.8	3.7	3.9[1]
Benefits	3.5	3.7	3.8	3.6	3.6	3.6
Executive Compensation	**3.8**	**3.9**	**3.7**	**3.9**	**3.7**	**3.9**
Employee Development	**3.6**	**3.9**	**3.9**	**3.8**	**3.8**	**3.6**
Training/education	3.5[6]	3.8	3.8	3.6	3.7	3.9
Management development	3.7	4.1	4.2[6]	3.9	3.9	3.7[3]
Performance appraisal	3.7	3.9	4.0	4.0	4.0	3.8
Career planning	3.4	3.5	3.3	3.4	3.5	3.3
Competency/Talent assessment	3.8[6]	3.9[6]	3.9[6]	4.0[6]	3.8[6]	3.4[1,2,3,4,5]
Recruitment & Selection	**3.6[6]**	**3.8**	**3.8**	**3.5[6]**	**3.8**	**3.9[1,4]**
Recruitment	3.6[6]	3.8	3.8	3.6[6]	3.8	4.0[1,4]
Selection	3.6	3.8	3.8	3.5[6]	3.8	3.8[4]
HR Metrics & Analytics	**3.8[6]**	**3.7[6]**	**3.7[6]**	**3.8[6]**	**3.8[6]**	**3.2[1,2,3,4,5]**
HR Information Systems	**3.8**	**3.8**	**3.7**	**3.9**	**3.7**	**3.7**
Union Relations	**2.9[2]**	**3.4[1,5]**	**3.0**	**3.3**	**2.8[2]**	**3.2**

Response scale: 1 = Greatly decreased; 3 = Stayed the same; 5 = Greatly increased

[a] "HR planning" prior to 2007

[1,2,3,4,5,6] Significant differences between countries ($p \le .05$).

Table 8.3. Relationship of HR activities change to strategic focuses

HR Activities	Strategic Focuses				
	Growth	Information-Based Strategies	Knowledge-Based Strategies	Sustainability	Innovation
Design & organizational development	.15*	.26***	.36***	.28***	.22**
Compensation & benefits	.10	.08	.21**	.09	.10
Employee development	.14[t]	.31***	.47***	.24***	.26***
Recruitment & selection	.13[t]	.20**	.28***	.11	.18*
HR metrics & analytics	.04	.22**	.21**	.08	.17*
HR information systems	−.01	.22***	.13[t]	.05	.02
Union relations	.01	.02	.02	−.04	−.04

Significance level: [t] $p \le .10$; * $p \le .05$; ** $p \le .01$; *** $p \le .001$

It is somewhat surprising that the growth focus is not strongly related to an increase in any of the HR activities. Growth, in particular, creates a number of challenges for HR and might be expected to be related to recruitment and selection. It is weakly related to employee development and to recruitment, which may reflect the need to develop competencies, particularly management and leadership skills, more quickly in a growing organization. Apparently, these two business strategies do not entail the kinds of changes that create the need for increased HR focuses.

All of the HR activities show some significant relationships to the strategic focuses except for union relations, which is not significantly related to any of them. This suggests that any strategic focus is likely to impact much of what HR does, once again affirming the important relationship between people and strategy.

Design and organization development is the only activity that is significantly related to all five strategic focuses. The employee development focus is related to four. The most likely cause of these relationships is that they are key HR activities regardless of the strategy adopted. They need to support these strategies in order for them to be effective. In some respects they are strategically neutral; they are likely to receive a decreasing focus only if there is no clear strategy.

Management Approach

There are some strong relationships between HR activities change and the management approach of companies (see Table 8.4). Not surprisingly, the bureaucratic approach and low-cost operator approach show a negative relationship to all of the activities except union relations.

Table 8.4. Relationship of HR activities change to management approach					
	Management Approach				
HR Activities	Bureaucratic	Low-Cost Operator	High Involvement	Global Competitor	Sustainable
Design & organizational development	−.25***	−.22**	.30***	.10	.13^t
Compensation & benefits	−.17*	−.04	.32***	−.11	.12
Employee development	−.24***	−.11	.43***	.02	.22**
Recruitment & selection	−.10	−.06	.20**	.05	.18*
HR metrics & analytics	−.26***	−.01	.27***	.04	.12
HR information systems	−.12	−.03	.09	−.03	.15*
Union relations	.08	.19*	.00	−.09	.11
Significance level: $^t p \leq .10$; $^* p \leq .05$; $^{**} p \leq .01$; $^{***} p \leq .001$					

People simply are not a major focus in bureaucratic and low-cost operator organizations unless they are disruptive. The high-involvement approach shows a positive relationship to five of the HR activities. The relationships to high involvement are not surprising. High-involvement organizations are talent focused and thus require HR functions that are broadly supportive of high-quality talent management.

Conclusion

Not surprisingly, HR executives report increases in the focus of their companies on almost all HR activities. In every survey we have done, HR executives have reported that they are more focused on organization design and development, and the data show that the more they are, the more likely they are to be involved in strategy. Particularly interesting is the increased activity in design and organizational development when the strategic focuses of information, knowledge, sustainability, and innovation are present. Organization design and development is an area that has not always been a focus of HR. It is, however, an area that is closely tied to organizational performance and business strategy. Providing expertise in this area appears to be a way for HR to become more of a business partner, particularly in information- and knowledge-based business. These same focuses are related to increased activity in employee development. Thus, regardless of their strategic focus, organizations that had strong ones increased all their HR activities except union relations.

CHAPTER 9

HR Metrics and Analytics: Uses and Comprehensiveness

Two one-liners are frequently used when HR measurement is discussed: "What's measured gets managed," and "Not everything that counts can be counted, and not everything that can be counted actually counts." The first has led business and HR leaders to strive for more measurement, in a belief that measures will produce increased attention and understanding of human resource issues in organizations. The second caution is that simply because something can be measured does not mean that it should be a major force. It may not "count," in terms of organizational goals. A key decision for HR and business leaders is what to measure and how measures will be used in decision making.

Organizations can collect and make use of three major HR measurement types: measures of efficiency, effectiveness, and impact (Boudreau and Ramstad 2007; Cascio and Boudreau 2011). Efficiency refers to measuring the resources used by HR programs, such as cost-per-hire. Effectiveness refers to the outcomes produced by HR activities, such as learning from training. Impact refers to measuring the business or strategic value created by the activity, such as higher sales.

All three types of measures can be useful, and indeed measuring all three is often required to fully understand how HR investments affect organizational performance. Each calls for somewhat different metrics and analytics. They can complement each other when they are used together.

Cost-benefit analysis most resembles efficiency and has often been referred to as the "holy grail" of HR measurement; it certainly has drawn the attention of many HR leaders and consultants. Understanding the return-on-investment of HR programs is similar to effectiveness and is highly useful, but may tell little about the synergies among HR programs and the overall value of measures in enhancing decisions about human capital, which is impact. A combination of efficiency, effectiveness, and impact measures is likely to be the most effective approach, but this combination does not exist in most organizations.

Efficiency measures are basic to the HR function, and they connect readily to the existing accounting system. There is growing attention being given to measuring effectiveness by focusing on such things as turnover, attitudes, and bench strength. Rarely do organizations consider impact (for example, the relative effect of improving the quality of different talent pools on organizational effectiveness). More important, rarely is HR measurement specifically directed to vital talent "segments," where decisions are most important. As we point out elsewhere in this book, our evidence suggests that the evolution of HR measurement, toward more comprehensive and analytically rigorous approaches based on a science for human capital, is very likely a requirement for HR to progress in such areas as strategic partnership and HRISs, as well as measurement and analytics.

Metrics and Analytics Use

Table 9.1 shows the pattern of HR's use of metrics and analytics for the U.S. sample. The results suggest that most of the measurement and

Table 9.1. HR analytics and metrics use, USA only

Measures	Percentages					Means[a]		2010 Correlation with HR Role in Strategy
	Not Currently Being Considered	Planning For	Being Built	Yes, Have Now		2007	2010	
				2007	2010			
Efficiency								
Measure the financial efficiency of HR operations (e.g. cost-per-hire, time-to-fill, training costs)?	11.5	15.9	18.7	50.5	53.8	3.1	3.1	.28***
Collect metrics that measure the cost of providing HR programs and processes?	10.6	25.0	21.1	39.8	43.3	3.0	3.0	.17*
Benchmark analytics and measures against data from outside organizations (e.g. Saratoga, Mercer, Hewitt, etc.)?	19.2	15.9	9.9	48.5	54.9	3.0	3.0	.19**
Effectiveness								
Use HR dashboards or scorecards?	8.8	17.0	22.5	37.8	51.6	2.9	3.2[1]	.30***
Measure the specific effects of HR programs (such as learning from training, motivation from rewards, validity of tests, etc.)?	23.1	28.6	15.9	19.2	32.4	2.4	2.6	.24***
Have the capability to conduct cost-benefit analyses (also called utility analyses) of HR programs?	26.4	25.3	22.0	18.4	26.4	2.3	2.5	.17*
Impact								
Measure the business impact of HR programs and processes?	17.7	27.1	27.6	20.4	27.6	2.6	2.7	.23**
Measure the quality of the talent decisions made by non-HR leaders?	39.6	28.0	14.3	10.1	18.1	1.9	2.1	.06
Measure the business impact of high versus low performance in jobs?	40.1	30.8	11.0	12.1	18.1	2.0	2.1	.14[t]

[a] Responses scored: 4 = Yes, have now; 3 = Being built; 2 = Planning for; 1 = Not currently being considered

[1] Significant differences ($p \leq .05$) between years.

Significance level: [t] $p \leq .10$; * $p \leq .05$; ** $p \leq .01$; *** $p \leq .001$

analytics elements remain relatively rare HR practices, with only four of them rated as "Yes, have now," for more than 40 percent of organizations. Three of these are clearly in the efficiency category. They include the financial efficiency of HR operations, the costs of HR programs, as well as creating traditional HR data benchmarks, which we include in efficiency because the vast majority of such benchmarks reflect costs and activity levels. The percentage of organizations that report having the three efficiency measures is slightly higher in 2010 than in 2007, but as Table 9.1 shows, it is still below 55 percent. The fourth item, rated as "have now" by 51.6 percent of organizations, is an effectiveness item, reflecting the use of dashboards or scoreboards.

Measures of effectiveness and impact are rarer than efficiency measures. Beyond scorecards, the other effectiveness measures are used by less than 35 percent of organizations, including the ability to measure the effects of specific HR programs and the ability to do cost-benefit analysis of HR programs.

Perhaps predictably, measures of impact are the least frequently used. Though about 27.6 percent of organizations report having measures of the business impact of HR programs and processes, only 18.1 percent have measures of the business impact of performance differences in jobs and actually measure the quality of talent decisions. The latter finding reinforces our results in Chapter 6, which showed that while HR and business leaders believe they are moderately good at talent decisions, HR systems generally do not educate leaders about their decision quality.

Indeed, even 27.6 percent may be an overestimate of the use of business impact measures. Our experience suggests that when HR leaders are asked if they measure "business impact," they often interpret it to mean the effects of specific programs on workforce changes such as skills, competencies, and attitudes, rather than the effects of such programs on business outcomes such as financial performance and sustainable effectiveness.

The results in Table 9.1 show some changes from the 2007 data. There are increases in the use of effectiveness and impact measures. The largest increase is in the use of HR scorecard (37.8 vs. 51.6 percent) and measures of the effects of HR programs (19.2 vs. 32.4 percent). These are measures that organizations said they were developing in 2007, so it is not surprising that they now have them and are using them. That said, a high proportion of the 2007 sample (31.6 percent) also said they were building the ability to measure the business impact of HR programs and processes, yet those saying "yes, have now" went from 20.4 to 27.6 percent between 2007 and 2010.

Use and Role in Strategy

The relationship between the use of HR metrics and HR's role in strategy is shown in Table 9.1. Most of the measurement items are significantly positively correlated with greater HR involvement in strategy. The non-significant measurement elements are two impact measures: the quality of talent measures and the business impact of jobs.

Measures of financial efficiency and program cost are strongly correlated with HR's strategic role. They focus on efficiency, but often draw on information from accounting reports. Measures of specific HR program effects are easy to understand because they associate particular programs with tangible outcomes such as performance ratings, turnover levels, or engagement scores. As a result, their existence helps to establish HR as business focused and a credible contributor to business strategy decisions. Overall, organizations that have efficiency measures rate HR's strategic role more highly. This was also true in the 2007 sample, though the 2010 sample associated benchmarks more strongly with strategic role than in 2007.

All three of the effectiveness measurement types are significantly related to HR's role in strategy, yet only scorecards are used by over 50 percent of companies; the other two are used by less than 33 percent. These proportions are higher than in 2007, when dashboards were used by less than 40 percent of companies and the other two items were in use by less than 20 percent. The level of correlation with HR's role in strategy in 2010 was substantially greater for the effectiveness measures, with the exception of measuring the specific effects of HR programs.

With regard to measuring impact, only the measures of the business impact of HR programs item significantly related to HR's role in strategy in Table 9.1. The percentages of "have now" for all three impact measures were somewhat higher in 2010 than in 2007. Measuring the quality of talent decisions and the value of performance differences in jobs are used by less than 20 percent of the companies, the lowest-rated measurement items. This was also true in 2007, when less than 15 percent of companies reported using these measures. A significant difference between the 2007 and 2010 samples was that in 2007 the correlations between the use of the impact measures in the bottom two rows were statistically significantly related to HR's role in strategy, while these correlations were non-significant in 2010.

We cannot say definitively that increased use of measures leads to higher HR strategy involvement, but there may be significant opportunities for HR to enhance its strategic involvement through greater use of these measures. Such measures are fundamental to the evolution of a more sophisticated decision science, as the historical evolution of marketing and finance have shown (Boudreau and Ramstad 2007). We believe that impact metrics can be both a precursor and a result of HR strategic involvement.

The 2010 results suggest that since 2007 the association with HR's strategic role has decreased for measures of the quality of non-HR leader talent decisions and understanding where performance differences are pivotal to strategic success. This may reflect the effects of the economic downturn, which also appears to have generally enhanced the association with HR's role in strategy of more traditional HR roles such as compliance and service delivery. It remains to be seen whether this is a trend toward defining HR more traditionally—rather than in terms of its decision support capability—or a short-term manifestation of recent events.

The finding that at least one measure in each category has a statistically significant relationship with HR's involvement in business strategy supports the proposition that the most effective measurement systems combine impact, effectiveness, and efficiency. The more common measurement elements (financial efficiency and efficiency) have high correlations, suggesting that they have credibility with business leaders. They may represent an attractive first step in the measurement journey. HR leaders then can move on to become more strategically effective by using and communicating the value of the less-common HR measures (such as the quality of talent decisions).

International Use

Table 9.2 shows the results for the use of HR metrics and analytics across the different national samples. All countries reflect the general pattern seen in the U.S. sample, that efficiency measures are more utilized than the effectiveness measures and impact measures. This pattern occurs in the U.S. sample, primarily due to significantly more developed efficiency measures. It occurs in Canada and Australia due to less development of impact measures. It is least pronounced in the China sample, where the averages are much more similar across the three measurement types. The use of dashboards or scorecards is significantly less developed in China relative to the U.S., Canada, and the U.K. Measures of the business impact of HR programs are rated as most developed in the U.S. and U.K. samples, particularly when compared to Europe and Canada.

Overall, the conclusion from all countries is that the average ratings are virtually all less than 3.0, suggesting that for the most part HR measures are in the planning or building stages on a global basis. The most pronounced cross-country pattern is that the China sample has very similar

Table 9.2. HR analytics and metrics use, by country

Measures	Means[a]					
	USA[1]	Canada[2]	Australia[3]	Europe[4]	UK[5]	China[6]
Efficiency						
Measure the financial efficiency of HR operations (e.g. cost-per-hire, time-to-fill, training costs)?	3.1[3,4,6]	2.8	2.3[1]	2.5[1]	3.0	2.6[1]
Collect metrics that measure the cost of providing HR programs and processes?	3.0[2,4,6]	2.3[1]	2.7	2.5[1]	2.5	2.5[1]
Benchmark analytics and measures against data from outside organizations (e.g. Saratoga, Mercer, Hewitt, etc.)?	3.0[6]	2.6	2.4	2.8	2.5	2.6[1]
Effectiveness						
Use HR dashboards or scorecards?	3.2[6]	3.0[6]	2.7	2.7	3.0[6]	2.3[1,2,5]
Measure the specific effects of HR programs (such as learning from training, motivation from rewards, validity of tests, etc.)?	2.6	2.2	2.0[6]	2.5	2.5	2.7[3]
Have the capability to conduct cost-benefit analyses (also called utility analyses) of HR programs?	2.5[4]	2.3	2.2	1.9[1,6]	2.4	2.3[4]
Impact						
Measure the business impact of HR programs and processes?	2.7[2,4]	2.0[1,3]	2.8[2,4]	2.1[1,3]	2.5	2.5
Measure the quality of the talent decisions made by non-HR leaders?	2.1	1.6[6]	1.8	1.8	2.1	2.2[2]
Measure the business impact of high versus low performance in jobs?	2.1	1.8[6]	1.6[6]	2.0	2.1	2.3[2,3]

[a]Responses scored: 4 = Yes, have now; 3 = Being built; 2 = Planning for; 1 = Not currently being considered

[1,2,3,4,5,6] Significant differences between countries ($p < .05$).

ratings for all three types of HR measures, at roughly 2.5 on the 4-point scale, while other countries showed a pattern of more use of measures of efficiency, moderate use of effectiveness measures, and the least use of impact measures. This may be due to the fact that HR in China has emerged more recently, and so progress on effectiveness and impact measures has been similar to efficiency, while in other countries the efficiency measures may have emerged earlier, before many of the current impact measurement technologies and frameworks were widespread.

Use and Strategic Focuses

Table 9.3 shows the relationship between the use of HR measurement systems and the strategic focuses of the organization. The pattern suggests that three of the strategic focuses (information-based, knowledge-based, and innovation) are strongly associated with HR measurement use, while pursuit of growth and sustainability are less so.

For the strategies that are correlated with HR metrics use, the pattern of correlations suggests that all three categories of HR measures are about equally correlated with the pursuit of the strategy, suggesting that a broadly balanced HR measurement approach characterizes the organizations with information-based, knowledge-based, and innovation focuses.

The extent to which organizations pursue a strategy of growth is significantly related to only one of the HR measurement items (measuring the quality of talent decisions by non-HR leaders), and even then the correlation is relatively small (.19). This finding reinforces the earlier observation that growth-focused strategic pursuits tend to have somewhat lower correlations with decision science elements generally. It may be that growth-focused organizations are at an earlier stage or focused on more traditional measures of financial growth, not on human capital.

The degree to which sustainability is pursued showed an interesting pattern, with non-significant correlations for all of the efficiency and most of the effectiveness measures, but relatively strong correlations for the use of cost-benefit analysis and all of the impact measures. It may be that a sustainability focus typically carries with it a stronger focus on non-financial outcomes, making traditional efficiency measures less emphasized. It may also be that this focus on non-traditional outcomes

Table 9.3. HR analytics and metrics use to strategic focuses					
Measures	**Strategic Focuses**				
	Growth	**Information-Based Strategies**	**Knowledge-Based Strategies**	**Sustainability**	**Innovation**
Efficiency					
Measure the financial efficiency of HR operations (e.g. cost-per-hire, time-to-fill, training costs)?	.01	.27***	.24***	.03	.20**
Collect metrics that measure the cost of providing HR programs and processes?	.04	.22**	.22**	.09	.22**
Benchmark analytics and measures against data from outside organizations (e.g. Saratoga, Mercer, Hewitt, etc.)?	.10	.30***	.26***	.10	.38***
Effectiveness					
Use HR dashboards or scorecards?	.09	.29***	.20**	.06	.18*
Measure the specific effects of HR programs (such as learning from training, motivation from rewards, validity of tests, etc.)?	.01	.17*	.25***	.14^t	.24***
Have the capability to conduct cost-benefit analyses (also called utility analyses) of HR programs?	.07	.27***	.21**	.24***	.23**
Impact					
Measure the business impact of HR programs and processes?	.09	.27***	.32***	.22**	.25***
Measure the quality of the talent decisions made by non-HR leaders?	.19*	.20**	.23**	.15*	.16*
Measure the business impact of high versus low performance in jobs?	.03	.28***	.31***	.25***	.23**
Significance level: $^t p \leq .10$; $^* p \leq .05$; $^{**} p \leq .01$; $^{***} p \leq .001$					

Table 9.4. HR analytics and metrics to management approach

Measures	Management Approach				
	Bureaucratic	Low-Cost Operator	High Involvement	Global Competitor	Sustainable
Efficiency					
Measure the financial efficiency of HR operations (e.g. cost-per-hire, time-to-fill, training costs)?	−.02	.02	.19*	.11	.12
Collect metrics that measure the cost of providing HR programs and processes?	.08	−.07	.07	.12	.14^t
Benchmark analytics and measures against data from outside organizations (e.g. Saratoga, Mercer, Hewitt, etc.)?	−.07	−.00	.16*	.11	.12
Effectiveness					
Use HR dashboards or scorecards?	−.12	.01	.11	.16*	.19*
Measure the specific effects of HR programs (such as learning from training, motivation from rewards, validity of tests, etc.)?	.01	.12	.10	.07	.17*
Have the capability to conduct cost-benefit analyses (also called utility analyses) of HR programs?	−.06	−.03	.12	.07	.30***
Impact					
Measure the business impact of HR programs and processes?	−.08	−.05	.23**	.16*	.19**
Measure the quality of the talent decisions made by non-HR leaders?	−.06	.02	−.06	.11	.16*
Measure the business impact of high versus low performance in jobs?	−.11	−.01	.10	.02	.19**

Significance level: $^t p \leq .10$; $^* p \leq .05$; $^{**} p \leq .01$; $^{***} p \leq .001$

extends to a greater focus and accountability for the employment relationship as an outcome in itself, leading to greater use of impact measures that focus on the pivotalness of performance and on the talent decisions of leaders.

Use and Management Approaches

Table 9.4 shows the correlation between the measurement use and the degree to which organizations pursue different organization and management approaches. Overall, there are relatively few significant correlations, suggesting that different management approaches are not associated with different HR measurement systems. There are a few notable exceptions for the high-involvement and sustainable management approaches.

The high-involvement approach shows significant positive correlations with three of the nine measurement uses, two of them related to efficiency and one related to measuring the business impact of HR programs. The sustainable management approach has seven significant correlations with all of the measurement items in the effectiveness and impact categories, with cost-benefit analysis being notably significant at a correlation of .30. This pattern reinforces the earlier findings that a focus on sustainability seems to associate with greater advancements in measures of impact and effectiveness, suggesting that such approaches may engender greater attention to employment issues generally and more accountability for the quality of those decisions among non-HR leaders.

Comprehensiveness and HR Activities

Table 9.5 shows the pattern of HR measurement use for thirteen specific types of HR programs and activities. The rows of the table reflect HR practices. The columns reflect whether respondents indicated they measured that program with none of the approaches, or with one or more of efficiency, effectiveness, and/or impact. For example, the number 16.9

Table 9.5. HR analytics and metrics measures (percentages)									
	Measures (Percentages)								**Correlation of Scale[†] with HR Role in Strategy**
HR Programs and Activities	**None**	**Efficiency**	**Effectiveness**	**Impact**	**Efficiency + Effectiveness**	**Efficiency + Impact**	**Effectiveness + Impact**	**Efficiency + Effectiveness + Impact**	
Compensation	6.2	24.7	16.3	16.9	5.6	9.0	9.0	12.4	**.30*****
Benefits	6.2	35.4	11.2	14.0	10.1	5.6	5.1	12.4	**.23****
Organization development	15.2	10.7	22.5	21.3	2.8	1.1	16.9	9.6	**.26*****
Organization design	21.9	14.0	23.6	20.8	2.2	1.7	7.9	7.9	**.21****
Training/Education	6.2	11.8	32.0	10.7	10.1	0.6	11.8	16.9	**.28*****
Leader development and succession	7.9	11.2	26.4	23.0	6.7	0.6	15.7	8.4	**.23****
HR information systems	11.2	37.1	12.9	5.1	16.9	3.4	2.8	10.7	**.19****
Performance management	8.4	18.5	24.7	15.7	10.1	2.2	14.0	6.2	**.21****
Career planning	22.5	16.9	34.3	10.1	3.9	0	7.9	4.5	**.12**
Diversity	16.9	16.9	24.7	19.7	3.9	2.2	7.9	7.9	**.15***
Employee assistance	18.0	36.5	21.3	7.9	9.0	1.1	1.1	5.1	**.19***
Staffing	5.1	28.7	19.1	9.6	12.4	2.8	3.4	19.1	**.24*****
Social and knowledge networks	33.1	24.7	27.5	4.5	1.7	0.6	3.4	4.5	**.16***

Efficiency: The resources used by the program, such as cost-per-hire.

Effectiveness: The changes produced by the program, such as learning from training.

Impact: The business or strategic value produced by the program.

[†] Scale: Number of measures (efficiency, effectiveness, impact) selected for each HR program or activity.

Significance level: [†] $p \leq .10$; * $p \leq .05$; ** $p \leq .01$; *** $p \leq .001$

in the Compensation row under Impact indicates that 16.9 percent of respondents checked only "Impact," and the 12.4 indicates that 12.4 percent of respondents checked all three measurement choices.

While the earlier results focused on the overall measurement practices at the level of the HR function, this analysis allows for approaches to vary depending on the type of HR program. It seems plausible that the use of efficiency, effectiveness, and impact measures might vary by program type. This could be due to the availability or feasibility of measures for different programs, the historical emphasis on measurement in certain areas, or the decision models used to evaluate HR activities of different types.

Most HR programs are measured on just one type of measure. It also appears that the sole use of effectiveness measures is somewhat more common than any other choice. That said, there are some interesting variations among the programs.

It is interesting to observe how many programs had a low frequency of the approaches. Career planning, organization design, and social and knowledge networks all had more than 20 percent of respondents who chose none of the three measurement approaches. These programs are frequently applied across the entire organization, or at least large proportions of it. They also often encompass effects that are complex combinations of building capabilities, motivation, and skills. Finally, they are often designed and implemented at the corporate level, rather than reflecting decisions by individual business units or individual managers and employees, unlike programs such as training. Thus, the tendency to forego measurement may be because complexity makes measurement difficult. The highest proportion (33.1 percent) choosing "None" was with regard to social and knowledge networks, which may reflect that this is a relatively new element of HR management.

Several programs show a strong tendency to be measured primarily with efficiency measures. More than 30 percent of companies use only efficiency measures for benefits, HRISs, and employee assistance. These programs tend to be organization-wide programs for which individual business units have little design impact. Thus, it may be that isolating the effectiveness and impact of such programs is difficult, so organizations focus on efficiency-level outcomes. Compensation also shows a strong tendency toward dominance by efficiency measurement (24.7 percent), but it shows some use of effectiveness and impact measures (16.3 and 16.9 percent). This may be because while a large array of compensation decisions are policy-based and applied across the entire employee population, some elements are more "local" decision-based, in that they are under the control of individual leaders and affect individual employees and groups.

Leader development, organization development, and organization design show a marked tendency to be measured on impact or effectiveness, not efficiency. These programs often originate with business leaders rather than with the HR function, and they often have extensive involvement by the top leadership team. This may not only draw attention to their impact on the business, but may also make cost less salient. The decision to begin them presumes that it is important enough to justify the budget for in-house and outside consultants, significant leader time commitment, etc. It may be that attention is drawn away from the administrative efficiency of such programs and toward their effects on employees and connection to the business.

Staffing is most frequently measured through a combination of all three approaches. This may reflect the recent attention to staffing as a more "strategic" activity in light of the prominence of global talent shortages and demographic changes that increase the need for a strong labor market presence. It is interesting that staffing does show more use of combining all three measures. Mathematical and statistical tools for calculating the monetary value of improved selection have existed for decades (Cascio and Boudreau 2011).

Training/education and career planning show a strong emphasis on effectiveness measures, and the highest frequency of such measurement (32.0 and 34.3 percent respectively). This may reflect the long history of attention to training evaluation and the popular emphasis on training return-on-investment and measures at several levels, such as reactions, learning, behaviors, and results (Cascio and Boudreau 2011). Career planning has a long history of measures of promotion rates and flows through the various organizational career paths that may explain the high level of effectiveness measures.

Comprehensiveness and Role in Strategy

Table 9.5 shows the correlations between the comprehensiveness of the measurement approaches for the HR programs and HR's role in strategy. Comprehensiveness is defined as the number of approaches used to measure the HR programs. Thus, it ranges from 0 to 3 for a program. The results suggest that comprehensiveness is significantly related to HR's strategic role for most of the HR programs, suggesting that more comprehensive HR measurement is generally associated with a stronger strategic role.

Comprehensiveness and Strategic Focuses

Table 9.6 shows the relationship between HR measurement comprehensiveness and the different strategic focuses. The growth focus stands out once again as notably uncorrelated with measurement comprehensiveness. For all the other strategic focuses there are significant correlations. Our data do not allow us to fully explain this pattern, but it may be that growth-oriented organizations are at earlier stages of development and thus have less developed HR measurement systems.

Leader development and performance management show the lowest correlations with the strategic focuses. It may be that measurement of these areas is expected as a minimum HR activity, or that these areas are satisfactorily measured using only one or two of the measurement categories. It is also interesting that comprehensive measurement of knowledge and social networks is significantly correlated with the knowledge-based, sustainability, and innovation focuses, but not with growth and information-based strategies. Social networks, and in particular their strategic impact, may be more vital to organizations pursuing strategies that require sharing knowledge, integrating multiple perspectives for sustainability, or spanning organization units to create innovation.

Table 9.6. HR analytics and metrics to strategic focuses					
	Strategic Focuses				
HR Programs and Activities[†]	Growth	Information-Based Strategies	Knowledge-Based Strategies	Sustainability	Innovation
Compensation	−.03	.23**	.26***	.10	.16*
Benefits	−.08	.22**	.20**	.13^t	.16*
Organization development	.01	.18*	.28***	.22**	.23**
Organization design	.02	.16*	.25***	.18*	.24**
Training/Education	.07	.14^t	.23**	.15^t	.15*
Leader development and succession	.04	.17*	.15^t	.13^t	.11
HR information systems	.03	.25***	.29***	.23**	.18*
Performance management	−.05	.18*	.12	.16*	.11
Career planning	−.03	.18*	.23**	.22**	.25***
Diversity	.07	.21**	.18*	.19*	.26***
Employee assistance	.06	.24***	.33***	.24***	.31***
Staffing	.07	.22**	.22**	.18*	.17*
Social and knowledge networks	−.01	.10	.22**	.28***	.21**

[†] Scale: Number of measures (efficiency, effectiveness, impact) selected for each HR program or activity.
Significance level: $^t p \le .10$; $^* p \le .05$; $^{**} p \le .01$; $^{***} p \le .001$

Overall, there is a tendency for the strategic focuses to be positively correlated with the measurement of HR programs. This is consistent with the general point that when organizations have strong strategic focuses they are more likely to have more developed HR measurement for their programs and practices.

Comprehensiveness and Management Approaches

Table 9.7 shows the relationship between the measurement comprehensiveness of HR program areas and the use of management approaches. The significant correlations are mainly with the sustainable management approach, which has five of the seven significant relationships. This is in contrast to the 2007 results, where the high-involvement approach showed significant positive correlations with measurement of compensation, organization development, organization design, training, and career planning. In the 2010 sample, comprehensiveness of HR measurement is not a hallmark of high-involvement approaches.

The sustainable management approach is positively correlated with the comprehensiveness of measurement for organization development, HR information systems, career planning, and in particular diversity and employee assistance. It is notable that these are areas that rate somewhat lower in the frequency of fully comprehensive measurement (see

Table 9.7. HR analytics and metrics to management approach					
HR Programs and Activities[†]	**Management Approach**				
	Bureaucratic	**Low-Cost Operator**	**High Involvement**	**Global Competitor**	**Sustainable**
Compensation	−.16*	−.04	.15[†]	.02	.08
Benefits	.02	−.07	.06	−.02	.05
Organization development	−.09	−.04	.12	.10	.15*
Organization design	−.06	−.12	.10	.08	.07
Training/Education	.01	−.01	.04	.05	.10
Leader development and succession	−.09	−.09	.05	.06	.01
HR information systems	−.08	−.12	.15[†]	.04	.18*
Performance management	−.04	−.11	.00	.06	.01
Career planning	.03	−.10	.11	.09	.17*
Diversity	−.01	.05	.11	.03	.25***
Employee assistance	−.12	−.07	.16*	.16*	.23**
Staffing	−.09	−.01	.07	.09	.17*
Social and knowledge networks	−.06	−.07	.12	.07	.14[†]

[†] Scale: Number of measures (efficiency, effectiveness, impact) selected for each HR program or activity.
Significance level: [†] $p \le .10$; * $p \le .05$; ** $p \le .01$; *** $p \le .001$

Table 9.5), suggesting that pursuing sustainable management approaches may associate with organizations that devote effort to comprehensively measuring areas that others do not. Also, career planning, diversity, and employee assistance tend to be important non-traditional elements of the employer value proposition. As a result they may be more prominent in organizations pursuing sustainable management approaches, due to its focus on long-term employment relationships and its employment brand.

The bureaucratic approach presents some intriguing results. Virtually all of the correlations are negative with the bureaucratic approach (though only the correlation with compensation measurement is significant); this approach places less emphasis on HR, including measurement of it. It is notable that the low-cost-operator management approach also shows very low and mostly negative correlations, suggesting a tendency for it to reject more comprehensive HR measurement. As noted earlier, it may be that the bureaucratic approach relies on formal rules and authority to oversee its HR activities, rather than comprehensive measurement.

Conclusion

There is significant variability in how much organizations use different types of HR measures. Efficiency measures are used the most, effectiveness measures next, and impact measures the least. Overall, no measurement type is used by much over 50 percent of all companies. This pattern holds across different national samples, with the U.S. showing greater implementation of efficiency measures and China showing consistent moderate use of measurements across all three categories. Compared to the 2007 survey, there has been a general increase in the percentages of organizations that report they now have measures in each of the categories; however, there is room for HR to do more measurement and there is reason to believe that it would have a positive impact.

The use of HR measures and analytics is significantly related to HR's role in strategy. It is also important to note that all measurement elements are not equal when it comes to strategy. In the 2010 data, in contrast to the 2007 data, impact measures reflecting non-HR talent decisions and the pivotalness of job performance were not significantly related to HR's role in strategy. More traditional measures such as benchmarks and scorecards were more strongly related to HR's strategic role in 2010 than in 2007. This may suggest a return to more traditional measures during this period.

The comprehensiveness of measurement is positively related to HR's role in strategy for virtually all HR programs, suggesting that more complete measurement is generally indicative of a strong strategic role. In contrast, HR measure comprehensiveness is not highly correlated with most management approaches except sustainability, suggesting that sustainability requires or leads to greater measurement attention. The comprehensiveness of HR programs varies significantly across strategic focuses, suggesting that it is not just that HR measurement is related to HR's role in strategy, but that the nature of the most strategically valuable measurement may vary for different strategic focuses.

Overall, the results present tantalizing evidence that there may be systematic variations in how HR measures are used, and that the pattern of use significantly relates to the strategies and management approaches of organizations, as well as HR's strategic role. There is no doubt that HR metrics and analytics remain underdeveloped and underutilized. Increasing the attention given to HR metrics and analytics seems to be called for, considering the potential for improvement and added value.

CHAPTER 10

HR Metrics and Analytics: Effectiveness

It is important to examine the effectiveness of the HR metrics and analytics used by organizations. This chapter does this in two ways. First we will focus on two broad areas of effectiveness: strategic contributions (such as contributing to strategy decisions, identifying where talent makes the greatest strategic impact, connecting human capital practices to organization performance, and supporting organization change) and HR functional and operational strategies (such as improving HR department operations and evaluating and investing in HR practices).

Second, we asked about four elements that contribute to the effectiveness of measures as catalysts for organizational change. These four elements comprise the LAMP framework, which identifies four vital features of measurement systems for driving strategic change (Boudreau and Ramstad 2007; Cascio and Boudreau 2011).

The four LAMP elements are:

1. Logic (frameworks that articulate the connections between talent and strategic success, as well as the principles and conditions that predict individual and organizational behavior)

2. Analytics (tools and techniques to transform data into rigorous and relevant insights, e.g. statistical analysis, research design)

3. Measures (the numbers and indices calculated from data system)

4. Process (communication and knowledge transfer mechanisms through which the information becomes accepted and acted upon by key organization decision makers)

HR Metrics and Analytics Effectiveness

Table 10.1 shows the results regarding the effectiveness of HR measurement systems in contributing to outcomes related to strategic contributions, HR functional and operational contributions, and the four LAMP elements. Overall, the picture shows rather low effectiveness ratings. For no outcomes are HR measures and analytics rated effective or very effective by more than 40 percent of the respondents. Indeed, for only four outcomes are HR measures and analytics rated as effective or very effective by more than 30 percent of respondents.

Two of the highest-rated outcomes are related to strategic contributions: supporting organizational change efforts, and contributing to decisions about business strategy and human capital management. The other two reflect assessing and improving the HR department operations and using logical principles that clearly connect talent to organization success. It is encouraging that some strategically related items are relatively effective, but again this is in the context of rather low effectiveness ratings overall. Overall, the effectiveness of HR metrics and analytics falls at or slightly below the midpoint (3.0 = somewhat effective) of the 5-point scale, suggesting improvement is possible in all areas. This pattern is similar to our results from the 2004 and 2007 surveys.

The means for the 2007 and 2010 samples are very similar with a slight upward trend. The only upward trend that reaches statistical significance is for the item "motivating users to take appropriate action." This is encouraging as that is a central but often overlooked aspect of

Table 10.1. HR analytics and metrics effectiveness, USA only								
	Percentages					Means		Correlation with HR Role in Strategy
Outcomes	Very Ineffective	Ineffective	Somewhat Effective	Effective	Very Effective	2007[1]	2010[2]	
Strategy Contributions								
Contributing to decisions about business strategy and human capital management	7.9	19.2	35.6	31.1	6.2	3.0	3.1	.47***
Identifying where talent has the greatest potential for strategic impact	9.0	27.0	36.5	25.8	1.7	3.0	2.8	.33***
Connecting human capital practices to organizational performance	10.7	38.4	36.2	14.1	0.6	2.5	2.6	.30***
Supporting organizational change efforts	5.6	16.3	41.6	26.4	10.1	3.1	3.2	.36***
HR Functional and Operational Contributions								
Assessing and improving the HR department operations	5.1	16.4	44.1	27.7	6.8	3.0	3.1	.33***
Predicting the effects of HR programs before implementation	14.1	31.1	40.7	13.0	1.1	2.7	2.6	.24***
Pinpointing HR programs that should be discontinued	14.1	30.5	36.7	17.5	1.1	2.6	2.6	.26***
Logic, Analysis, Measurement, and Process (LAMP)								
Using logical principles that clearly connect talent to organization success	8.5	21.5	38.4	26.6	5.1	2.8	3.0	.34***
Using advanced data analysis and statistics	14.9	34.3	32.0	13.7	5.1	2.4	2.6	.26***
Providing high-quality (complete, timely, accessible) talent measurements	8.5	37.9	32.8	18.6	2.3	2.5	2.7	.34***
Motivating users to take appropriate action	9.0	22.6	42.4	22.6	3.4	2.6[2]	2.9[1]	.28***
[1,2] Significant differences (p ≤ .5) between years.								
Significance level: [1] p ≤ .10; * p ≤ .05; ** p ≤ .01; *** p ≤ .001								

effective measurement. The 2007 ratings were also higher than in 2004, suggesting steady improvement in measurement effectiveness, albeit at a rather moderate rate.

The four items reflecting the LAMP framework show the highest effectiveness ratings for the logic element and for motivating users to take action, with slightly lower ratings for the elements of data analysis and high-quality measures. The results concerning data analysis and measures are interesting in that they contradict much of the anecdotal evidence we encounter. Most organizations we study report that their ability to generate measurements is well-developed, and they have good data-analysis capabilities. Failure to effectively use measures is usually attributed to those receiving the information not having the cognitive frameworks to make sense of the information (such as understanding how an engagement score or a turnover rate connects to business success), and/or the information being conveyed in ways that fail to motivate and direct the right decisions and actions. Still, the ratings in Table 10.1 are low for all four LAMP areas, leaving significant opportunity for improvement both in the HR measures and analyses and on the part of managers using the data.

Role in Strategy

Table 10.1 also contains the correlations between the rated effectiveness of HR measures and analytics and HR's role in strategy. All of the outcomes show a positive and significant relationship with HR's role in strategy. The highest correlation is for contributing to decisions about business strategy and human capital management. In 2010 that correlation was much higher than the others, while in 2007 it was more similar to the others. Similarly, it is notable that all four elements of the LAMP framework are positively related to HR's role in strategy. This suggests that the four elements may work together to support or to help advance HR's strategic role, as suggested by Boudreau and Ramstad (2007) and by Cascio and Boudreau (2011).

Overall, the main conclusion is that all the correlations are relatively high and statistically significant. Indeed, compared to the 2004 and 2007 samples, the 2010 correlations are somewhat higher and more frequently statistically significant. This suggests that over time both the level of effectiveness of these measurement areas has increased as has their association with HR's strategic role.

We often encounter HR and business leaders who believe that the HR profession must first "get its own house in order" by improving its measurement capability and achieving functional effectiveness, and that only after doing so should it focus on strategic effectiveness. The results reported here suggest that strategy and HR functional measurement effectiveness both contribute to a strong strategic role. Thus, they support the idea of developing measurement systems that are effective at strategic outcomes, even if HR functional and operational outcomes are not yet perfect.

International

The international results for measurement effectiveness are shown in Table 10.2. Overall, the results are quite similar to those for the U.S. sample, both in terms of the level of effectiveness and the relative effectiveness across the different measures.

One notable exception to the pattern of similar results is the results from China; for several items the effectiveness ratings are significantly higher than for other countries. The Chinese executives consistently rate the effectiveness of their metrics slightly above the scale midpoint on all items. In the U.S. and other countries the ratings are more varied, with some items receiving lower effectiveness ratings. From our data we cannot determine if the Chinese companies are more effective at HR measurement in more

Table 10.2. HR analytics and metrics effectiveness, by country						
	Means					
Outcomes	USA[1]	Canada[2]	Australia[3]	Europe[4]	UK[5]	China[6]
Strategy Contributions						
Contributing to decisions about business strategy and human capital management	3.1	3.1	3.3	3.1	3.0	3.2
Identifying where talent has the greatest potential for strategic impact	2.8	3.0	3.1	3.0	2.8	3.0
Connecting human capital practices to organizational performance	2.6[6]	2.6	2.9	2.7	2.5[6]	3.0[1,5]
Supporting organizational change efforts	3.2	3.3	3.2	3.2	3.2	3.1
HR Functional and Operational Contributions						
Assessing and improving the HR department operations	3.1	3.3	3.2	3.1	3.0	3.2
Predicting the effects of HR programs before implementation	2.6[6]	2.8	2.8	2.7	2.6[6]	3.1[1,5]
Pinpointing HR programs that should be discontinued	2.6	2.7	2.8	2.8	2.6	2.9
Logic, Analysis, Measurement, and Process (LAMP)						
Using logical principles that clearly connect talent to organization success	3.0	3.0	3.3	3.0	2.7	3.1
Using advanced data analysis and statistics	2.6[6]	2.3[6]	2.8	2.8	2.6[6]	3.1[1,2,5]
Providing high-quality (complete, timely, accessible) talent measurements	2.7[6]	2.6	2.8	2.8	2.5[6]	3.0[1,5]
Motivating users to take appropriate action	2.9[6]	2.7[6]	3.0	2.9	2.7[6]	3.2[1,2,5]
[1,2,3,4,5,6] Significant differences between countries ($p \leq .05$).						

Table 10.3. HR analytics and metrics effectiveness to strategic focuses					
	Strategic Focuses				
Outcomes	**Growth**	**Information-Based Strategies**	**Knowledge-Based Strategies**	**Sustainability**	**Innovation**
Strategy Contributions					
Contributing to decisions about business strategy and human capital management	.05	.38***	.41***	.29***	.35***
Identifying where talent has the greatest potential for strategic impact	.16*	.42***	.50***	.29***	.34***
Connecting human capital practices to organizational performance	.15ᵗ	.44***	.42***	.20**	.31***
Supporting organizational change efforts	.09	.27***	.40***	.23**	.28***
HR Functional and Operational Contributions					
Assessing and improving the HR department operations	.10	.40***	.49***	.28***	.34***
Predicting the effects of HR programs before implementation	.02	.31***	.36***	.24***	.32***
Pinpointing HR programs that should be discontinued	–.04	.26***	.33***	.20**	.27***
Logic, Analysis, Measurement, and Process (LAMP)					
Using logical principles that clearly connect talent to organization success	.11	.36***	.40***	.26***	.31***
Using advanced data analysis and statistics	.10	.39***	.40***	.26***	.34***
Providing high-quality (complete, timely, accessible) talent measurements	.12	.41***	.50***	.26***	.34***
Motivating users to take appropriate action	.14ᵗ	.37***	.45***	.18*	.34***

Significance level: ᵗ $p \le .10$; * $p \le .05$; ** $p \le .01$; *** $p \le .001$

areas, or if this is a response for differences that is due to the recency with which HR measurement systems have been implemented in China. In other countries these systems have a longer history, and as a result HR executives are more critical about effectiveness levels.

Strategic Focuses

Table 10.3 shows the relationship between the effectiveness of HR metrics and analytics, and the different strategic focuses. Once again, the growth strategy focus shows no significant correlations with any of the measurement effectiveness areas. Apparently, when the focus is on growth an organization may not require or benefit from systemic enhancements of HR effectiveness, in this case the effectiveness of HR measures.

In marked contrast to the correlations for growth are its correlations for the other four strategic focuses, which are all strong. This is consistent with the point made earlier that for HR to be effective an organization needs a strategy that is clear and related to a competitive advantage that is partly based on talent.

The correlations for knowledge-based strategies are particularly strong. This pattern parallels the results in Chapter 9 for metrics and analytics usage. It is somewhat different from the 2007 results, where only the knowledge-based strategic focus showed strong correlations. The 2010 results show strong relationships between measurement effectiveness and the strategic focuses of information, sustainability, and innovation. It appears that over time the relationship between measurement effectiveness and other focuses has strengthened and generalized.

Our data are not sufficient to explain why the correlations for the knowledge-based strategic focus are particularly strong, but it is possible that knowledge-based strategies rely more upon organizational integration and employee understanding and involvement and thus they put an emphasis on metrics and analytics. Certainly, knowledge-based strategies are explicitly built upon human capital, and this may lead them to develop more advanced HR practices and strategies.

Management Approaches

The correlations between the five management approaches and the effectiveness of HR measures and analytics are shown in Table 10.4. Once again, the high-involvement and sustainability approaches show strong correlations with HR effectiveness—in this case the effectiveness of HR measures. The global competitor approach shows positive associations

Table 10.4. HR analytics and metrics effectiveness to management approach					
	Management Approach				
Outcomes	**Bureaucratic**	**Low-Cost Operator**	**High Involvement**	**Global Competitor**	**Sustainability**
Strategy Contributions					
Contributing to decisions about business strategy and human capital management	−.19*	−.10	.27***	.11	.38***
Identifying where talent has the greatest potential for strategic impact	−.14ᵗ	−.13ᵗ	.32***	.20**	.35***
Connecting human capital practices to organizational performance	−.09	−.04	.21**	.17*	.33***
Supporting organizational change efforts	−.21**	−.09	.23**	.10	.31***
HR Functional and Operational Contributions					
Assessing and improving the HR department operations	−.22**	−.04	.29***	.23**	.37***
Predicting the effects of HR programs before implementation	−.09	−.00	.23**	.07	.32***
Pinpointing HR programs that should be discontinued	−.10	−.07	.16*	.05	.21**
Logic, Analysis, Measurement, and Process (LAMP)					
Using logical principles that clearly connect talent to organization success	−.22**	−.05	.22**	.14ᵗ	.38***
Using advanced data analysis and statistics	−.06	.06	.12	.17*	.38***
Providing high-quality (complete, timely, accessible) talent measurements	−.07	−.06	.25***	.13ᵗ	.45***
Motivating users to take appropriate action	−.16*	−.16*	.28***	.19*	.37***
Significance level: ᵗ $p \le .10$; * $p \le .05$; ** $p \le .01$; *** $p \le .001$					

with most effectiveness measures, but they fail to reach statistical significance as often as those for the high-involvement and sustainability approaches. These results are consistent with the 2004 survey. The addition of the sustainability management approach in the 2010 survey provided intriguing results; it shows the highest and most comprehensive positive correlations with the effectiveness of HR metrics and analytics.

The other two management approaches, bureaucratic and low-cost operator, show an interesting pattern that parallels prior results for the development of the HR decision science and for measurement usage. Specifically, both approaches show negative correlations with most elements of measurement effectiveness, and in the case of the bureaucratic approach many of these negative correlations are statistically significant. These results are consistent with the 2007 sample, though in the 2010 sample the trend is even more comprehensive and statistically significant.

It appears that when organizations emphasize a bureaucratic or low-cost operator management approach, they are significantly less likely to report that measurement effectiveness contributes to strategic decisions, supporting organization change efforts, improving HR department operations, using logical principles, and motivating action. The causal direction could go either way, but it seems most likely that pursuit of the bureaucratic or the low-cost operator approach leads to less attention to HR measurement and thus less effective HR measures. Considering the strong association between HR measurement effectiveness and HR's role in strategy (see Table 10.1), this may suggest that HR leaders wishing to pursue state-of-the-art measures and strategic roles need to avoid organizations emphasizing bureaucratic or low-cost operator approaches.

In contrast, organizations with high-involvement and sustainable management approaches have higher-quality HR measurement across all items. It appears that the focus of high-involvement organizations on making employees and the employment relationship a key element of competitive success, and the focus of sustainability on the employment relationship as a key performance driver, may lead both to value and to investment in improved HR measurement.

Conclusion

The results for HR measurement systems effectiveness indicate low average effectiveness, but slight effectiveness improvement since 2007, and consistently strong relationships with HR's strategic role. This is an important area for HR and one where improvement is needed in order for HR to have a meaningful role in business strategy. The results for the effectiveness of HR measures and analytics in many ways reinforce the findings from Chapter 9 on measure use and strategy. Not only did strategy measurement effectiveness relate to HR's strategic role; effectiveness in HR functional and operational areas was found to be related to the strength of HR's strategic role.

Our results show a strong relationship between the four LAMP elements and HR's strategic role, supporting the point that all four elements are necessary for a strategically effective measurement system. Of course the causal direction cannot be discerned from our data, so it may be that as HR organizations become more strategically involved and relevant, organizations perceive and support more effective HR measures. It seems plausible, however, that at least some of the effect may be through more effective measures leading to a greater strategic contribution from HR.

The results for strategic focuses suggest that organizations pursuing knowledge, information, sustainability, and innovation-based strategies are likely to have measurement effectiveness across a wide array of outcomes. While not definitive, these results suggest that effective HR measurement may be more readily accepted and used in organizations that rely on broad-based talent understanding and involvement to achieve competitive advantage, innovation, or sustainability.

It appears that some management approaches such as the bureaucratic and low-cost operator ones may actually discourage HR measurement excellence. Just the opposite appears to be true of the high-involvement and sustainable management approaches.

Overall, the current findings reinforce the conclusion from our prior surveys—that the potential for HR metrics and analytics to contribute to HR's strategic value is significant, while the perceived effectiveness levels remain stubbornly moderate. Our 2010 results also suggest even more strongly that the association of measurement excellence with HR's strategic role generalizes across all measurement dimensions, particularly when organizations pursue human-capital-centric strategies and management approaches. Leaders both inside and outside of HR may find great value in pursuing HR measurement effectiveness both at a strategic and functional level, and through a balanced approach of logic, analytics, measures, and process.

CHAPTER 11

Outsourcing

Outsourcing is a possible way to improve the effectiveness of an HR function and make it more strategic. Outsourcing transactional work can reduce the work load of HR organizations, increase quality, and reduce costs (Lawler, Ulrich, Fitz-enz, and Madden 2004). In the best-case scenario, transaction outsourcing companies can provide better and cheaper services because they are focused on a particular process or area of expertise that is their core competency. In addition, when they provide transaction services, they can capture economies of scale by servicing multiple organizations. They also can improve the processes of organizations because of the knowledge they have.

At the very least, outsourcing can reduce the number of employees who are on the HR department payroll and can create a flexible cost structure when services are needed occasionally or for short periods of time. They also can allow companies to relatively easily increase or decrease the number of people who are working on their HR programs.

By outsourcing professional and knowledge work, organizations can acquire expertise and strategic information that may not be available internally. Here the hoped-for advantages are not as much related to scale as they are expertise in areas like HR strategy, organization development, and training. Particularly in the case of the large consulting firms, they are able to provide a depth of expertise in their areas of specialization that most companies cannot hope to achieve.

Use of Outsourcing

Table 11.1 shows the degree to which eighteen HR activities are currently being outsourced in the U.S. Activities are grouped by the three factors that our statistical analysis produced; ten items did not group. In 1995, 1998, 2001, 2004, 2007, and 2010 the use of outsourcing varied widely among the activities, but in no case were any of these activities even close to being completely outsourced by a majority of the companies.

At one extreme in 2010, over 90 percent of the companies did not outsource HC forecasting, career planning, and organization design, all areas in which HR can add considerable strategic value and act as a strategic partner. However, as was noted in Chapter 5, they are not all areas where HR is particularly active (strategic planning and organization design). They represent areas of opportunity for HR given their importance.

Table 11.1. Outsourcing use, USA only

Type of Outsourcing	Percentages			Means						Correlation with HR Role in Strategy 2010
	Not at All	Partially	Completely	1995[1]	1998[2]	2001[3]	2004[4]	2007[5]	2010[6]	
Overall Outsourcing (mean for all items except union relations)									1.4	.15[t]
Human Capital Forecasting and Planning[a]	98.3	1.7	0.0	1.0	1.1	1.0	1.0	1.0	1.0	.05
Organization Design/ Development				1.2[6]	1.2	1.2	1.1		1.2[2]	.01
Organization development	81.5	18.5	0.0	1.3[5,6]	1.3[6]	1.2	1.2	1.2[1]	1.2[1,2]	.12
Organization design	89.1	10.3	0.6		1.2[5]	1.1	1.1	1.1[2]	1.1	−.11
Training				1.6[2]	1.7[1,6]	1.7[6]	1.7	1.6	1.5[2,3]	.19*
Training/ Education	39.0	59.9	1.1	1.6[2]	1.9[1,6]	1.8[6]	1.8	1.8	1.6[2,3]	.15[t]
Management development	56.0	42.3	1.7	1.5	1.6[6]	1.6[6]	1.6	1.5	1.5[2,3]	.16*
HR Information Systems	54.5	41.5	4.0	1.3[2,5]	1.6[1]	1.5	1.5	1.6[1]	1.5	.07
Staffing & Career Development				1.2	1.2	1.2	1.3	1.2	1.2	.08
Performance appraisal	84.2	15.3	0.6	1.0[5,6]	1.1	1.1	1.1	1.2[1]	1.2[1]	.04
Recruitment	48.9	51.1	0.0	1.4	1.6	1.5	1.6	1.6	1.5	.07
Selection	78.3	21.7	0.0	1.2	1.2	1.2	1.2	1.2	1.2	.04
Career planning	92.0	8.0	0.0	1.1	1.2	1.2[5]	1.1	1.0[3]	1.1	−.05
HR Metrics and Analysis	86.7	13.3	0.0				1.2	1.1	1.1	.15[t]
Benefits	27.0	65.7	7.3	1.7[4,5,6]	1.9[6]	1.9[6]	2.0[1,6]	2.0[1,6]	1.8[1,2,3,4,5]	.08
Compensation	74.4	25.6	0.0	1.2[2,3]	1.5[1,6]	1.5[1,6]	1.4	1.4	1.3[2,3]	.09
Legal Affairs	48.6	51.4	0.0	1.4[2]	1.6[1]	1.6	1.6	1.5	1.5	.20**
Executive Compensation	67.4	31.4	1.1						1.3	.11
Employee Assistance	25.8	34.8	39.3		2.2[6]	2.3[6]	2.5[6]	2.3[6]	2.1[2,3,4,5]	.00
Competency/Talent Assessment	74.7	24.1	1.1			1.3	1.5[6]	1.3	1.3[4]	.14[t]
Union Relations	90.8	8.0	1.2	1.1	1.1	1.1	1.2	1.1	1.1	−.01

[a]"HR planning" prior to 2007

[1,2,3,4,5,6] Significant differences ($p \leq .05$) between years.

Significance level: [t] $p \leq .10$; * $p \leq .05$; ** $p \leq .01$; *** $p \leq .001$

By a large margin, the most likely area to be completely outsourced is employee assistance, with 39.3 percent of the companies completely outsourcing it in 2010. This is hardly surprising given its personal and confidential nature. Benefits was the next most likely to be outsourced; 73 percent of the companies partially or completely outsourced it. The frequency of outsourcing benefits probably reflects the combination of transactional and specialized knowledge work that it involves. In over

50 percent of companies, training, recruitment, and legal were partially or completely outsourced. Management development was partially outsourced by almost 50 percent of the companies.

Overall, outsourcing occurs both in areas where specialized expertise is involved, such as legal affairs, and areas where primarily transactional work occurs, such as benefits administration. This result provides confirmation that organizations are outsourcing to gain both transactional efficiency and expertise.

A comparison between the 1995 and 2010 results shows some areas where there is a small increase in the use of outsourcing. Specifically, there are increases in the use of outsourcing from 1995 to 2010 in the following areas: HRISs, compensation, recruitment, performance appraisal, and legal affairs. Organizational development was less likely to be outsourced in 2010 than in 1995.

The comparison between the 2004 and 2010 data shows essentially no change in the frequency of outsourcing. Thus, although outsourcing has increased slightly since 1995, our data show little evidence of a recent increased use of outsourcing; the obvious conclusion at this point is that there is no current trend toward greater use of outsourcing.

Clearly the opportunity exists for more outsourcing to take place, since few companies completely outsource any of their HR activities and many HR activities are barely outsourced. This finding raises the question of whether there will be a new wave of outsourcing that will, in fact, lead to a significant increase in the amount of outsourcing that takes place.

One possibility is that outsourcing will increase because more and more organizations will decide to outsource their HR administration to the growing number of HR business process outsourcing (HRBPO) firms that exist (Lawler, Ulrich, Fitz-enz, and Madden 2004). To check on this for the first time in 2007 we asked whether the companies had a multiple process HR outsourcing contract: 21 percent said they did, and another 10 percent said they were considering it. We asked this question again in 2010 and got slightly lower answers. Apparently, multi-process outsourcing is not growing even though it promises to reduce costs—and the period from 2007 to 2010 was a period during which many companies tried to reduce their costs. Overall, there is little reason to believe there will be a significant increase in most of the types of outsourcing that are shown in Table 11.1.

Table 11.1 also shows the relationship between outsourcing and the role that HR plays in strategy. There is little indication that these two issues are related. Only the correlations with management development and legal affairs are significant.

International

The amount of outsourcing does not vary greatly among the countries in our international survey. As can be seen in Table 11.2, only three areas show a significant difference: executive compensation, employee assistance, and benefits. They are all areas where national laws and practices differ, so it is not surprising there is a difference in the degree to which they are outsourced. For example, China is low in outsourcing benefits and employee assistance, in part because suppliers do not exist in these areas.

Table 11.2. Outsourcing use, by country						
	Means					
Type of Outsourcing	USA[1]	Canada[2]	Australia[3]	Europe[4]	UK[5]	China[6]
Overall Outsourcing (all items except union relations)	1.4[6]	1.4[6]	1.4	1.3	1.3	1.3[1,2]
Human Capital Forecasting and Planning[a]	1.0[6]	1.0[6]	1.0	1.0[6]	1.1[6]	1.2[1,2,4,5]
Organization Design/ Development	1.2	1.1	1.1	1.1	1.0	1.2
Organization development	1.2	1.2	1.2	1.1	1.1	1.2
Organization design	1.1	1.0[6]	1.1	1.0[6]	1.0[6]	1.2[2,4,5]
Training	1.5	1.7[6]	1.6	1.5	1.6	1.4[2]
Training/ Education	1.6	1.8	1.7	1.7	1.7	1.5
Management development	1.5	1.7[6]	1.5	1.4	1.5	1.4[2]
HR Information Systems	1.5	1.4	1.4	1.5	1.5	1.5
Staffing & Career Development	1.2	1.3	1.2	1.2	1.2	1.3
Performance appraisal	1.2	1.2	1.0	1.1	1.1	1.2
Recruitment	1.5	1.5	1.6	1.6	1.5	1.5
Selection	1.2	1.2	1.2	1.3	1.3	1.2
Career planning	1.1	1.1	1.0	1.1	1.1	1.2
HR Metrics and Analysis	1.1	1.1	1.2	1.2	1.1	1.2
Benefits	1.8[3,4,6]	1.7[6]	1.4[1]	1.5[1,6]	1.5[6]	1.2[1,2,4,5]
Compensation	1.3	1.3	1.3	1.3	1.3	1.2
Legal Affairs	1.5	1.7	1.7	1.6	1.6	1.6
Executive Compensation	1.3[6]	1.5[5,6]	1.3	1.2	1.1[2]	1.1[1,2]
Employee Assistance	2.1[2,4,5,6]	2.5[1,4,5,6]	2.2[4,5,6]	1.5[1,2,3]	1.6[1,2,3,6]	1.2[1,2,3,5]
Competency / Talent Assessment	1.3	1.3	1.4	1.3	1.2	1.4
Union Relations	1.1	1.1	1.2	1.1	1.0	1.1

[a]"HR planning" prior to 2007
Response scale: 1 = Not at all; 2 = Partially; 3 = Completely
[1,2,3,4,5,6] Significant differences between countries ($p \le .05$).

Table 11.3. Relationship of outsourcing to strategic focuses					
	Strategic Focuses				
Type of Outsourcing	Growth	Information-Based Strategies	Knowledge-Based Strategies	Sustainability	Innovation
Overall Outsourcing (all items except union relations)	.13[t]	.14[t]	.09	.00	.13
Human Capital Forecasting and Planning[a]	–.00	.01	.13[t]	.05	.07
Organization Design/ Development	.09	.02	–.05	.06	.09
Training	.12	.17*	.09	.07	.18*
HR Information Systems	.23**	.06	.07	–.03	.12
Staffing & Career Development	.21**	.17*	.04	.02	.07
HR Metrics and Analysis	.04	.08	.06	.13[t]	.01
Benefits	–.04	–.06	–.05	–.04	–.01
Compensation	.11	.15[t]	.02	–.02	.07
Legal Affairs	.03	.10	.20**	–.03	.17*
Executive Compensation	–.12	.15*	.04	–.00	.11
Employee Assistance	.03	–.01	.00	–.06	.02
Competency / Talent Assessment	.09	.11	.04	.07	.09
Union Relations	.07	.02	.18*	.01	.13

[a] "HR planning" prior to 2007

Response scale: 1 = Not at all; 2 = Partially; 3 = Completely

Significance level: [t] $p \le .10$; * $p \le .05$; ** $p \le .01$; *** $p \le .001$

Strategic Focuses and Management Approaches

Table 11.3 shows that there are very few significant relationships between the strategic focuses and outsourcing. In general, this result is not surprising. The strongest relationship is with growth. Growth puts a stress on the human resource delivery capabilities of an organization, and outsourcing can provide a quick way to acquire additional support for an HR function that is under pressure to serve a larger organization.

There is little relationship between outsourcing and the management approach of the organization. This is not surprising, since the five management approaches do not differ in how appropriate outsourcing is.

Impact of HR Outsourcing

In 2007, questions were asked about the impact of outsourcing. The questions were not asked in 2010. Table 11.4 presents the results for 2007. In general, outsourcing does seem to help HR be a business partner, contribute to strategy, and perform high-value-added activities. It seems to have only a small positive impact in virtually every area. The

Table 11.4. Effectiveness of outsourcing HR services (2007, percentages)						
How has the outsourcing of HR services affected the following?	Greatly Decreased	Decreased	Stayed the Same	Increased	Greatly Increased	Mean
Overall effectiveness of the HR function	1.2	9.5	31.0	52.4	6.0	3.5
Ability of HR to be a business partner	0.0	8.3	31.0	52.4	8.3	3.6
Ability of HR to contribute to business strategy	0.0	3.7	42.7	47.6	6.1	3.6
The cost of HR services	0.0	32.9	40.2	20.7	6.1	3.0
The quality of HR services	3.6	15.7	34.9	37.3	8.4	3.3
The value HR adds to the organization	0.0	7.0	36.0	47.7	9.3	3.6
Satisfaction of company employees with HR services	1.2	23.8	39.3	26.2	9.5	3.2
Satisfaction of HR staff	2.4	19.0	34.5	36.9	7.1	3.3
Commitment of HR staff	1.2	14.1	47.1	27.1	10.6	3.3
Mining of employee data by HR	0.0	12.7	60.8	20.3	6.3	3.2
Time spent on HR strategy	0.0	4.8	40.5	50.0	4.8	3.5
Use of metrics by HR	1.3	1.3	54.4	38.0	5.1	3.4
Time spent on business strategy by HR	0.0	2.5	43.2	46.9	7.4	3.6
Availability of HR metrics	0.0	9.0	46.2	35.9	9.0	3.4
Use of HR analytic models	1.3	7.9	63.2	23.7	3.9	3.2

most positive responses are to questions concerned with HR being more strategic and a business partner. Apparently to a limited extent, it does free up HR to be more strategic and perhaps provide HR with the expertise it needs to be a strategic partner. Overall, 58 percent of the HR executives surveyed report it has a positive impact; only 11 percent report it has a negative impact; while 31 percent report no change.

Amount of Outsourcing

A new question in 2007 asked about the effectiveness of different amounts of outsourcing. Table 11.5 presents the U.S. results for 2010, and Table 11.6 presents the international results. The clear winners in the opinion of HR executives are very limited and moderate outsourcing to either a single vendor or multiple vendors. They get a relatively high rating in the U.S. and U.K., but are not rated as highly in the other countries. The worst option is perceived to be no outsourcing. Somewhat surprising are the low effectiveness ratings for substantial outsourcing to a single vendor or to multiple vendors.

HR Outsourcing Approaches

In order to better understand HR outsourcing, for the first time in 2007 we asked about multi-process HR outsourcing contracts. As can be seen in Table 11.7, in the U.S. less than 20 percent of the firms have one, a

Table 11.5. HR outsourcing approaches, USA only (percentages)

In general, how effective do you think the following approaches to HR outsourcing are?	Very Ineffective	Ineffective	Neither	Effective	Very Effective	Mean
No outsourcing	26.4	36.8	25.3	10.3	1.1	2.2
Very limited: only a few transactional services (e.g. payroll)	5.2	23.7	22.5	40.5	8.1	3.2
Moderate outsourcing to *multiple* vendors	2.9	13.5	34.5	46.8	2.3	3.3
Moderate outsourcing to a single vendor	2.9	16.4	34.5	40.4	5.8	3.3
Substantial outsourcing to *multiple* vendors	9.3	33.7	34.3	20.3	2.3	2.7
Substantial outsourcing to a single vendor	14.0	25.7	33.9	24.0	2.3	2.7

Table 11.6. HR outsourcing approaches, by country

In general, how effective do you think the following approaches to HR outsourcing are?	Means					
	USA[1]	Canada[2]	Australia[3]	Europe[4]	UK[5]	China[6]
No outsourcing	2.2[6]	2.4	2.4	2.6	2.7	2.6[1]
Very limited: only a few transactional services (e.g. payroll)	3.2	3.9[6]	3.5	3.6[6]	3.5[6]	3.0[2,4,5]
Moderate outsourcing to *multiple* vendors	3.3[4,6]	3.8[3,4,6]	2.9[2]	2.8[1,2]	3.0	2.9[1,2]
Moderate outsourcing to a single vendor	3.3	2.9	2.8	3.2	3.1	3.0
Substantial outsourcing to *multiple* vendors	2.7	2.6	2.4	2.5	2.6	2.4
Substantial outsourcing to a single vendor	2.7	2.5	2.3	2.6	2.9	2.7

Response scale: 1=Very ineffective; 2=Ineffective; 3=Neither, 4=Effective; 5=Very effective

[1,2,3,4,5,6] Significant differences between countries ($p \le .05$).

Table 11.7. Use of HRBPO

	Percentages						
	USA[1]		Canada[2]	Australia[3]	Europe[4]	UK[5]	China[6]
	2007	2010					
Yes	22.1	18.9[6]	10.0[6]	11.1[6]	7.5[6]	10.5[6]	23.0[1,2,3,4,5]
No, but seriously considering	9.6	7.0	5.0	0.0	9.4	15.8	32.4
No, not seriously considering	68.3	74.1	85.0	88.9	83.0	73.7	44.6

[1,2,3,4,5,6] Significant differences between countries ($p \le .05$).

Table 11.8. Satisfaction with HRBPO (percentages)							
	USA[1]		Canada[2]	Australia[3]	Europe[4]	UK[5]	China[6]
	2007	2010					
Very dissatisfied	9.1	8.0[2]	0.0[1,6]	0.0	0.0	0.0	0.0[2]
Dissatisfied	0.0	8.0	0.0	0.0	25.0	25.0	8.3
Somewhat dissatisfied	13.6	8.0	0.0	33.3	0.0	25.0	27.1
Neither satisfied nor dissatisfied	22.7	8.0	0.0	33.3	25.0	0.0	22.9
Somewhat satisfied	27.3	44.0	0.0	0.0	25.0	25.0	27.1
Satisfied	27.3	20.0	25.0	33.3	25.0	25.0	14.6
Very satisfied	0.0	4.0	75.0	0.0	0.0	0.0	0.0

[1,2,3,4,5,6] Significant differences between countries ($p \leq .05$).

slight drop from 2007. Almost 75 percent say they are not considering one. China, like the U.S., shows a relatively high adoption rate with 23 percent reporting they have a contract and a high percentage (32 percent) saying they are considering one.

The satisfaction data in Table 11.8 show a mixed picture. In all the countries with the exception of Canada where only four organizations have a contract, some organizations report they are dissatisfied with their HRBPO relationship. In the U.S., 24 percent say they are dissatisfied. It is clear that most firms that do not have an HRBPO contract may be a "hard sell" for an industry that is committed to growth.

Conclusion

Overall, there is little evidence that outsourcing is in a strong growth mode. As a result, organizations may be missing an opportunity to improve their HR activities. Outsourcing can allow them to access knowledge and expertise that they lack and are not in a good position to develop. They may also be missing a chance to realize economies of scale.

An obstacle to the growth of outsourcing may be the number of problems associated with it, including the apparent difficulty of getting sustained cost and quality advantages. The evidence is mixed on whether it helps HR be more of a strategic partner. HR executives say it can, but the amount of it is only slightly correlated with the degree to which HR plays a role in strategy. There remains the possibility that outsourcing will grow in the future, but given its failure to grow during the recession, it is not clear what could happen that would cause it to increase. One possibility is strong economic growth; it is slightly correlated with the degree to which firms have a growth strategy.

CHAPTER 12

Use of Information Technology

Information technology (IT) is potentially a way to accomplish HR record-keeping, HR transactions, and many other administrative tasks more quickly, efficiently, and accurately, thus enabling HR to save money and spend more time on strategic business support. IT can do more than serve as an administrative tool. It can be a way to deliver expert advice to managers and employees in areas such as selection, career development, talent management, and compensation. It can also facilitate change efforts by assessing the capabilities of the workforce and by providing information and training that supports change. Finally, it can support the development and implementation of business strategy by providing important information about the capabilities and core competencies of the organization, as well as creating transparency with respect to organizational performance.

Amount of Use

Table 12.1 shows the state of IT-based human resource processes from 1995 to 2010. In 2010, 66 percent of companies were using human resource information systems (HRISs) for most or all of their human resource processes, a relatively high level of use. Although there is not a significant increase in 2010 from 2004 to 2007, there is a significant increase in comparison to 1995, 1998, and 2001. This is not surprising, particularly in light of the great amount of activity occurring in the HRIS world. In many respects, the increase almost had to occur, given the increased popularity of business software and the fact that the major business software companies have HR applications (e.g. SAP, Oracle). It is somewhat surprising, given the growth in the use of IT by companies, that there was not an increase in use from 2004 and 2007; it

Table 12.1. State of human resources information system (HRIS), USA only						
	Percentages					
State of Information System	1995[1]	1998[2]	2001[3]	2004[4]	2007[5]	2010[6]
Little or no information technology/ automation present in the HR function	6.3	8.4	8.3	6.1	7.8	3.8
Some HR processes are information technology-based/ automated	45.3	40.3	48.3	32.3	32.0	30.1
Most processes are information technology-based/ automated but not fully integrated	40.6	42.9	35.9	48.5	51.5	49.7
Completely integrated HR information technology/ automated system	7.8	8.4	7.6	13.1	8.7	16.4
Mean[a]	3.50[6]	3.50[6]	3.41[6]	3.69	3.59	3.79[1,2,3]

[a]Response scale: 1=No information technology; 2=Little information technology; 3=Some processes integrated; 4=Most processes integrated; 5=Completely integrated
[1,2,3,4,5,6]Significant differences ($p \leq .05$) between years.

is not surprising that in 2010 66 percent of U.S. companies report that most or all of their processes are IT based.

International Results

The international results in Table 12.2 show some significant differences in the state of HRISs. Not surprisingly, China has by far the lowest rate of utilization. The U.K. and Australia have a lower rate than the other developed countries studied, while the U.S. has the highest. The data for the U.S. are not surprising and most likely are the results of it being an early adopter. The low use in the U.K. and Australia is harder to understand and explain. The low rate in China is not surprising; it lags somewhat behind in the adoption of information technology for most business processes.

Activities

In 1998, a series of questions on the use of company HRISs was added to our survey in order to obtain a more complete picture of the capabilities and uses of the systems. We asked about the degree to which employees and managers could do certain HR tasks via an HRIS. Table 12.3 shows the results for 1998, 2001, and 2004, grouped on the basis of a statistical factor analysis of the questions. Because of survey length limitations, we did not ask this question in 2007 or 2010 so our discussion will be limited to data collected in previous surveys.

Perhaps the most striking finding is the variation in the extent to which these HR activities are done by employees and managers on HRISs. Posting job openings, applying for a job, personal information changes, and changing benefit coverage are done completely on HRISs by employees or managers in over 60 percent of the companies. At the other extreme, there are six activities, primarily in the area of management tools, that in 40 percent or more of the companies are not done on HRISs at all.

Table 12.2. State of human resources information system (HRIS), by country						
	Percentages					
State of Information System	USA[1]	Canada[2]	Australia[3]	Europe[4]	UK[5]	China[6]
Little or no information technology/automation present in the HR function	3.8	13.6	23.3	11.3	18.6	41.8
Some HR processes are information technology-based/ automated	30.1	31.8	23.3	33.9	39.5	19.2
Most processes are information technology-based/automated but not fully integrated	49.7	43.2	43.3	38.7	30.2	27.7
Completely integrated HR information technology/automated system	16.4	11.4	10.0	16.1	11.6	11.3
Mean[a]	3.79[6]	3.50[6]	3.40	3.58[6]	3.35	3.02[1,2,4]

[a]Response scale: 1=No information technology; 2=Little information technology; 3=Some processes integrated; 4=Most processes integrated; 5=Completely integrated
[1,2,3,4,5,6] Significant differences between countries ($p \leq .05$).

Table 12.3. Information system HR activities done by employees or managers	Means[2]		
Activities	1998	2001	2004
Personnel Records	**2.1**	**2.1**	**2.5[1]**
Change benefit coverage	2.2	2.2	2.5[1]
Change address and/or other personal information	2.0	2.1	2.4[1]
Job Information		**2.1**	**2.4[1]**
Apply for a job (external applicants)	1.9	2.2	2.5[1]
Apply for a job (internal applicants)		2.2	2.6[1]
Post job openings	2.3	2.5	2.5
Post personal resume/bio		1.5	1.9[1]
Employee Training		**1.7**	**1.9[1]**
New hire orientation		1.5	1.7[1]
Skills training		1.7	1.9[1]
Scheduling training		2.0	2.2[1]
Management Tools			**1.7**
Career development planning	1.4	1.5	1.6[1]
Obtain advice and information on handling personnel issues	1.5	1.5	1.7[1]
Management development training		1.5	1.7[1]
Search for employees with specified skills/competencies		1.5	1.6
Assess skills/competencies/knowledge			1.7
Access knowledge communities or experts			1.5
Access managers tool kit			1.8
Salary Planning/ Administration	**1.9**	**2.0**	**2.1**
Performance Management	**1.6**	**1.9**	**1.9**
Financial Transactions		**1.6**	**1.9[1]**

[1] Significant difference ($p \leq .05$) between 2001 and 2004.
[2] Response scale: 1 = Not at all; 2 = Partially; 3 = Completely
Significance level: [1] $p \leq .10$; * $p \leq .05$; ** $p \leq .01$; *** $p \leq .001$

What most clearly distinguishes the tasks that are frequently done from those that are done infrequently or not at all is the degree to which the activities are transactional. Transactional activities are particularly likely to be done on an HRIS, whereas those involving expert advice and decision making (e.g. all the management tool items) are either done not at all or done only partially via an HRIS. The difference in findings between transactional and advice tools is hardly surprising, since transactions are particularly suited to self-service. It takes much more sophisticated software support to offer advice and training, and it often takes much more skilled users.

Since 1998, more and more companies have invested in HR information systems that can perform virtually all the activities in Table 12.3. A comparison between the 2001 and 2004 results shows significant increases in the use of HRISs for a wide range of activities. A particularly large increase occurred from 1998 to 2004 in the ability to use HRISs for job information. Apparently, organizations have increasingly adopted the web as a way to handle the entire job application and job posting processes.

There also is evidence of increased use of HRISs for performance management purposes. This finding may well reflect the use of HRISs for 360-degree appraisals and for gathering of performance data throughout an organization. The emergence of standard modules for such data in the major software packages being sold to organizations may well be driving this increase.

Overall, it is clear that organizations are making greater use of self-service HRISs in the HR function, at least in the number of activities that are carried out on them. Most likely there has been continued growth since 2004 in both the areas where individuals can service themselves via an HRIS and in the number of companies that use such a system.

IT System Effectiveness

Because of the relative newness of HRISs, there is relatively little information available about their overall effectiveness, or about their impact on the effectiveness of organizations and their HR systems. In order to measure their effectiveness, beginning in 2001 we asked questions about both the effectiveness of HRISs in general and their effectiveness in key areas.

As can be seen in Table 12.4, a statistical factor analysis grouped the outcome questions asked since 2001 into two clusters: efficiency and business effectiveness. Six other items did not cluster. The results for items asked for the first time in 2007 about overall effectiveness, human capital decision making, and impact on the business are also shown in Table 12.4. Two network questions which were asked for the first time in 2010 are shown as well.

The HRISs did not receive very high performance ratings on any of the outcomes. The highest ratings are in the areas of speed, costs, and service, but even there, the highest-rated item received a rating in the middle of the 5-point rating scale. It is hardly surprising that high ratings came in the efficiency area, since efficiency is an area where short-term payoffs should be achieved by an IT system. Nevertheless, it is significant that we now have data that confirm that the systems do, to some extent, improve HR services, reduce costs, and increase speed.

The ratings concerned with business effectiveness are among the lowest. HR executives do not see their HRISs strongly affecting organizational performance, strategic decision making, HR's impact on the business, or human capital decision making. The effectiveness item gets the highest rating, while improving human capital decisions and measuring HR's impact get low ratings. Overall, it is clear that HRISs are not yet doing a good job of providing the information that HRIS executives need to be strategic business partners. This is disappointing since there are good reasons to believe that HRISs can have a big impact in these areas. The failure of HRISs to have an impact may be in part due to the newness of the systems and the fact that organizations are just beginning to learn how to use HRISs as a strategic tool.

We added two new "networks" items in 2010. They both received very low effectiveness ratings. It is clear that the HRISs in these companies are not doing a great deal to create networks that help employees share knowledge and facilitate getting work done.

Table 12.4. HRIS outcomes, USA only

HRIS Outcomes	Percentages					Means				Correlation with HR Role in Strategy 2010
	Little or No Extent	Some Extent	Moderate Extent	Great Extent	Very Great Extent	2001[1]	2004[2]	2007[3]	2010[4]	
Overall Effectiveness[a]						2.6	2.8	2.7	2.7	.22**
Employee Satisfaction	12.0	27.7	40.2	18.5	1.6	2.4	2.7	2.6	2.7	.11
Efficiency						2.9	3.0	2.8	2.8	.19*
Improve HR services	10.4	20.8	36.1	24.6	8.2	3.0	3.0	2.9	3.0	.14[t]
Reduce HR transaction costs	13.6	21.7	26.6	28.3	9.8	2.9	3.0	2.8	3.0	.16*
Speed up HR processes	13.6	22.8	27.7	24.5	11.4	3.1	3.2	3.0	3.0	.15*
Reduce the number of employees in HR	27.9	30.1	26.8	10.9	4.4	2.4	2.6	2.4	2.3	.17*
Business Effectiveness						2.2	2.3	2.5	2.5	.23**
Provide new strategic information	23.5	25.7	29.5	16.4	4.9	2.1[4]	2.3	2.5	2.5[1]	.24***
Integrate HR processes (e.g. training, compensation)	25.7	26.8	29.5	14.2	3.8	2.4	2.4	2.5	2.4	.17*
Measure HR's Impact on the Business	31.0	29.3	25.0	12.0	2.7		2.1	2.3	2.3	.26***
Improve Human Capital Decisions of Managers Outside HR	33.2	26.6	25.0	12.5	2.7			2.4	2.3	.22**
Effective	7.7	24.0	38.3	25.7	4.4			2.9	3.0	.11
Create Knowledge Networks	48.9	25.8	18.1	5.5	1.6				1.9	.19*
Build Social Networks That Help Get Work Done	60.1	19.7	14.8	3.8	1.6				1.7	.15*

[1,2,3,4] Significant difference ($p \le .05$) between years.

[a] Includes items from Employee Satisfaction, Efficiency, and Business Effectiveness scales only.

Significance level: [t] $p \le .10$; * $p \le .05$; ** $p \le .01$; *** $p \le .001$

The relationships between the effectiveness of HRISs and the role of HR in strategy are shown in Table 12.4. Most are statistically significant although the correlations are relatively low. Nevertheless, it does suggest that HRISs can lead to HR playing a more important role in strategy.

Only time will tell what impact HRISs will have on HR and organizations. As Boudreau and Ramstad (2003) have noted, a decision science for HR remains elusive, yet it is essential for guiding decision makers through the increasingly daunting amount of information available in HRISs. They note that having such a decision science is one reason that data systems in finance, marketing, supply chain, and other areas have been so influential. As the HR profession develops a deeper and more precise decision science, HRISs may become more effective in the HR arena.

International

There are some differences among the countries in our international sample. As can be seen in Table 12.5, Canada and the U.K. have the lowest scores. In the case of the U.K. this is not surprising; it also is a

Table 12.5. HRIS outcomes, by country						
	Means					
HRIS Outcomes	USA[1]	Canada[2]	Australia[3]	Europe[4]	UK[5]	China[6]
Overall Effectiveness[a]	**2.7**[2]	**2.2**[1,4]	**2.5**	**2.9**[2]	**2.4**	**2.6**
Employee Satisfaction	**2.7**[2,6]	**2.1**[1,4]	**2.5**	**2.9**[2,5,6]	**2.4**[4]	**2.4**[1,4]
Efficiency	**2.8**[2]	**2.3**[1,4]	**2.7**	**2.9**[2]	**2.4**	**2.7**
Improve HR services	3.0[2]	2.4[1,4]	2.8	3.2[2]	2.7	2.8
Reduce HR transaction costs	3.0[5]	2.5	2.8	3.1[5]	2.4[1,4]	2.8
Speed up HR processes	3.0	2.5[4]	2.9	3.2[2,5]	2.5[4]	2.8
Reduce the number of employees in HR	2.3[2]	1.8[1]	2.3	2.2	2.1	2.2
Business Effectiveness	**2.5**	**2.1**[4]	**2.1**	**2.7**[2]	**2.3**	**2.5**
Provide new strategic information	2.5	2.2	2.1	2.7	2.4	2.4
Integrate HR processes (e.g. training, compensation)	2.4	2.0[4,6]	2.1	2.8[2]	2.2	2.6[2]
Measure HR's Impact on the Business	**2.3**[2]	**1.7**[1,4,6]	**2.2**	**2.3**[2]	**2.3**	**2.3**[2]
Improve Human Capital Decisions of Managers Outside HR	**2.3**[4]	**1.9**[4]	**2.4**	**2.7**[1,2]	**2.3**	**2.4**
Effective	**3.0**	**2.6**[4]	**2.8**	**3.2**[2,5,6]	**2.6**[4]	**2.7**[4]
Create Knowledge Networks	**1.9**[6]	**1.5**[4,6]	**1.9**	**2.3**[2]	**1.9**[6]	**2.5**[1,2,5]
Build Social Networks That Help Get Work Done	**1.7**[6]	**1.4**[4,6]	**1.7**[6]	**2.0**[2]	**1.6**[6]	**2.3**[1,2,3,5]

Response scale: 1=Little or no extent; 2=Some extent; 3=Moderate extent; 4=Great extent; 5=Very great extent

[a] Includes items from Employee Satisfaction, Efficiency, and Business Effectiveness scales only.

[1,2,3,4,5,6] Significant differences between countries ($p < .05$).

Table 12.6. Relationship of HRIS outcomes to strategic focuses

HRIS Outcomes	Strategic Focuses				
	Growth	Information-Based Strategies	Knowledge-Based Strategies	Sustainability	Innovation
Overall effectiveness (all items)[a]	.11	.36***	.30***	.22**	.22**
Employee satisfaction	–.06	.30***	.15*	.10	.12[t]
Efficiency	.11	.31***	.26***	.20**	.19*
Business effectiveness	.15*	.37***	.35***	.24***	.25***
Measures HR's impact on the business	.14[t]	.36***	.39***	.23**	.28***
Improve human capital decisions of managers outside HR	.15*	.27***	.36***	.16*	.21**
Effective	.10	.36***	.23**	.11	.17*
Create knowledge networks	.09	.24***	.36***	.14[t]	.24***
Build social networks that help get work done	.09	.21**	.38***	.20**	.30***

Response scale: 1=Little or no extent; 2=Some extent; 3=Moderate extent; 4=Great extent; 5=Very great extent

[a] Includes items from Employee Satisfaction, Efficiency, and Business Effectiveness scales only.

Significance level: [t] $p \leq .10$; * $p \leq .05$; ** $p \leq .01$; *** $p \leq .001$

low user of HRISs. Canada's low score is somewhat surprising since it is not one of the lowest users. The highest scores are those for the U.S. and Europe. Given the high adoption rate in these countries, this result is not surprising. Finally, China's results are interesting: it is a low user, but its scores are relatively positive particularly with respect to networks. The high score for networks most likely is the result of a translation problem with the questions' wording in Mandarin. After the survey was complete, we were told that these two items were not clear.

Strategic Focuses and Management Approach

As we see in Table 12.6, there are a number of significant relationships between HRIS effectiveness and the strategic focuses. All of the strategic focuses show some significant relationships. The strongest relationships involve knowledge-based strategies and information-based strategies. The next strongest set is with sustainability and innovation. These results are not surprising since all four of these strategies are ones that can be aided by an effective HRIS. Only a weak relationship with growth exists. This fits the pattern we have seen with respect to growth. It seems to be a strategic focus that is quite different from the other four.

There are only a few significant correlations between the management approach items and the HRIS effectiveness items. High-involvement management is associated with HRISs improving the human capital decisions of managers, once again making the point that HR has a potential positive and important role in high-involvement organizations.

Table 12.7. Relationship of HRIS outcomes to state of HRIS	
HRIS Outcomes	**HRIS[1]**
Overall Effectiveness[a]	**.58***
Employee satisfaction	.52***
Efficiency	.57***
Business effectiveness	.47***
Measures HR's impact on the business	.33***
Improve human capital decisions of managers outside HR	.31***
Effective	.59***
Create knowledge networks	.20**
Build social networks that help get work done	.21**

Response scale: 1=Little or no extent; 2=Some extent; 3=Moderate extent; 4=Great extent; 5=Very great extent

[1] Amount of use (Table 12.1)

[a] Includes items from Employee Satisfaction, Efficiency, and Business Effectiveness scales only.

Significance level: [1] $p \leq .10$; * $p \leq .05$; ** $p \leq .01$; *** $p \leq .001$

Effectiveness and Use

Table 12.7 shows the relationship of HRIS effectiveness to the state of information technology use (see Table 12.1). There clearly is a strong relationship here, as there was in 2001, 2004, and 2007. Completely integrated HRISs are rated much higher in all areas. Less strongly related, but still significantly related, are the two network items. This is not surprising since networks can be created without an integrated HRIS and most are not designed to facilitate the development of networks.

The strong relationships to HRIS outcomes undoubtedly reflect the power that integrated systems have. They offer the opportunity to do many things with an HRIS, including doing analyses related to business effectiveness and business strategy. For example, it is possible to assess the practicality of a business strategy by determining whether the organization has the capability to execute it. It is also possible to determine the impacts of HR programs and to more effectively develop and place employees.

Conclusion

Our findings bear out that HRISs are most effective at providing transaction tools for HR administration. When these findings are combined with the data we collected on usage, we can see that HRISs are used the most to do the thing that they do best: administration. There is a slow but sure movement toward companies having integrated HR information systems that improve decision making and organizational performances, but there is a long way to go.

HRISs are not rated as more effective in 2010 than they were in 2001. They also are not rated as very effective in an absolute sense. There are many possible reasons for this result, including the fact that they are relatively new and that companies and managers are just beginning to learn how to utilize them effectively. The technology is advancing rapidly, and many companies may be experiencing difficulties dealing with a technology that is not well developed.

The evidence is quite clear that HRISs are most effective when they fit the strategy of an organization. They are particularly likely to be perceived as successful in companies with knowledge and information-based strategies. Perhaps the strongest finding is that the more things an HRIS can do, and the more services it performs, the more effective it is perceived to be. As a result, the future of HR is dependent upon it developing comprehensive HRISs.

CHAPTER 13

Human Resources Skills

The skills and knowledge of the members of an organization's HR function are perhaps the most important determinant of what it does and how well it performs (Ulrich et al. 2008). Much of the high-value-added work HR does is knowledge work that requires considerable expertise in a wide variety of areas. In today's rapidly changing global economy, the knowledge and skill requirements for the members of an organization's staff functions are continuing to evolve, just as they are for the firm's core business and technical units. Key issues for HR are what skills and knowledge do HR professionals need, and what is the current level of their skills and knowledge.

Skill Importance

For the first time in 2007, we asked both HR executives and managers to rate the importance of a variety of HR skills and knowledge. For survey length reasons we did not ask this question in 2010. Table 13.1 shows the results based on a statistical analysis that yielded four factors and one item. There is some similarity between our factors and the HR competencies Ulrich and his partners identified in their study of competencies (Ulrich et al. 2008). However, ours are more focused on the content knowledge needed by HR executives, while theirs include personal traits (e.g. "credible activist"), and as a result there are significant differences.

Although there is some variation in how highly they are rated, most of the skills are rated as high in importance by both HR executives and managers. The skills that are rated particularly highly by both groups include business understanding and skills having to do with interpersonal dynamics and change management. Managers rate HR technical skills and communication skills highest. HR executives rate business understanding, team skills, and interpersonal skills highest. Metrics skills and managing contractor skills are rated lowest in importance by both managers and HR executives. The relatively low rating for managing contractors/vendors is not surprising or concerning. The relatively low rating of metrics skills is another story. It is an area of growing importance and certainly is one that HR functions need to have.

A few skills are rated higher by HR executives (e.g. information technology), and a few are rated higher by managers (e.g. organization design). However, when we correlated the mean importance given to the skills by HR executives with those given by managers, we found they are strongly

Table 13.1. Importance of HR skills (2007)					
	HR Executive Percentages			Mean	
Skills	Not Important	Somewhat Important	Very Important	HR Executives	Managers
HR Technical Skills				**2.7**	**2.7**
HR technical skills	1.0	26.8	72.2	**2.7**	**2.9**[1]
Process execution and analysis	2.1	29.2	68.8	**2.7**	**2.5**[1]
Interpersonal Dynamics				**2.8**	**2.7**[1]
Team skills	0	12.4	87.6	**2.9**	**2.7**
Interpersonal skills	0	14.4	85.6	**2.9**	**2.8**
Consultation skills	1.0	20.6	78.4	**2.8**	**2.6**
Coaching and facilitation	1.0	22.7	76.3	**2.8**	**2.7**
Leadership/Management	1.0	15.5	83.5	**2.8**	**2.7**
Business Partner Skills				**2.6**	**2.6**
Business understanding	0	7.2	92.8	**2.9**	**2.8**
Strategic planning	0	38.1	61.9	**2.6**	**2.4**[1]
Organization design	3.1	53.6	43.3	**2.4**	**2.7**[1]
Change management	0	20.6	79.4	**2.8**	**2.8**
Cross-functional experience	8.2	51.5	40.2	**2.3**	**2.2**
Global understanding	18.6	39.2	42.3	**2.2**	**2.2**
Communications	0	19.6	80.4	**2.8**	**2.9**
Metrics Skills				**2.4**	**2.3**
Information technology	9.3	55.7	35.1	**2.3**	**2.0**[1]
Metrics development	5.2	48.5	46.4	**2.4**	**2.4**
Data analysis and mining	6.2	48.5	45.4	**2.4**	**2.3**
Managing Contractors/Vendors	12.4	58.8	28.9	**2.2**	**2.1**

[1] Significant difference ($p \leq .05$) between HR executives and managers.

related ($r = .85$, $p \leq .001$). Apparently, HR executives and managers do agree on what skills the HR staff of an organization need to have.

Overall, it is clear that these results support the argument that HR professionals need to have a range of business skills—it is not enough for them to just be good HR technicians. They need to understand the business and what makes it effective. Further, they need to be able to help design the organization, develop teams and leaders, and support change efforts.

Skill Satisfaction

Table 13.2 shows the level of satisfaction with the skills of the HR staff as rated by HR executives. Not surprisingly, one of the two highest levels of satisfaction is with HR technical skills. The other highest level of satisfaction is with skills that pertain to interpersonal dynamics, including interpersonal skills, team skills, consulting, coaching, and leadership/management skills. This is the only area where all the individual skills show an increased level of satisfaction when the 2010 data are compared to earlier data. Business understanding is the only other individual skill that shows a significant increase in satisfaction. The high level of satisfaction with interpersonal skills is a positive, but it may reflect HR being an eager-to-please "nice guy" when it could add more value by being an effective business partner and/or metrics expert.

A relatively low area of satisfaction is business partner skills. A comparison of the data from 1998 with the data from 2010 shows a significant increase in satisfaction with business understanding and organization design. However, there still is not a positive level of satisfaction with the

Table 13.2. Satisfaction with skills of HR staff, USA only											
	Percentages					Mean					
Skills	Very Dissatisfied	Dissatisfied	Neutral	Satisfied	Very Satisfied	1995[1]	1998[2]	2001[3]	2004[4]	2007[5]	2010[6]
HR Technical Skills									3.8	3.6	3.6
HR technical skills	1.1	9.6	18.6	50.3	20.3				4.0	3.7	3.8
Process execution and analysis	4.0	16.7	31.0	40.2	8.0				3.5	3.4	3.3
Interpersonal Dynamics						3.3[3,4,5,6]	3.1[3,4,5,6]	3.6[1,2]	3.7[1,2]	3.6[1,2]	3.6[1,2]
Team skills	2.2	7.9	25.8	53.9	10.1	3.3[3,4,5,6]	3.2[3,4,5,6]	3.7[1,2]	3.7[1,2]	3.7[1,2]	3.6[1,2]
Interpersonal skills	0.6	6.2	14.7	57.6	20.9	3.7[3,4,5]	3.5[3,4,5,6]	4.0[1,2]	4.1[1,2]	4.0[1,2]	3.9[2]
Consultation skills	3.9	18.0	30.3	38.8	9.0	3.0[3,4]	2.9[3,4,5,6]	3.3[1,2]	3.4[1,2]	3.3[2]	3.3[2]
Leadership/Management	2.8	11.2	26.4	48.3	11.2	3.0[4,5,6]	2.9[3,4,5,6]	3.3[2]	3.5[1,2]	3.5[1,2]	3.5[1,2]
Business Partner Skills									3.0	3.0	3.1
Business understanding	2.8	13.5	29.8	46.1	7.9	3.0[3,4,5,6]	2.9[3,4,5,6]	3.3[1,2]	3.3[1,2]	3.3[1,2]	3.4[1,2]
Cross-functional experience	5.6	27.1	33.9	29.4	4.0	2.9	2.8	2.9	2.9	2.8	3.0
Strategic planning	5.6	27.1	33.9	28.8	4.5		2.8	2.9	3.0	2.9	3.0
Organization design	5.1	25.8	37.6	28.1	3.4		2.7[4,6]	2.8	3.1[2]	3.0	3.0[2]
Global understanding	8.0	28.4	37.5	21.0	5.1		2.6	2.7	2.8	2.8	2.9
Change management	6.2	17.4	30.3	39.3	6.7			3.1	3.3	3.2	3.2
Metrics Skills									2.8	2.7[6]	2.9[5]
Information technology	6.2	23.7	36.2	28.2	5.6			3.1	3.0	2.9	3.0
Metrics development	7.9	28.8	32.2	24.3	6.8				2.7	2.7	2.9
Data analysis and mining	9.6	33.3	29.9	20.9	6.2				2.8	2.5[6]	2.8[5]

[1,2,3,4,5,6] Significant difference ($p \leq .05$) between years.

substantive business support areas of strategic planning, organization design, and global understanding. Satisfaction with change management skills remains at slightly above the neutral point. Finally, the HR staff continues to have a low level of cross-functional experience, a factor that may well contribute to the relatively low scores in the business partner area.

It is encouraging that HR professionals increasingly understand the business. However, they still do not appear to bring substantive business expertise to the table. This deficit clearly has to change if HR is to influence an organization's strategic direction. It is a critical weakness with respect to HR's performing as an effective strategic contributor. Fixing this deficit requires going well beyond simple business acumen, to being able to create a truly unique perspective on strategy through the lens of HR and human capital.

As in 2004 and 2007, the lowest satisfaction level is with metrics and information technology skills and there is not an increase in satisfaction with them from 2004 to 2010. Apparently, HR managers are not improving their skills in this area. They are critical skill areas. Metrics skills are particularly critical in terms of the ability of the HR function to play a major business strategy role. Bringing data and performing data analyses are critical in many business decisions; thus, it is particularly important that HR executives have good skills in these areas.

International Results on Skills Satisfaction

Except for China, the skills satisfaction results for the international samples are very similar to those for the U.S. (see Table 13.3). No other country stands out as having a particularly high or low level of skills satisfaction. There is a relatively large difference with respect to global understanding; not surprisingly, Europe has the highest satisfaction level in this area.

China has lower satisfaction levels with HR technical skills, interpersonal dynamics skills, and business partner skills. It has similar satisfaction levels with respect to metrics skills. There are some positives: China scores well on cross-functional experience, for example, but it does not have any satisfaction levels, except in metrics, that exceed the level of any other country.

Overall, the satisfaction with skills scores is low for all countries on an absolute basis. This is particularly true for business partner skills and metrics skills. These clearly are areas that HR professionals in all countries need to improve.

Skills	Means					
	USA[1]	Canada[2]	Australia[3]	Europe[4]	UK[5]	China[6]
HR Technical Skills	**3.6[6]**	**3.7[6]**	**3.4**	**3.6[6]**	**3.6[6]**	**3.1[1,2,4,5]**
HR technical skills	3.8[6]	3.9[6]	3.8[6]	3.8[6]	4.0[6]	3.0[1,2,3,4,5]
Process execution and analysis	3.3	3.4	3.1	3.3	3.2	3.1
Interpersonal Dynamics	**3.6[6]**	**3.8[6]**	**3.6[6]**	**3.5[6]**	**3.5[6]**	**3.0[1,2,3,4,5]**
Team skills	3.6[6]	3.9[6]	3.5	3.7[6]	3.6	3.3[1,2,4]
Interpersonal skills	3.9[6]	4.0[6]	3.8[6]	3.7[6]	3.8[6]	3.3[1,2,3,4,5]
Consultation skills	3.3[6]	3.6[6]	3.5[6]	3.2	3.2[6]	2.8[1,2,3,5]
Leadership/Management	3.5[6]	3.6[6]	3.4[6]	3.4[6]	3.3[6]	2.8[1,2,3,4,5]
Business Partner Skills	**3.1[6]**	**3.1[6]**	**3.2[6]**	**3.1[6]**	**3.0[6]**	**2.7[1,2,3,4,5]**
Business understanding	3.4[6]	3.3	3.6[6]	3.2	3.2	3.0[1,3]
Cross-functional experience	3.0	3.0	3.1	2.7	2.9	2.9
Strategic planning	3.0[6]	3.0[6]	3.2[6]	2.9[6]	2.9	2.5[1,2,3,4]
Organization design	3.0	3.0	3.0	3.1[6]	3.0	2.7[4]
Global understanding	2.9[4,6]	2.8[6]	2.9[6]	3.3[1,6]	2.8[6]	2.3[1,2,3,4,5]
Change management	3.2[6]	3.3[6]	3.2[6]	3.2[6]	3.3[6]	2.5[1,2,3,4,5]
Metrics Skills	**2.9**	**2.8**	**2.8**	**2.9**	**2.8**	**2.9**
Information technology	3.0	2.9	2.8	2.9	3.0	2.8
Metrics development	2.9	2.8	2.9	2.9	2.7	3.0
Data analysis and mining	2.8	2.7	2.8	2.9	2.6	2.9

Table 13.3. Satisfaction with skills of HR staff, by country

Response scale: 1=Very dissatisfied; 2=Dissatisfied; 3=Neither; 4=Satisfied; 5=Very satisfied
[1,2,3,4,5,6] Significant differences between countries ($p \le .05$).

Managers' Satisfaction with Skills

Table 13.4 presents skill satisfaction data, comparing the responses of HR executives with those of other managers. It yields a rather surprising result: in every skill area, HR executives are actually less satisfied with the skills of the HR staff than are other managers. Interestingly, this trend was also found in our 2004 and 2007 surveys, which were the first surveys that gathered data from managers on skill satisfaction. We have no data in the survey that identify the cause of this pattern, but it may be that HR suffers from a bit of an inferiority complex, because it is often on the defensive and is criticized by other employees and in the press.

The differences between the views of HR executives and managers are particularly striking in the area of metrics and business partner skills. As in 2004 and 2007, managers rate HR as significantly more skillful vis-à-vis metrics development and data analysis and mining than do HR executives. We suspect that this result may arise in part because managers have low expectations and may be impressed with the mere existence of measures, data, and scorecards. HR executives, in contrast, may be better able to see the untapped potential in such systems.

All of the business partner skill areas are rated considerably lower by HR executives than they are by managers. This appears to be one area where HR definitely underestimates its skills. What may need to happen for HR to become more of a business partner is for it to realize that it often has something to contribute in this area and that others see it as capable of adding value. Perhaps it needs to knock on the business partner door more often; our data suggest that if it does, it is likely to find a more favorable reception than it expects.

Table 13.4. Satisfaction with skills and knowledge of HR staff				
	HR Executives		Managers	
Skills	Mean	Correlation with HR Role in Strategy	Mean	Correlation with HR Role in Strategy
HR Technical Skills	**3.6**	**.33*****	**4.0[1]**	**.48****
HR technical skills	3.8	.24***	4.3[1]	.28
Process execution and analysis	3.3	.33***	3.8[1]	.55***
Interpersonal Dynamics	**3.6**	**.36*****	**4.1[1]**	**.41***
Team skills	3.6	.39***	4.1[1]	.34*
Interpersonal skills	3.9	.27***	4.2[1]	.20
Consultation skills	3.3	.20**	4.0[1]	.42*
Leadership/Management	3.5	.34***	4.1[1]	.36*
Business Partner Skills	**3.1**	**.38*****	**3.8[1]**	**.54*****
Business understanding	3.4	.23**	4.0[1]	.39*
Cross-functional experience	3.0	.21**	3.6[1]	.49**
Strategic planning	3.0	.38***	3.6[1]	.52**
Organization design	3.0	.33***	3.9[1]	.27
Global understanding	2.9	.24**	3.7[1]	.55***
Change management	3.2	.33***	3.7[1]	.43*
Metrics Skills	**2.9**	**.31*****	**3.5[1]**	**.56*****
Information technology	3.0	.16*	3.4[1]	.43*
Metrics development	2.9	.35***	3.6[1]	.62***
Data analysis and mining	2.8	.28***	3.3[1]	.51**

Response scale: 1=Very dissatisfied; 2=Dissatisfied; 3=Neither; 4=Satisfied; 5=Very satisfied

[1] Significant difference ($p \leq .05$) between HR executives and managers.

Significance level: [1] $p \leq .10$; * $p \leq .05$; ** $p \leq .01$; *** $p \leq .001$

Despite the fact that HR executives and managers differ in just how satisfied they are with certain HR skills, they are in general agreement when it comes to which skills they are most and least satisfied with. When we correlated the mean satisfaction levels for managers and HR executives, we found a very high correlation ($r = .88, p \leq .001$). Thus it seems HR executives and managers are in general agreement about what HR can do well and what it cannot do well.

Role in Strategy

The relationship between HR skills satisfaction and HR's role in strategy is shown in Table 13.4. Let's look first at the correlations for the HR executives' data. The correlations for HR technical skills, interpersonal dynamics, business partner skills, and metrics skills are statistically significant.

The significant correlations between HR technical skills and its role in strategy support the view that HR technical skills are required in order to get involved in business strategy. The correlations of role in strategy with interpersonal dynamics and business partner skills were expected to be high, given that they are truly the foundation for contributing to business strategy both from an implementation and a development point of view. The correlations with metrics skills are the lowest, but they are significant. These skills certainly are potentially useful in strategy development and implementation, so it is not surprising that they are related.

A similar picture of the relationship of HR skills and HR's role in strategy exists in the data from managers. All the skills areas are significantly related to managers' perception of HR, and the relationships are stronger than they are for HR executives. Not surprisingly, business partner skills are strongly related to managers' perceptions of HR being involved with strategy. Metrics skills also are strongly related to HR's role in strategy. Not related to HR's role in strategy are interpersonal skills and organization design skills.

Overall, our findings about the relationship of HR skill satisfaction and the strategic role of HR strongly suggest that technical, interpersonal, metrics, and business partner skills are all critical to HR's role in strategy. This is not surprising since, with the exception of HR technical skills, these are skills that are related to the development and implementation of business strategies.

Overall Skill Levels

Despite the improvement in satisfaction with skills in some areas, as we see in Table 13.5, the percentage of HR professionals with the necessary overall skills has not changed significantly from 1995 to 2010

Table 13.5. Human resources professionals with skill set, USA only									
	Percentages								
				2004		2007		2010	
Have Skills	1995	1998	2001	HR Executives	Managers	HR Executives	Managers	HR Executives	Managers
None	0.0	0.0	0.0	0.0	0.0	0.0	0.0	0	0
1–20%	0.0	1.7	4.7	2.1	5.3	2.0	5.0	6.3	5.9
21–40%	18.6	15.1	18.9	12.4	17.1	17.3	15.0	16.0	5.9
41–60%	34.9	38.7	33.1	37.1	27.6	33.7	25.0	29.7	20.6
61–80%	37.2	40.3	33.1	34.0	36.8	36.7	52.5	35.4	35.3
81–99%	8.5	4.2	10.1	11.3	13.2	10.2	2.5	11.4	32.4
100%	0.8	0.0	0.0	3.1	0.0	0.0	0.0	1.1	0.0
Mean	4.38	4.30	4.25	4.49	4.33	4.36	4.28	4.33	4.74

Response scale: 1 = None; 2 = 1–20%; 3 = 21–40%; 4 = 41–60%; 5 = 61–80%; 6 = 81–99%; 7 = 100%

No significant differences ($p \leq .05$) between HR executives and managers within year.

in the judgment of HR executives. Very few HR executives report that over 80 percent of their staff have the necessary skills. In 2004 and 2007, the same conclusion was reached by the line managers, who gave a slightly lower appraisal of the skills of HR professionals in those years. There is a change in the 2010 data: managers rate HR professionals higher than they have in the past and than do HR executives. This is a real positive for HR and is consistent with the earlier point that HR executives may underestimate the skills of HR professionals.

International Results on Skill Sets

The international results on skill sets is shown in Table 13.6. All the countries show the same result with two exceptions: Australia and China. Australia shows that a slightly higher percentage of HR professionals has the necessary skill set, while China shows a much lower percentage having the necessary skill set. This is not surprising given the low skill satisfaction scores in Table 13.3. Together they provide strong evidence that HR professionals in China need to greatly improve their skills.

Strategic Focuses

The relationships between the strategic focuses and HR skill satisfaction as rated by HR executives are shown in Table 13.7. All the correlations, except for three with growth, are significant.

Overall, organizations with stronger strategic focuses definitely have HR functions with better skill sets. It is easy to see why the information, knowledge sustainability, and innovation focuses would lead to better

Table 13.6. Human resources professionals with skill set, by country						
Have Skills	USA[1]	Canada[2]	Australia[3]	Europe[4]	UK[5]	China[6]
None	0.0	0.0	0.0	0.0	0.0	1.0
1–20%	6.3	2.3	6.7	3.2	7.9	14.7
21–40%	16.0	16.3	6.7	17.7	21.1	34.6
41–60%	29.7	30.2	30.0	33.9	21.1	31.4
61–80%	35.4	41.9	33.3	32.3	36.8	15.2
81–99%	11.4	7.0	23.3	12.9	13.2	2.6
100%	1.1	2.3	0.0	0.0	0.0	0.5
Mean	**4.33[6]**	**4.42[6]**	**4.60[6]**	**4.34[6]**	**4.26[6]**	**3.55[1,2,3,4,5]**

Response scale: 1 = None; 2 = 1–20%; 3 = 21–40%; 4 = 41–60%; 5 = 61–80%; 6 = 81–99%; 7 = 100%

[1,2,3,4,5,6] Significant difference ($p \leq .05$) between countries.

Table 13.7. Relationship of HR skills satisfaction to strategic focuses					
	Strategic Focuses				
Skills	Growth	Information-Based Strategies	Knowledge-Based Strategies	Sustainability	Innovation
HR technical skills	.27***	.33***	.38***	.22**	.29***
Interpersonal dynamics	.13[t]	.26***	.35***	.32***	.34***
Business partner skills	.14[t]	.33***	.39***	.35***	.43***
Metrics skills	.10	.41***	.40***	.26***	.33***

Significance level: [t] $p \leq .10$; * $p \leq .05$; ** $p \leq .01$; *** $p \leq .001$

skills in the HR area. They often require HR functions that are able not only to do HR technical work, but also to design systems and develop talent that supports organizational performance and knowledge development.

Management Approach

The pattern of correlation between HR skills satisfaction and the five management approaches shown in Table 13.8 is very interesting. The bureaucratic and low-cost operator approaches are negatively related. This most likely is due to the low importance they place on human capital, thus leading to their having HR functions with low skill levels.

The two management approaches which focus the most on human capital—high involvement and sustainability—have significant positive relationships with HR skills satisfaction. This is not surprising since they place a major emphasis on talent and talent management, and therefore need skilled managers.

Chapter 13

Table 13.8. Relationship of HR skills satisfaction to management approaches					
	Management Approach				
Skills	Bureaucratic	Low-Cost Operator	High Involvement	Global Competitor	Sustainable
HR technical skills	−.23**	−.15^t	.33***	.14^t	.25***
Interpersonal dynamics	−.27***	−.11	.28***	.00	.26***
Business partner skills	−.19*	−.20*	.29***	.04	.33***
Metrics skills	−.12	−.06	.15^t	.19*	.30***
Significance level: $^t p \le .10$; * $p \le .05$; ** $p \le .01$; *** $p \le .001$					

Finally, the global competitor approach falls in the middle. It does not place a major emphasis on talent, and therefore it is not surprising that it is unrelated to HR skills, except for metrics. The metrics relationship is interesting since it fits with the global competitor's analytic approach to talent management.

Conclusion

The results suggest that HR professionals suffer from a skills deficit and that this limits their role in business strategy development and implementation. It is notable that there is at best only moderate satisfaction with all HR skills; no rating by HR executives was higher than a mean of 3.9 on a 5-point scale, and that was on interpersonal skills. Most ratings in all the countries studied fall around the neutral point. Of particular concern are the relatively low ratings given to business partner skills, since they are related to HR playing a significant role in strategy. On the encouraging side, there has been an improvement in some business partner skills. Still, there is much work to be done on enhancing HR skills, as well as developing a common understanding about the level those skills need to be at in order to have an effective HR organization.

CHAPTER 14

Effectiveness of the HR Organization

Determining the effectiveness of an HR organization must be based upon an assessment of its performance in a number of areas. The most obvious area is service delivery, but as the results we have presented so far show, good service delivery is not enough. To be an effective contributor to organizational performance effectiveness, HR also has to support current business performance by contributing to effective employment relationships and good staffing and training decisions. In addition, to be a strategic contributor, it needs to deliver value with respect to business strategy, organizational change, and human capital decision making. How is HR doing?

HR Effectiveness

HR executives and managers were asked to judge the overall effectiveness of their HR organizations and to judge their effectiveness in performing eleven activities. As shown in Table 14.1, our statistical analysis produced three groups of effectiveness items: services, corporate roles, and business and strategy.

The results for HR executives show ratings for 2010 that are generally at the same level as the 2007 and slightly lower than the 2004 level. Many of the ratings are higher than they were in 1998 and 2001. Given these results, the best conclusion is that HR's performance is not improving in the opinion of HR executives.

The effectiveness results for managers in 2010 show a clear pattern of improvement from 2004, when managerial data were first collected, and from 2007. A comparison of 2010 with 2007 shows that all the managers ratings increased in 2010 from their level in 2007. The largest increase is in the business and strategy activities group. The activity that shows the biggest improvement from 2007 to 2010 is working with the corporate board. Also showing large increases are decisions about human capital and developing business strategies. These increases in effectiveness suggest that at least in the opinion of managers, HR is becoming a more effective strategic contributor.

The effectiveness ratings from 2001, 2004, 2007, and 2010 are highest for the HR services area. This is true of the ratings by both HR executives and managers. The highest-rated item in the survey is providing HR services. Also highly rated by both HR executives and managers is being an employee advocate. This finding is consistent with other studies, which have found that HR tends to be rated particularly highly when it comes to the delivery of basic HR services (Csoka and Hackett 1998).

HR receives its lowest activity effectiveness ratings when it comes to the business and strategy area. The ratings by both HR executives and managers are lowest on the developing business strategy item. However, being a business partner is rated relatively high. This finding supports the point made in Chapter 1 that there is a difference between being a business partner and having an active role in strategy development.

Table 14.1. Effectiveness of HR organization, USA only

| Activities | 1995 | 1998 | 2001 | 2004 | | 2007 | | 2010 | | | |
| | Means | | | Means | | Means | | Mean | Correlation with HR Role in Strategy | Mean | Correlation with HR Role in Strategy |
	HR Executives	HR Executives	HR Executives	HR Executives	Managers	HR Executives	Managers	HR Executives		Managers	
Overall Effectiveness (all items)				6.8	6.7	6.4	6.5	6.4	.55***	7.3[1]	.65***
HR Services				7.0	7.0	6.7	7.1	6.9	.44***	7.6[1]	.67***
Providing HR services	7.1	7.0	7.3	7.8	7.2[1]	7.4	7.6	7.7	.33***	7.7	.63***
Being an employee advocate		6.8	7.2	7.4	7.3	7.3	7.5	7.1	.31***	7.7	.68***
Analyzing HR and business metrics				5.9	6.4	5.3	6.0[1]	5.9	.42***	7.2[1]	.66***
Corporate Roles				6.9	6.7	6.5	6.1	6.2	.46***	7.0[1]	.51**
Managing outsourcing				7.3	6.8	6.1	6.1	5.9	.31***	6.6	.57***
Operating HR centers of excellence		5.5	5.6	6.8	6.0[1]	6.7	5.8	6.3	.40***	6.6	.73***
Operating HR shared service units		5.7	6.0	6.9	6.5	6.3	6.4[1]	6.6	.28***	6.9	.30[t]
Working with the corporate board				7.1	7.1	6.8	6.4	6.2	.44***	7.5[1]	.42*
Business and Strategy				6.5	6.3	6.1	6.3	6.4	.55***	7.2[1]	.67***
Providing change consulting services	5.8	5.5	5.7	6.5	6.1	5.9	6.0	6.1	.40***	6.7	.52**
Being a business partner	6.3	6.5	6.4	7.1	6.8	6.8	7.2	6.9	.52***	7.5	.73***
Helping to develop business strategies		6.2	5.8	6.0	5.7	5.8	5.4	5.9	.55***	6.5	.73***
Improving decisions about human capital				6.7	6.7	6.1	6.7	6.4	.45***	7.7[1]	.76***
Overall Performance				7.2	6.7	6.7	7.1	6.9	.51***	7.5	.74***

Response scale: 1 = Not meeting needs; 10 = All needs met

[1] Significant differences ($p \le .05$) between HR executives and managers within each year.

Significance level: [t] $p \le .10$; * $p \le .05$; ** $p \le .01$; *** $p \le .001$

When managers and HR executives consider what makes for a successful business partnership, they don't seem to see it as synonymous with playing an active role in developing business strategies.

The ratings by HR executives and managers of HR's performance in its corporate roles are mixed. HR gets low ratings from HR executives and managers on managing outsourcing; it gets higher ratings on work with the board.

A comparison of the ratings in 2010 by HR executives and those by managers shows some large differences and a clear trend. Managers rate HR more highly on ten of the eleven activities and on overall performance. One activity, providing HR services, is a tie.

The higher ratings by managers is a surprising result. It was also true in 2007, but the difference is greater in 2010, in large part because of the more favorable rating by managers. One explanation for the higher ratings by managers is that HR executives are increasingly becoming aware of what it means to be an effective HR function and are raising the performance bar and being more self-critical. It is also possible that HR underrates its performance, possibly as a result of it being criticized by managers and the press. The rise in ratings by managers suggests that perhaps HR is becoming more effective and that even though HR executives do not think so, others do.

Although there is a strong trend for HR executives to give lower ratings, there is a high level of agreement between HR executives and managers on which activities HR performs well and poorly. The mean ratings of performance by HR executives correlate highly with those by managers ($r = .78$, $p \leq .001$). This is a positive for HR, since it means that it is not at odds with the rest of the organization when it comes to this aspect of how well it is performing.

In order to better understand the overall performance ratings HR executives and managers gave to the HR function, we analyzed these ratings further. We did a regression analysis in order to see how their ratings of specific activities were related to their ratings of overall performance. For HR executives, the most important determinant of their overall rating is their rating of HR's performance in delivering services. Next in line was change consulting services. Very different results were obtained for managers. For them, the best predictors were being a business partner and developing business strategies. Put together, these findings suggest that when it comes to HR effectiveness, HR executives think of how HR does as a service deliverer, while managers think of how it does as a business partner. One implication of this is that in order to be seen by others as a good performer, HR needs to perform better as a strategic partner, which is a relatively low performance area for it.

One final way to look at the scores on effectiveness concerns their absolute level. The ratings are on a 10-point scale; thus, even the highest ratings in 2010, 7.7 for HR executives and 7.7 for managers, fall significantly short of the top of the scale. Clearly, there is still plenty of room for HR to improve its effectiveness, particularly in those activities that are related to the business and strategy.

International

The international data show some significant differences in HR organization effectiveness ratings (Table 14.2). In all three areas (services, roles, and strategy) and overall effectiveness, the results are much lower for China. This is not surprising given the low ratings that were given to the skills of the HR managers in China. That said, the ratings are somewhat lower than might have been expected. Overall, the difference between China and the other countries is larger here than anywhere else, and this is the most important area since it is concerned with the effectiveness of the function.

Table 14.2. Effectiveness of HR organization, by country						
	Means					
Activities	USA[1]	Canada[2]	Australia[3]	Europe[4]	UK[5]	China[6]
Overall Effectiveness (all items)	**6.4[6]**	**6.5[6]**	**5.9**	**5.7**	**6.1**	**5.2[1,2]**
HR Services	**6.9[4,6]**	**6.7**	**6.4**	**6.2[1]**	**6.3**	**6.0[1]**
Providing HR services	7.7[6]	7.6[6]	7.4	7.1	7.2	6.5[1,2]
Being an employee advocate	7.1[4,6]	7.3[6]	6.6[6]	6.1[1]	6.3	5.4[1,2,3]
Analyzing HR and business metrics	5.9	5.2	5.2	5.4	5.5	6.0
Corporate Roles	**6.2[4,6]**	**6.4[6]**	**5.4**	**5.1[1]**	**5.6**	**4.7[1,2]**
Managing outsourcing	5.9[4,6]	6.3[4,6]	4.7	4.2[1,2]	4.9	4.0[1,2]
Operating HR centers of excellence	6.3[6]	6.9[6]	6.4[6]	5.6[6]	6.1[6]	4.6[1,2,3,4,5]
Operating HR shared service units	6.6[5,6]	6.6[6]	6.0	5.6	5.3[1]	5.0[1,2]
Working with the corporate board	6.2[6]	5.6	5.7	5.8	6.3	5.1[1]
Business and Strategy	**6.4[6]**	**6.3[6]**	**6.3[6]**	**5.9**	**6.5[6]**	**5.2[1,2,3,5]**
Providing change consulting services	6.1[6]	5.9[6]	5.6	5.6[6]	6.3[6]	4.7[1,2,4,5]
Being a business partner	6.9[6]	6.9[6]	7.2[6]	6.7[6]	7.1[6]	5.2[1,2,3,4,5]
Helping to develop business strategies	5.9[6]	5.9	6.4[6]	5.4	6.2[6]	5.0[1,3,5]
Improving decisions about human capital	6.4[6]	6.5	6.2	5.8	6.6[6]	5.5[1,5]
Overall Performance	**6.9[6]**	**7.1[6]**	**6.6**	**6.4**	**7.0[6]**	**5.9[1,2,5]**

Response scale: 1 = Not meeting needs; 10 = All needs met
[1,2,3,4,5,6] Significant differences between countries (p<.05).

The U.S. shows the most positive data overall, but the rest of the countries, with one exception, Europe, are very close. Europe is rated lower on the average of all items, and it is rated much lower in three areas. Europe has a particularly low rating on managing outsourcing. As noted earlier, it is not particularly popular in Europe. It is impossible to determine from our study the degree to which its lack of popularity is due to poor management. All we can say is that it is not as popular or successful elsewhere in the world as it is in the U.S. and Canada.

Role in Strategy

Table 14.1 shows the correlations between the role that HR plays in strategy and its effectiveness. There are many high correlations here with the data from HR executives and those from managers. Not surprisingly, the strongest pattern of relationships has to do with the effectiveness of HR performance in the business and strategy area. The more effective HR is in this area, the more it plays an active role in strategy formulation. The implication of this is clear: if HR wants to play a more important role in strategy formulation, it needs to be more effective when it comes to the business and strategy activities in Table 14.1.

In the data from both HR executives and managers, effectiveness in providing HR services is significantly related to the strategic role of HR; the relationship is particularly strong for managers. It is impossible to tell from the data whether the correlations with service effectiveness mean that providing good services is a prerequisite to playing a strategic role, or simply mean that effective HR organizations that are doing a good job at service delivery are also partners in strategy. However, it may be an important indicator that the correlations are much higher for managers than for HR executives. This may indicate that as is often said, delivering high-quality services is a must-do if HR wants to be a strategic contributor.

The Importance of HR Performance

The results for the ratings of the importance of HR performance in Table 14.3 show generally high ratings in 2004, 2007, and 2010 (asked for the first time in 2004). Both HR executives and managers see overall HR performance as very important. The highest 2010 importance ratings by HR executives concern improving decisions about human capital, being a business partner, and providing HR services, a pattern that is similar to the one found in 2007. Managers give their highest rating to the same three items. The lowest ratings by both HR executives and managers are given to the corporate roles items.

It is interesting that both HR executives and managers rate providing HR services very highly, with managers rating it the highest. This

Table 14.3. Importance of HR performance, USA only

Activities	2004 Means		2007 Means		2010			
	HR Executives	Managers	HR Executives	Managers	Mean	Correlation with HR Role in Strategy	Mean	Correlation with HR Role in Strategy
					HR Executives		Managers	
Overall Importance (all items)	**8.1**	**8.0**	**8.0**	**7.7**	**7.9**	**.48*****	**8.1**	**.55****
HR Services	**8.2**	**8.3**	**8.0**	**8.2**	**8.2**	**.34*****	**8.6¹**	**.41***
Providing HR services	9.0	8.8	8.5	9.2¹	8.7	.20**	9.0	.42*
Being an employee advocate	7.9	7.9	7.5	7.7	7.9	.26***	8.5¹	.46**
Analyzing HR and business metrics	7.9	8.1	8.2	7.8	8.2	.32***	8.4	.20
Corporate Roles	**7.6**	**7.6**	**7.3**	**7.0**	**7.2**	**.34*****	**7.5**	**.47****
Managing outsourcing	7.6	7.5	6.6	6.8	6.5	.06	7.1	.38*
Operating HR centers of excellence	7.7	7.6	7.9	7.2	7.9	.27***	7.6	.45**
Operating HR shared service units	7.6	7.4	7.4	7.3	7.6	.24**	7.5	.29
Working with the corporate board	8.0	8.0	7.2	7.1	7.2	.40***	7.8	.53**
Business and Strategy	**8.4**	**8.2**	**8.6**	**8.1¹**	**8.3**	**.41*****	**8.3**	**.60*****
Providing change consulting services	8.2	8.1	8.3	7.7¹	7.9	.23**	7.8	.62***
Being a business partner	9.0	8.7	9.1	8.6	8.8	.42***	8.8	.40*
Helping to develop business strategies	8.0	7.3¹	8.4	7.2¹	7.9	.43***	7.9	.56***
Improving decisions about human capital	8.3	8.8¹	8.8	8.6	8.6	.36***	8.8	.21
Overall Performance	**8.9**	**8.8**	**9.1**	**8.6¹**	**8.8**	**.37*****	**8.8**	**.60*****

Response scale: 1 = Not important; 10 = Very important
¹Significant difference (p ≤ .05) between HR executives and managers.
Significance level: ¹ p ≤ .10; * p ≤ .05; ** p ≤ .01; *** p ≤ .001

finding once again makes the point that HR must not lose sight of the importance of delivering basic HR services.

There are multiple items where there is a significant disagreement between HR executives and managers, although only one difference reaches statistical significance. In most cases the difference is because managers rate them as more important. All the HR services items are rated higher by managers, as is improving decisions about human capital. This result reinforces the pattern we saw earlier: business leaders value more highly HR's contribution to decisions about human capital than they do its developing business strategies. One implication of this pattern is that HR leaders may need to do some selling to the non-HR community with respect to what they can contribute to business strategy.

As for the correlations between HR's role in strategy and the HR activity importance ratings, a number of items are statistically significant and some of the correlations are high. The majority of the strongest relation-ships involve responses from managers. Not surprisingly, playing a major role in strategy is associated with placing high importance on the various corporate roles and on the business and strategy items. This is particularly true for managers; those who feel it is important for HR to play a corporate role and to be involved in business and strategy report that HR is more involved in strategy. In this case, it may well be that the reason HR is involved is because managers see the importance of HR performance in these areas.

International

The ratings of the importance of HR performance show some interest-ing country differences. As can be seen in Table 14.4, the HR services items are rated as particularly important by the U.S. and Canadian HR executives. This may be one of the reasons the HR functions in the U.S. continue to spend time on service even though they want to become business partners. There are differences with respect to outsourcing. It

Table 14.4. Importance of HR performance, by country						
	Means					
Activities	USA[1]	Canada[2]	Australia[3]	Europe[4]	UK[5]	China[6]
Overall Importance (all items)	**7.9[4,6]**	**7.9[6]**	**7.0**	**6.9[1]**	**7.2**	**6.8[1,2]**
HR Services	**8.2[4,6]**	**8.3[4,6]**	**7.4**	**7.4[1,2]**	**7.8**	**7.3[1,2]**
Providing HR services	8.7[6]	8.9[6]	8.0	8.3[6]	8.0	7.2[1,2,4]
Being an employee advocate	7.9[3,4,6]	7.9	6.7[1]	6.8[1]	7.4	7.1[1]
Analyzing HR and business metrics	8.2[4,6]	8.2[4]	7.4	7.0[1,2]	7.9	7.4[1]
Corporate Roles	**7.2[4,6]**	**7.2[4]**	**6.5**	**6.0[1,2]**	**6.4**	**6.3[1]**
Managing outsourcing	6.5[4,5,6]	6.4[4,5,6]	5.1	4.8[1,2]	4.9[1,2]	5.0[1,2]
Operating HR centers of excellence	7.9[4,6]	7.9[6]	7.5	6.8[1]	7.2	6.6[1,2]
Operating HR shared service units	7.6[4,6]	7.8[6]	7.0	6.5[1]	6.5	6.6[1,2]
Working with the corporate board	7.2	6.7	6.9	7.2	7.5	6.8
Business and Strategy	**8.3[6]**	**8.2[6]**	**7.9**	**7.7**	**7.9[6]**	**7.1[1,2,5]**
Providing change consulting services	7.9[6]	7.8[6]	7.6	7.2	7.5	6.7[1,2]
Being a business partner	8.8[6]	8.8[6]	8.2[6]	8.4[6]	8.7[6]	7.1[1,2,3,4,5]
Helping to develop business strategies	7.9[4,6]	8.0	7.9	7.0[1]	7.3	7.2[1]
Improving decisions about human capital	8.6[6]	8.3[6]	8.0	8.0[6]	8.0	7.0[1,2,4]
Overall Performance	**8.8[6]**	**9.0[6]**	**8.4**	**8.2**	**9.0[6]**	**8.0[1,2,5]**

Response scale: 1 = Not important; 10 = Very important
[1,2,3,4,5,6] Significant differences between countries ($p < .05$).

is rated much more highly by the U.S. and Canada than it is by other countries. This most likely reflects its more extensive use in these countries.

The relatively high importance rating for all the performance areas except outsourcing highlights again the challenge HR faces. It needs to provide services as well as contribute to corporate strategy and business effectiveness. In every country except China, the highest importance rating goes to "being a business partner."

Once again the results for China are very different. Particularly striking are the low importance ratings given to the corporate roles items. This clearly is an area that HR managers in China do not see as important as other executives feel it is. They do agree with HR executives from other countries that it is the least important of the three areas.

Effectiveness and Importance

The results of a comparison between the importance assigned to HR activities and their effectiveness are shown in Table 14.5. To create this table, the effectiveness ratings were subtracted from the importance ratings. Thus, the larger the number, the bigger the gap between importance and effectiveness and the greater the cause for concern, because it means HR is doing an important thing poorly.

The results for HR executives and managers are relatively similar in both 2007 and 2010. The scores for managers are generally lower in 2010 because of the higher ratings they gave to effectiveness. For both groups, most of the largest numbers are in the business and strategy area. One outlier is the analyzing HR and business metrics activity. It shows the largest difference for HR executives, but doesn't have a particularly large difference in the case of managers. This may well be due to HR having a better understanding of what can be done and isn't being done in this area.

Both managers and HR executives show small gaps in the case of being an employee advocate. It is not surprising that managers feel this way. They are known to complain that HR sometimes is too much of an employee advocate. Perhaps HR has gotten the message, since there is a relatively small gap here for HR executives.

Finally, it is interesting that there is a very small gap for working with corporate boards. This is an important area where it often seems HR could do much more and be more effective. Apparently that is not the way HR executives and managers see things.

Table 14.5. HR importance and effectiveness rating differences				
	2007 Means*		2010 Means*	
Activities	**HR Executives**	**Managers**	**HR Executives**	**Managers**
Overall Importance/ Effectiveness (all items)	**1.6**	**1.0**[1]	**1.5**	**0.9**[1]
HR Services	**1.3**	**1.1**	**1.3**	**1.0**
Providing HR services	1.0	1.6	1.0	1.3
Being an employee advocate	0.1	0.3	0.8	0.8
Analyzing HR and business metrics	2.9	1.7[1]	2.3	1.1[1]
Corporate Roles	**0.8**	**0.8**	**1.1**	**0.6**
Managing outsourcing	0.5	0.8	0.5	0.6
Operating HR centers of excellence	1.2	1.7	1.6	1.0
Operating HR shared service units	1.1	1.2	1.1	0.6
Working with the corporate board	0.5	0.6	1.0	0.5
Business and Strategy	**2.5**	**1.8**[1]	**2.0**	**1.1**[1]
Providing change consulting services	2.3	1.7	1.9	1.1[1]
Being a business partner	2.3	1.4[1]	1.9	1.2
Helping to develop business strategies	2.6	1.8[1]	2.1	1.4[1]
Improving decisions about human capital	2.8	2.0	2.2	1.2[1]
Overall Performance	**2.3**	**1.5**[1]	**2.0**	**1.3**[1]

*Mean difference between Importance and Effectiveness ratings for each activity.

Importance response scale: 1 = Not important; 10 = Very important

Effectiveness response scale: 1 = Not meeting needs; 10 = All needs met

[1]Significant difference ($p \leq .05$) between HR executives and managers within each year.

Conclusion

HR executives and other managers seem to be in general agreement about where HR is effective. Both say it is particularly effective at delivering HR services. However, delivering HR services is not seen by HR executives as its only important contribution area. The other important area, according to HR executives, is business and strategy. It also appears that HR has improved its effectiveness since 1995.

HR executives and managers say that a strong emphasis needs to be placed on HR's role as a business partner and on improving decisions about human capital. These are areas of relatively low effectiveness for HR, and thus there is a tremendous opportunity for improvement on the part of HR. They are also areas that are related to the strategic involvement of the HR function. Thus, by making improvements in these areas, HR is likely to become much more of a strategic contributor.

CHAPTER 15

Determinants of HR Effectiveness

What determines how effective an HR organization is? To answer this question, we need to look at the relationship between the effectiveness of the HR organization in companies and the HR practices and activities that are likely to influence its effectiveness.

Time Spent

The amount of time spent on HR roles relates significantly to HR effectiveness. As can be seen in Table 15.1, our results for 2010 show a strong negative relationship between effectiveness and the amount of time HR executives report their function spends maintaining records, auditing, and providing services. There is a significant positive relationship between spending time as a strategic business partner and HR effectiveness. These results are consistent with what we found in the 2004 and 2007 surveys. Despite this, as we saw in Chapter 3, the amount of time spent on the major HR roles has not changed since at least 1995.

The strong positive correlation between time spent on being a business partner and HR effectiveness is consistent with the positive correlation between HR effectiveness and the role HR plays in strategy, as reported in Chapter 14. The more HR is involved in business strategy, the more

Table 15.1. Relationship of HR roles (time spent) and HR effectiveness			
	HR Executives' Rating of HR Effectiveness[1]		
HR Roles[2]	2004	2007	2010
Maintaining Records Collect, track, and maintain data on employees	–.47***	–.33**	–.42***
Auditing/Controlling Ensure compliance to internal operations, regulations, and legal and union requirements	–.04	–.18	–.30***
Human Resources Service Provider Assist with implementation and administration of HR practices	–.05	.05	–.24**
Development of Human Resources Systems and Practices Develop new HR systems and practices	.24[t]	.02	.12
Strategic Business Partner Member of the management team. Involved with strategic HR planning, organizational design, and strategic change	.30*	.27*	.54***
[1] Based on total score for all eleven effectiveness items as rated by HR executives.			
[2] Based on percentage of time spent on HR roles as rated by HR executives.			
Significance level: [t] $p \le .10$; * $p \le .05$; ** $p \le .01$; *** $p \le .001$			

effective HR is seen to be, a relationship that is significant for HR executive ratings and for the ratings by managers (see Table 14.1).

Our findings paint a consistent picture suggesting that more effective HR organizations spend less time on record-keeping and controlling activities, and are more involved in human capital and business strategy issues than less effective HR organizations. It is interesting that in Table 15.1 the only significant positive correlations are with time spent being a strategic partner, the more the better.

Business Strategy

HR's role in the business strategy process is significantly related to the effectiveness of the HR function as rated by both HR executives and managers (see Table 15.2). Indeed, when compared to the 2004 and 2007 results, the relationships in 2010 are even stronger and more consistent. In 2010, all but one of the correlations are statistically significant for both HR executives and managers. None of the strategic activities shows a pattern of being consistently more strongly related to effectiveness; they all seem to be activities that are related to HR effectiveness. The biggest difference between 2004 and 2010 is that the absolute level of the correlations is generally higher in 2010 than in 2004. This suggests that over this time period the strategy activities of HR have become more important in determining its effectiveness.

Table 15.2. Relationship of business strategy activities to HR effectiveness						
	HR Effectiveness					
	2004		**2007**		**2010**	
Activities[3]	**HR Executives[1]**	**Managers[2]**	**HR Executives[1]**	**Managers[2]**	**HR Executives[1]**	**Managers[2]**
Help identify or design strategy options	.32*	.33*	.31**	.55**	.45***	.44*
Help decide among the best strategy options	.45***	.38**	.35**	.65**	.53***	.56**
Help plan the implementation of strategy	.31*	.24[t]	.35**	.53**	.55***	.38*
Help identify new business opportunities	.27*	.39**	.28*	.51**	.47***	.64***
Assess the organization's readiness to implement strategies	.30*	.31*	.32**	.58**	.59***	.45*
Help design the organization structure to implement strategy	.42***	.40**	.35**	.69***	.62***	.29
Assess possible merger, acquisition, or divestiture strategies	.23[t]	.25[t]	.17	.57**	.55***	.40*
Work with the corporate board on business strategy	.32*	.28*	.19	.49*	.51***	.36[t]

[1] Based on total score for all eleven effectiveness items as rated by HR executives.
[2] Based on total score for all eleven effectiveness items as rated by managers.
[3] Based on response scale: 1 = Little or no extent; 2 = Some extent; 3 = Moderate extent; 4 = Great extent; 5 = Very great extent
Significance level: [t] $p \leq .10$; * $p \leq .05$; ** $p \leq .01$; *** $p \leq .001$

Table 15.3. Relationship of HR strategy to HR effectiveness			
	HR Effectiveness[1]		
HR Strategy	2004	2007	2010
Data-based talent strategy	.50***	.44***	.50***
A human capital strategy that is integrated with business strategy	.48***	.51***	.54***
Provides analytic support for business decision making	.38**	.67***	.58***
Provides HR data to support change management	.46***	.61***	.60***
Drives change management	.48***	.59***	.65***
Makes rigorous data-based decisions about human capital management	.47***	.62***	.60***

[1] Based on total score for all eleven effectiveness items as rated by HR executives.
Significance level: [1]$p \le .10$; * $p \le .05$; ** $p \le .01$; *** $p \le .001$

HR Strategy

The extent to which the HR function has a well developed HR strategy is strongly related to HR executives' ratings of HR effectiveness. Table 15.3 shows that all the relationships between the HR strategy items and HR effectiveness are statistically significant in the 2004, 2007, and 2010 data. The weakest relationship in 2004 concerned analytics support for business decision making. In 2007 and 2010, however, this correlation is among the highest. This suggests an increasing realization of the value of a decision science paradigm for HR, in which the mandate is extended to the quality of decision support, not just services and compliance.

Taken together, the results in Tables 15.2 and 15.3, indicate that HR is most effective when it focuses on both contributing to business strategy and developing a robust human capital and HR functional strategy. The best overall conclusion is that HR is most effective when it plays a major role in business strategy development and implementation as well as having a well developed HR strategy that is aligned with the business strategy.

HR Organization

The effectiveness of the HR organization is clearly related to certain features of how it is organized and managed. As can be seen in Table 15.4, the results from 2001, 2004, 2007, and 2010 are similar. The use of service teams is strongly related to HR effectiveness, as is the use of information technology. Service teams and information technology have shown consistently positive relationships with HR's strategic role, so these results reinforce the importance of these approaches.

Table 15.4. Relationship of HR organization to HR effectiveness

HR Organization[2]	HR Effectiveness[1]			
	2001	2004	2007	2010
HR service units	.44***	.43***	.36***	.54***
Decentralization	−.01	−.09	−.17	−.00
Resource efficiency	—	.16	.15	.04
Information technology	—	.52***	.43***	.35***
HR talent development	.32***	−.04	.30**	.51***

[1] Based on total score for all eleven effectiveness items as rated by HR executives.
[2] See Table 7.1 for items in scales.
Significance level: [1]$p \leq .10$; *$p \leq .05$; **$p \leq .01$; ***$p \leq .001$

Table 15.5. Relationship of HR activity changes to HR effectiveness

HR Activities[2]	HR Effectiveness[1]			
	2001	2004	2007	2010
Design and organizational development	.20*	.21	.37***	.35***
Compensation and benefits	.30**	−.08	.11	.23**
Employee development	.13	.17	.22[1]	.38***
Recruitment and selection	.08	.13	.08	.25**
HR metrics and analytics	—	.12	.26*	.34***
HR information systems	.11	−.14	−.01	.15[1]
Union relations	−.05	.18	−.12	−.01

[1] Based on total score for all eleven effectiveness items as rated by HR executives.
[2] See Table 8.1 for items in scales.
Significance level: [1]$p \leq .10$; *$p \leq .05$; **$p \leq .01$; ***$p \leq .001$

It is somewhat surprising that doing talent development for the HR staff is not related to the effectiveness of the HR organization in 2004. There is a somewhat stronger relationship in 2007 and a much stronger relationship in 2010, a result that is understandable since HR needs a talented workforce.

It is notable that decentralization is not correlated with HR effectiveness in 2001, 2004, 2007, or 2010. Much has been written advocating locating HR centrally for efficiency and control, and similarly strong positions are often taken in favor of decentralizing it for responsiveness and flexibility. Our results with respect to the positive effects of service teams suggest that HR organizations do need to have a strong corporate center, and our result for decentralization suggest that in general decentralization is not a positive approach.

Activity Changes

The relationship between HR activity changes in the last five to seven years and HR effectiveness is shown in Table 15.5. The results for 2001 and 2004 show no strong relationship. In 2007, HR effectiveness is strongly related to increasing time on design and organization development and on metrics and analytics. The results for 2010 show five significant relationships. Design and organization development, metrics, and employee development show the strongest relationships in 2010, suggesting that spending more time on them has created more effective HR organizations.

Notice that Table 15.5 deals not with the absolute amount of time nor the effectiveness of these activities, but the change in time spent. Table 15.2 showed that the amount of time spent on recruiting and developing talent was related to HR effectiveness; Table 15.5 shows that increasing the time spent on development is more strongly related to effectiveness than is spending more time on recruitment. This might mean that efforts devoted to recruitment were already at appropriate levels, but that recently employee development has become an area where increased time makes a significant difference in effectiveness.

From 2004 to 2010, the relationship of increased attention to metrics with HR effectiveness has become much stronger. As we saw earlier, the effectiveness of HR measurement and analytics is related to HR having a strategic role as well. This suggests that metrics have now reached the point where increased attention makes a significant difference in the impact of the HR function, perhaps because of an increasing ability to develop effective HRISs and meaningful metrics that tie closely to functional and organizational performance effectiveness.

Outsourcing

Table 15.6, which focuses on the relationship between outsourcing and HR effectiveness, shows no statistically significant relationships ($p \leq .05$) in 2004 and only one in 2007 and 2010. The degree to which individual activities are outsourced clearly is not a significant predictor or cause of HR effectiveness. Given this result, an organization's decisions about what to outsource probably should be based on its situation with respect to costs, logistics, and internal capabilities. There is no compelling evidence that it is either generally best to outsource or not to outsource.

Information Technology

The results from 2001, 2004, 2007, and 2010 show a positive relationship between IT use and HR effectiveness. As can be seen in Table 15.7, there is a clear trend: the greater the presence of IT and the more HR

Table 15.6. Relationship of outsourcing to HR effectiveness			
	HR Effectiveness[1]		
Outsourcing[2]	2004	2007	2010
Overall Outsourcing (except Union relations)	**.26[t]**	**–.05**	**.15**
Human capital forecasting and planning[a]	.00	–.29**	.02
Organization design/development	–.09	–.05	.03
Training	.13	.12	.16[t]
HR information systems	.18	.10	.10
Staffing and career development	.23[t]	–.01	.03
HR metrics and analysis	.02	–.16	–.05
Benefits	–.01	–.09	.10
Compensation	.11	–.03	–.01
Legal affairs	.24[t]	–.03	.29***
Executive compensation			.12
Employee assistance	.20	–.13	.01
Competency / Talent assessment	.26[t]	.14	.12
Union relations	–.18	–.01	–.02

[a] "HR planning" prior to 2007.

[1] Based on total score for all eleven effectiveness items as rated by HR executives.

[2] See Table 11.1 for items in scales.

Significance level: [t] $p \le .10$; * $p \le .05$; ** $p \le .01$; *** $p \le .001$

Table 15.7. Relationship of information system use to HR effectiveness				
	Mean HR Effectiveness[1]			
Information System	2001*	2004*	2007	2010
Completely integrated HR IT system	6.6	7.7	7.5	7.4
Most processes are IT-based but not fully integrated	6.5	6.9	6.6	6.5
Some HR processes are IT-based	6.0	6.5	5.9	5.4
Little IT present in the HR function	4.6	6.4	6.0	6.0
No IT present	5.1	No Respondents	4.7	No Respondents

Response scale: 1 = Not meeting needs; 10 = All needs met

[1] Based on total score for all eleven effectiveness items as rated by HR executives.

*Significant difference in HR effectiveness ($p \le .05$) among information system use levels.

processes are IT-based, the greater the effectiveness of HR. This finding is consistent with the finding (see Chapter 12) that those HR functions which use information technology for most HR processes tend to be perceived as the most effective.

Table 15.8 provides more detail concerning the relationship between information technology and HR effectiveness. In this table, we examine not the use of IT, but the outcomes of the HRIS as they relate to HR effectiveness. Here our results show strong positive correlations in 2004, 2007, and 2010. The more positive the outcomes in the areas, the more effective HR is judged to be. In 2004, efficiency generated the highest correlation, while in 2007 the correlations are very similar (though somewhat lower) across all the outcomes. The correlations in 2010 again are high for all HRIS outcomes. This suggests that today HRISs contribute to HR effectiveness across a wide spectrum of outcomes, ranging from efficiency to effectiveness and impact.

Two new items, knowledge networks and social networks, show significant relationships to HR effectiveness in 2010. Apparently, creating HRISs that aid networks is a positive for most HR functions. One reason for this may be that it helps individuals in HR deal with aspects of their work.

It is also notable that the new 2007 item reflecting the HRIS's effectiveness in improving human capital decisions among those outside HR shows a positive relationship with HR effectiveness in both 2007 and 2010. This may well be because good decisions by everyone in an organization are needed in order to have an effective HR organization.

Metrics and Analytics

The use of HR metrics and analytics is significantly related to HR effectiveness. As can be seen in Table 15.9, this is true in 2004, 2007, and 2010. In 2010, the greater use of HR metrics is concerned with efficiency, effectiveness, and impact significantly associated with greater HR

Table 15.8. Relationship of HRIS outcomes to HR effectiveness			
	HR Effectiveness[1]		
HRIS Outcomes [2]	**2004**	**2007**	**2010**
Overall Effectiveness[a]	**.61*****	**.47*****	**.49*****
Employee satisfaction	.55***	.40***	.34***
Efficiency	.63***	.46***	.48***
Business effectiveness	.40**	.42***	.47***
Improve human capital decisions of managers outside HR	—	.37***	.38***
Effective	.44***	.39***	.33***
Create knowledge networks	—	—	.40***
Build social networks that help get work done	—	—	.34***

[a] Includes items from Employee Satisfaction, Efficiency, and Business Effectiveness scales only.

[1] Based on total score for all eleven effectiveness items as rated by HR executives.

[2] See Table 12.4 for items in scales.

Significance level: [1] $p \leq .10$; * $p \leq .05$; ** $p \leq .01$; *** $p \leq .001$

effectiveness. This supports the position that, like other disciplines such as finance and marketing, attention to all three areas is an important determinant of HR effectiveness.

The only use that did not show a strong significant relationship in 2004 and 2007 is benchmarking analytics and measures against data from outside organizations. In 2010, however, it does show a significant relationship, making a stronger case for efficiency being an important measure.

Table 15.10 examines the relationship between the effectiveness of metrics and analytics and overall HR effectiveness. The results for 2010 are very similar to those for 2004 and 2007. They show that the effectiveness of HR is strongly related to the effectiveness of an organization's HR metrics and analytics activities. As can be seen in Table 15.10, all of the items concerned with metrics and analytics effectiveness are strongly related to HR effectiveness, including the strategic and HR functional features. This is also true for all the elements of the LAMP framework.

Table 15.9. Relationship of HR analytics and metrics use to HR effectiveness			
	HR Effectiveness[1]		
Measures	2004	2007	2010
Efficiency			
Measure the financial efficiency of HR operations (e.g. cost-per-hire, time-to-fill, training costs)?	.53***	.42***	.39***
Collect metrics that measure the cost of HR programs and processes?	.45***	.49***	.35***
Benchmark analytics and measures against data from outside organizations (e.g. Saratoga, Mercer, Hewitt, etc.)?	.17	.22[t]	.38***
Effectiveness			
Use HR dashboards or scorecards?	.37**	.29*	.48***
Measure the specific effects of HR programs (such as learning from training, motivation from rewards, validity of tests, etc.)?	—	.32**	.28**
Have the capability to conduct cost-benefit analyses (also called utility analyses) of HR programs?	.53***	.19[t]	.28***
Impact			
Measure the business impact of HR programs and processes?	.44***	.24*	.36***
Measure the quality of the talent decisions made by non-HR leaders?	—	.33**	.18*
Measure the business impact of high versus low performance in jobs?	—	.24*	.34***
[1] Based on total score for all eleven effectiveness items as rated by HR executives. Significance level: [t] $p \leq .10$; * $p \leq .05$; ** $p \leq .01$; *** $p \leq .001$			

Table 15.10. Relationship of HR analytics and metrics effectiveness to HR effectiveness			
	HR Effectiveness[1]		
Effectiveness	2004	2007	2010
Strategy Contributions			
Contributing to decisions about business strategy and human capital management	.52***	.55***	.58***
Identifying where talent has the greatest potential for strategic impact	.47***	.49***	.51***
Connecting human capital practices to organizational performance	.42***	.57***	.40***
Supporting organizational change efforts	.47***	.56***	.45***
HR Functional and Operational Contributions			
Assessing and improving the HR department operations	.61***	.63***	.50***
Predicting the effects of HR programs before implementation	—	.50***	.43***
Pinpointing HR programs that should be discontinued	.52***	.52***	.46***
Logic, Analysis, Measurement, and Process (LAMP)			
Using logical principles that clearly connect talent to organization success	—	.55***	.53***
Using advanced data analysis and statistics	—	.54***	.52***
Providing high-quality (complete, timely, accessible) talent measurements	—	.49***	.51***
Motivating users to take appropriate action	—	.52***	.45***

[1] Based on total score for all eleven effectiveness items as rated by HR executives.

Significance level: [1]$p \leq .10$; *$p \leq .05$; **$p \leq .01$; ***$p \leq .001$

Somewhat surprisingly, there is little difference in the size of the correlations in Table 15.10. This suggests that having effective HR analytics and metrics in almost any area is a way to improve the effectiveness of the HR function—possibly because it helps to make the HR organization more strategic, and that, in turn, makes it more effective. It is also possible that even for metrics that are not used directly to advance strategic decisions (such as those focusing on HR department operations), their existence signals rigor and effectiveness. Perhaps at this point in the evolution of the HR profession, demonstrating the effective use of metrics and analytics in virtually any HR area is a significant contributor to HR effectiveness.

The best conclusion concerning the use of metrics and analytics is that effective use is clearly tied to the effectiveness of the HR function and that the HR function needs to make increasing use of them. It is particularly important that HR develop greater effectiveness in the metrics and analytics area, considering the relatively low effectiveness ratings the metrics and analytics items received from HR executives (see Table 10.1). The typical response was "somewhat effective" to all of these items.

Decision Science

The sophistication of managers' decisions about human capital is clearly and strongly related to HR effectiveness, as was the case in 2004 and 2007. As can be seen in Table 15.11, most of the decision science items are highly correlated with effectiveness as rated by both HR executives and managers.

Table 15.11. Relationship of decision science sophistication to HR effectiveness						
	HR Effectiveness [1]					
	2004		2007		2010	
Decision Making	HR Executives[1]	Managers[2]	HR Executives[1]	Managers[2]	HR Executives[1]	Managers[2]
We excel at competing for and with talent where it matters most to our strategic success	—	—	.47***	.66***	.58***	.40*
Business leaders' decisions that depend upon or affect human capital (e.g. layoffs, rewards, etc.) are as rigorous, logical, and strategically relevant as their decisions about resources such as money, technology, and customers	.44***	.66***	.51***	.57**	.57***	.59***
Business leaders understand and use sound principles when making decisions about:						
1. Motivation	.45***	.37**	.50***	.62***	.52***	.39[t]
2. Development and learning	.44***	.43***	.53***	.49*	.50***	.56*
3. Culture	.45***	.62***	.52***	.65***	.37***	.56**
4. Organization design	.61***	.71***	.49***	.70***	.36***	.53*
5. Business strategy	.52***	.49***	.49***	.32	.35***	.47*
6. Finance	—	—	.30**	.06	.22*	.44[t]
7. Marketing	—	—	.39***	.36[t]	.29***	.41[t]
HR leaders have a good understanding about where and why human capital makes the biggest difference in their business	.52***	.60***	.58***	.76***	.61***	.50**
Business leaders have a good understanding about where and why human capital makes the biggest difference in their business	.44***	.51***	.60***	.42*	.46***	.28
HR systems educate business leaders about their talent decisions	—	—	.46***	.76***	.55***	.64***
HR adds value by insuring compliance with rules, laws, and guidelines	—	—	.20[t]	.54**	.34***	.67***
HR adds value by delivering high-quality professional practices and services	—	—	.56***	.75***	.72***	.71***
HR adds value by improving talent decisions inside and outside the HR function	—	—	.56***	.75***	.64***	.80***

Response scale: 1 = Little or no extent; 2 = Some extent; 3 = Moderate extent; 4 = Great extent; 5 = Very great extent

[1] Based on total score for all eleven effectiveness items as rated by HR executives.

[2] Based on total score for all eleven effectiveness items as rated by managers.

Significance level: [t] $p \leq .10$; * $p \leq .05$; ** $p \leq .01$; *** $p \leq .001$

For HR executives, all of the business skill areas (e.g. culture, organization design) are significantly related to their perceptions of HR effectiveness. Two areas, finance and marketing, do have relatively low correlations. Perhaps HR executives, working hard to connect to business decisions, vividly see the difficulty of being effective if business decisions are not well grounded and sophisticated.

For managers, HR effectiveness is significantly related to most of the ratings of the extent to which business leaders use sound principles in decisions. All but one of the correlations in 2010 are higher for managers.

The item reflecting HR adding value through compliance is much more strongly related for managers than for HR executives (this item was also the only one that was not significantly correlated with HR effectiveness among the HR executives in 2007). Managers also rated this item significantly higher in effectiveness than HR executives did (see Table 6.1). Perhaps compliance is seen as passé among HR executives, but other leaders perceive significant value in doing it well.

The highest correlation in Table 15.11 is with talent decisions. This is further confirmation of the importance managers put on talent decisions.

The pattern of correlations for 2010 in Table 15.11 is interesting. The responses of HR executives to its items concerning business leaders' decisions are consistently less correlated with HR effectiveness than are the responses of managers. They also are more variable. One explanation is that HR executives are more aware of the different skill sets managers have and judge them more independently of each other. Support for this view is provided by the fact that their ratings for financial and marketing have the lowest relationship to HR effectiveness.

Skill Satisfaction

Table 15.12 shows the relationships between HR effectiveness and the satisfaction of HR executives and managers with the HR and business skills of HR professionals. In 2004, 2007, and 2010, there are strong correlations for all the skills. The strong relationships for all these skills once again confirms the importance of HR professionals having skills beyond just HR technical skills. As we noted earlier, interpersonal, business partner, and metrics skills are rated only moderately present and effective by both HR executives and managers. This means that there is a great opportunity to enhance HR effectiveness by the skills of HR professionals.

Table 15.12. Relationship of HR skill satisfaction to HR effectiveness						
	HR Effectiveness[1]					
	2004		2007		2010	
HR Skills[3]	HR Executives[1]	Managers[2]	HR Executives[1]	Managers[2]	HR Executives[1]	Managers[2]
HR technical skills	.64***	.65***	.55***	.63***	.66***	.74***
Interpersonal dynamics	.62***	.77***	.66***	.77***	.65***	.71***
Business partner skills	.65***	.78***	.76***	.75***	.64***	.74***
Metrics skills	.56***	.55***	.68***	.53**	.56***	.81***

[1] Based on total score for all eleven effectiveness items as rated by HR executives.

[2] Based on total score for all eleven effectiveness items as rated by managers.

[3] See Table 12.3 for items in scales.

Significance level: [1] $p \leq .10$; * $p \leq .05$; ** $p \leq .01$; *** $p \leq .001$

Importance of HR Practices and Activities

In order to determine the relative importance of the many practices, structures, and skills that are associated with HR effectiveness, a final analysis was performed. A regression analysis was run using key items from Tables 15.1 to 15.12. The following items (in the order of predictive power) were the best predictors of HR effectiveness:

1. Satisfaction with business partner skills

2. Provides analytics support for business decision making

3. HRIS that improves HR operations

4. Increased activity in organization design and development

Once again, our data suggest that HR needs to perform well in its administrative activities and to be an effective business and strategic partner. In terms of relative importance, the data suggest that HR's business and strategic performance are the most important.

Conclusion

Our results show a number of strong relationships between the effectiveness of the HR function and the way it is organized, managed, and staffed. Among the most important findings are the following:

- Spending time on maintaining records is negatively related to effectiveness, while being a strategic partner is positively related.

- Strategic activities such as helping plan the implementation of strategy and choosing strategy options are strongly related to HR effectiveness.

- Using information technology and service teams as delivery mechanisms for HR services are strongly related to HR effectiveness.

- Increased focus on organization design and development is related to HR effectiveness.

- Having a completely integrated HRIS system leads to the highest level of HR effectiveness.

- The effectiveness of the HRIS system is strongly related to the overall effectiveness of the HR organization.

- Having a wide array of effective HR metrics and analytics is strongly related to HR effectiveness.

- The decision science sophistication of business leaders is strongly related to the effectiveness of the HR function.

- There is a clear relationship between the skills of HR managers and the effectiveness of the HR function.

Overall, the findings tell an important story. HR effectiveness is associated with a wide array of HR activities, structures, systems, and skills that are within the control of human resources. HR can do a lot to make HR more effective. It needs to be sure its administrative processes work well, but its best opportunities for improvement appear to be in the business partner role and in strategy.

CHAPTER 16

Determinants of Organizational Performance

How do the design and operation of HR influence organizational performance? To answer this question we need to look at the relationship between the performance of organizations and the HR practices and activities that are likely to influence it.

The obvious HR practices and activities to look at are those that influence the effectiveness of HR; these were the focus of the previous chapter. Although they are the best place to look, there are some reasons why they may have a different relationship to organizational performance than they have to HR effectiveness.

In the case of our sample of companies there is only a moderate relationship between the HR executives' ratings of organizational performance and their rating of HR effectiveness ($r = .31$, $p \leq .001$). The primary reason for this is that HR effectiveness and HR practices are just one determinant of organizational performance. The performance of marketing, finance, operations, and the other groups in a corporation also influences organizational performance. Thus, the relationship between organizational performance and HR practices should be much weaker than those between HR effectiveness and HR practices. It is likely that some HR practices and activities that are significantly related to HR effectiveness will not be related to organizational performance at all. Because of its role in many companies, HR does some things that do not directly impact the bottom line of organizations, and as a result activities which influence HR effectiveness may not impact organizational performance.

Time Spent

The results in Table 16.1 show that the amount of time spent on maintaining records, auditing, controlling, and human resources service provision is negatively related to organizational performance. Of these results, only the human resources service provider correlation is statistically significant. Development of human resource systems and strategic business partner are both positively related to organizational performance. The largest and most significant correlation for organizational performance is with being a strategic business partner. This reinforces the importance of HR being involved in the strategic decisions of corporations.

The pattern of correlations in Table 16.1 is very similar to the pattern in Table 15.1, which has data on HR effectiveness. In both cases the key to effectiveness is spending more time on being a strategic contributor and less time on traditional HR service activities. The major difference among them is the strength of the correlations; as expected, they are much lower for organizational performance (.27, $p \leq .01$) than for HR effectiveness (.54, $p \leq .001$).

Business Strategy

The extent of HR's involvement in specific business strategy activities shows low relationships with organizational performance. As can be seen in Table 16.2, the correlations for all of business strategy activities are positive but low. Given the overall positive pattern, it is reasonable to suggest that having HR involved in business strategy activities is a positive, but it certainly does not make a compelling case for its

Table 16.1. Relationship of HR roles (time spent) and organizational performance	
HR Roles[1]	Organizational Performance[2]
Maintaining Records Collect, track, and maintain data on employees	–.17
Auditing/Controlling Ensure compliance to internal operations, regulations, and legal and union requirements	–.13
Human Resources Service Provider Assist with implementation and administration of HR practices	–.23*
Development of Human Resources Systems and Practices Develop new HR systems and practices	.16ᵗ
Strategic Business Partner Member of the management team. Involved with strategic HR planning, organizational design, and strategic change	.27**

[1] Based on percentage of time spent on HR roles as rated by HR executives.

[2] Based on response: 1 = Much below average; 2 = Somewhat below average; 3 = About average; 4 = Somewhat above average; 5 = Much above average.

Significance level: ᵗ$p \leq .10$; *$p \leq .05$; **$p \leq .01$; ***$p \leq .001$

Table 16.2. Relationship of business strategy activities to organizational performance	
Activities	Organizational Performance
Help identify or design strategy options	.15
Help decide among the best strategy options	.14
Help plan the implementation of strategy	.11
Help identify new business opportunities	.12
Assess the organization's readiness to implement strategies	.13
Help design the organization structure to implement strategy	.12
Assess possible merger, acquisition, or divestiture strategies	.18ᵗ
Work with the corporate board on business strategy	.09

Significance level: ᵗ$p \leq .10$; *$p \leq .05$; **$p \leq .01$; ***$p \leq .001$

involvement in any specific strategy activity. In many respects this is not surprising. There is a considerable distance between HR participating in a business strategy activity and an organization performing more effectively than its competitors. Even at its best the HR role in strategy development and implementation is likely to be relatively minor, and having an effective business strategy is only part of what it takes to create an effective organization, there is still execution of the strategy!

HR Strategy

Results for the HR strategy items tend to show that there is a relatively strong, positive relationship between a number of features of the HR strategy and organizational performance. The strongest correlation in Table 16.3 is with human capital strategies that are integrated with the business strategy. This is not surprising given the potential advantage of this type of integration. Four other elements of HR strategy are also significantly related to organizational performance. Data-based talent strategy, analytic support, change management support, and driving change management all have statistically significant relationships with organizational performance.

Overall, the results indicate that a well designed HR strategy can in fact influence organizational performance. Again, the results are not as strong as they are for HR effectiveness, but this is hardly surprising given the many factors that determine organizational performance.

HR Organization

Organizational performance is not closely related to the features of the HR organization in the corporations we studied. As can be seen in Table 16.4, although all the correlations are positive, only HR talent development reaches statistical significance. The fact that HR talent development is significantly correlated with organizational performance again

Table 16.3. Relationship of HR strategy to organizational performance	
HR Strategy	**Organizational Performance**
Data-based talent strategy	.22*
A human capital strategy that is integrated with business strategy	.33***
Provides analytic support for business decision making	.24**
Provides HR data to support change management	.23*
Drives change management	.20*
Makes rigorous data-based decisions about human capital management	.18^t
Significance level: $^t p \le .10$; $^* p \le .05$; $^{**} p \le .01$; $^{***} p \le .001$	

Table 16.4. Relationship of HR organization to organizational performance	
HR Organization[1]	Organizational Performance
HR service units	.11
Decentralization	.06
Resource efficiency	.08
Information technology	.09
HR Talent development	.18*
[1] See Table 7.1 for items in scales. Significance level: [1] $p \leq .10$; * $p \leq .05$; ** $p \leq .01$; *** $p \leq .001$	

Table 16.5. Relationship of HR activity changes to organizational performance	
HR Activities[1]	Organizational Performance
Design and organization development	.30***
Compensation and benefits	.18*
Employee development	.34***
Recruitment and selection	.35***
HR metrics and analytics	.13
HR information systems	.11
Union relations	.05
[1] See Table 8.1 for items in scales. Significance level: [1] $p \leq .10$; * $p \leq .05$; ** $p \leq .01$; *** $p \leq .001$	

points to the value of having a well staffed and run HR organization. Also positively related to organizational performance is service units. This provides some support for the argument that it is useful to have corporate resource teams that service the rest of the organization.

HR Activity Changes

Multiple changes in HR activity levels are significantly related to organizational performance. As can be seen in Table 16.5, three activity level changes have particularly strong relationships. Design and organization development, employee development, and recruitment and selection all show relatively large significant relationships with organizational performance. This indicates that shifting more time and effort into these areas proved to be a high-payoff activity for these organizations. Particularly, interesting are the relationships with the amount of activity having to do with talent. Increasing the focus on talent management is potentially a high-payoff activity for many organizations, as talent has become more and more a driver of organizational performance.

Outsourcing

The results for HR outsourcing show no strong relationship with organizational performance. There is one significant correlation in Table 16.6, which shows the relationship between organizational performance and thirteen different types of outsourcing. Training is the only outsourcing activity that actual shows a statistically significant relationship with organizational performance, and even it is a weak relationship. Some types of activities, such as benefits, even show a negative relationship to organizational performance. Overall, the data suggest that outsourcing HR activities is not necessarily the right way to improve organizational performance—just as it is not necessarily a way to improve the performance of the HR organization.

Table 16.6. Relationship of outsourcing to organizational performance	
Outsourcing[1]	Organizational Performance
Overall Outsourcing (except Union relations)	**.16**[t]
Human capital forecasting and planning	.13
Organization design/development	.16[t]
Training	.20*
HR information systems	.02
Staffing and career development	.12
HR metrics and analysis	.12
Benefits	–.08
Compensation	.14
Legal affairs	.13
Executive compensation	–.02
Employee assistance	–.01
Competency / Talent assessment	.11
Union relations	.06
[1] See Table 11.1 for items in scales. Extent of outsourcing. Significance level: [t] $p \leq .10$; * $p \leq .05$; ** $p \leq .01$; *** $p \leq .001$	

Table 16.7. Relationship of information system use to organizational performance	
Information System	Organizational Performance[1]
Completely integrated HR IT system	4.3
Most processes are IT-based but not fully integrated	3.8
Some HR processes are IT-based	3.7
Little IT present in the HR function	3.8
No IT present	No Responses
[1] Based on response: 1 = Much below average; 2 = Somewhat below average; 3 = About average; 4 = Somewhat above average; 5 = Much above average	

Table 16.8. Relationship of HRIS outcomes to organizational performance	
HRIS Outcomes[1]	Organizational Performance
Overall Effectiveness[a]	**.21***
Employee satisfaction	.13
Efficiency	.22*
Business effectiveness	.18*
Improve human capital decisions of managers outside HR	.20*
Effective	.13
Create knowledge networks	.22*
Build social networks that help get work done	.24**

[a] Includes items from Employee Satisfaction, Efficiency, and Business Effectiveness scales only.

[1] See Table 12.4 for items in scales.

Significance level: [†] $p \leq .10$; * $p \leq .05$; ** $p \leq .01$; *** $p \leq .001$

Information Technology

The results for the use of information technology by HR show a clear relationship between its use and organizational performance. As can be seen in Table 16.7, those HR functions that have completely integrated IT systems have a significantly higher performance rating than those with lesser amounts of information technology use. The relationship is not as strong as is the one for HR effectiveness, but it is strong enough to establish the importance of having IT-based HR systems.

Table 16.8 shows the relationship between HRIS outcomes and organizational performance. The results generally show a positive relationship between how effective the HRIS system is and the overall performance of organizations. Although the correlations are low, six of them reach statistical significance and the other two are positive. This provides further evidence that information technology, when properly used by the HR function, can have a positive impact on organizational performance. This finding is particularly interesting with respect to the network questions. They are both significantly related to organizational performance, suggesting that they may be a new and potentially powerful way to improve organizational performance.

Metrics and Analytics

There are a number of significant relationships between the use of HR metrics and organizational performance (Table 16.9). As a general rule, the greater the use of metrics and analytics, the more effective an organization is. The statistically significant relationships are all in the effectiveness and impact areas. None of the efficiency items are significant. This once again makes the point that it is not how administratively efficient or effective the HR function is in doing its basic transactions work that determines organizational performance. Rather it is the degree to which it is able to put in place programs and make decisions that influence the way the organization develops and manages talent.

The highest correlation is between being able to measure the impact of HR programs and processes and organizational performance. The next highest correlations all have to do with the ability to make informed business decision about HR activities. They include measuring the business effects of HR programs, conducting cost-benefit analyses and measuring the business impact of performance in jobs. All these have direct implications for the bottom line of corporations.

The effectiveness of an organization's HR metrics and analytics is significantly related to organizational performance (Table 16.10). Three of the four strategy contributions measures, one of the functional and operational measures, and all of the LAMP items are significantly related to organizational performance. There is a strong correlation between identifying where talent has the greatest potential for strategic impact and organizational effectiveness. This once again reinforces the point that informed decision making about talent is something that HR functions can do that contributes to organizational performance. These significant relationships further reinforce the point that decision making and

Table 16.9. Relationship of HR analytics and metrics use to organizational performance	
Measures[1]	**Organizational Performance**
Efficiency	
Measure the financial efficiency of HR operations (e.g. cost-per-hire, time-to-fill, training costs)?	.13
Collect metrics that measure the cost of HR programs and processes?	.14
Benchmark analytics and measures against data from outside organizations (e.g. Saratoga, Mercer, Hewitt, etc.)?	.09
Effectiveness	
Use HR dashboards or scorecards?	.13
Measure the specific effects of HR programs (such as learning from training, motivation from rewards, validity of tests, etc.)?	.20*
Have the capability to conduct cost-benefit analyses (also called utility analyses) of HR programs?	.23*
Impact	
Measure the business impact of HR programs and processes?	.34***
Measure the quality of the talent decisions made by non-HR leaders?	.04
Measure the business impact of high versus low performance in jobs?	.24**
[1] Response scale: 1 = Yes, have now; 2 = Being built; 3 = Planning for; 4 = Not currently being considered Significance level: [1] $p \le .10$; * $p \le .05$; ** $p \le .01$; *** $p \le .001$	

Table 16.10. Relationship of HR metrics and analytics effectiveness to organizational performance	
Effectiveness[1]	Organizational Performance
Strategy Contributions	
Contributing to decisions about business strategy and human capital management	.19*
Identifying where talent has the greatest potential for strategic impact	.38***
Connecting human capital practices to organizational performance	.19*
Supporting organizational change efforts	.10
HR Functional and Operational Contributions	
Assessing and improving the HR department operations	.16[t]
Predicting the effects of HR programs before implementation	.16[t]
Pinpointing HR programs that should be discontinued	.19*
Logic, Analysis, Measurement, and Process (LAMP)	
Using logical principles that clearly connect talent to organization success	.26**
Using advanced data analysis and statistics	.23*
Providing high-quality (complete, timely, accessible) talent measurements	.32***
Motivating users to take appropriate action	.30***

[1] Response scale: 1 = Very ineffective; 2 = Ineffective; 3 = Somewhat effective; 4 = Effective; 5 = Very effective
Significance level: [t] $p \leq .10$; * $p \leq .05$; ** $p \leq .01$; *** $p \leq .001$

analysis by the HR function has the largest impact on organizational performance of all the things HR can do. For example, using the logical principles that connect talent to organizational success is significantly related to organizational performance. Similarly, providing high-quality talent measurements is significantly related.

Decision Science

The decision-making results are shown in Table 16.11. All the types of decisions studied are significantly related to organizational performance. The two highest correlations concern business leaders making decisions about strategy and finance, but the human capital decisions (e.g. where and why human capital makes a difference) are only slightly lower. Overall, the data strongly suggest that having managers both within and outside of the HR function who understand talent management leads to high organizational performance. It does not prove this, because these are correlational data and there is the possibility that because an organization is performing well it is seen as making good decisions. Perhaps the best explanation for why this relationship exists is one based on a kind of virtuous spiral in which good decisions drive good performance, which in turn encourages managers to focus on making good talent management decisions (Lawler 2008).

Table 16.11. Relationship of decision science sophistication to organizational performance

Decision Making[1]	Organizational Performance
We excel at competing for and with talent where it matters most to our strategic success	.32***
Business leaders' decisions that depend upon or affect human capital (e.g. layoffs, rewards, etc.) are as rigorous, logical, and strategically relevant as their decisions about resources such as money, technology, and customers	.27**
Business leaders understand and use sound principles when making decisions about:	
1. Motivation	.30***
2. Development and learning	.32***
3. Culture	.33***
4. Organization design	.31***
5. Business strategy	.40***
6. Finance	.39***
7. Marketing	.22*
HR leaders have a good understanding about where and why human capital makes the biggest difference in their business	.33***
Business leaders have a good understanding about where and why human capital makes the biggest difference in their business	.24*
HR systems educate business leaders about their talent decisions	.27**
HR adds value by insuring compliance with rules, laws, and guidelines	.27**
HR adds value by delivering high-quality professional practices and services	.30***
HR adds value by improving talent decisions inside and outside the HR function	.29**

[1] Response scale: 1 = Little or no extent; 2 = Some extent; 3 = Moderate extent; 4 = Great extent; 5 = Very great extent
Significance level: [1] $p \le .10$; * $p \le .05$; ** $p \le .01$; *** $p \le .001$

Table 16.12. Relationship of HR skill satisfaction to organizational performance

HR Skills[1]	Organizational Performance
HR technical skills	.25**
Interpersonal dynamics	.29***
Business partner skills	.23*
Metrics skills	.17[1]

[1] See Table 13.3 for items in scales.
Significance level: [1] $p \le .10$; * $p \le .05$; ** $p \le .01$; *** $p \le .001$

HR Skills

Satisfaction with HR skills is significantly related to organizational performance. As can be seen in Table 16.12, three of the four skills areas have statistically significant relationships. The fourth, metrics skills, has a positive relationship but does not reach the .05 level of significance. The overall pattern is clear: the more skills HR has, the more effective the organization is.

It is surprising that the metrics skills area is not more strongly related to organizational performance. Since the presence of metrics is related to organizational performance, it is logical to expect that the HR functions skills in this area would also be related to organizational performance. The overall positive relationship between HR skills and organizational performance does argue for staffing HR with competent individuals and for investing in the development of the HR staff. It reinforces the point made earlier that developing the HR staff has an impact on organizational performance.

Conclusion

Our results show a number of moderately strong relationships between organizational performance and the way HR is organized, managed, and staffed. As expected, the relationships are not as strong as those involving the effectiveness of HR as a function. Among the most important are the following:

- The amount of time spent on strategic issues is positively related to organizational performance.

- A number of HR strategy activities are related to organizational performance. The strongest relationship is with having a human capital strategy that is integrated with the business strategy.

- The amount of HR talent development that is done by an organization is positively related to its performance, as is the skill level in HR.

- Increasing HR's focus on talent is associated with high organizational performance.

- Having an integrated HR IT system is associated with high organizational performance.

- Employing metrics and analytics that measure the impact and quality of HR programs, processes, and talent decisions is associated with organizational performance.

- High performance organizations have a high level of decision science sophistication with respect to talent and its impact on organizational performance.

Overall, the results tell an important story about how HR can contribute to organizational performance. Talent management is clearly an area where by improving its data, analytics, and decision making HR can have a very positive impact on organizational performance. HR also can make important contributions to organizational performance by developing its role as a strategic contributor.

CHAPTER 17

How HR Has Changed

Our study provides unique data that answer questions about whether and how HR is changing. Other studies have asked about the importance of HR taking a new direction, adding new skills, and offering new services, and they have asked HR managers to report on the amount and kind of change they think has occurred. Our study is the only one that has examined change by measuring the activities and effectiveness of HR functions since 1995.

Reports of change are almost always less valid than are comparisons among data collected at two or more points in time. The former are influenced by memory and other factors. The problem with reports of change is demonstrated in our study by the responses to our question concerning how HR time is spent. HR executives responding to each of our six surveys report that there has been a significant shift in the way HR time is being spent. However, when we examine changes in activity levels using reports of current practice from different time periods, the percentages have not shifted. This is much better evidence about the kind and amount of change that is happening than are reports of whether changes have occurred.

There is no question that the business environment has changed dramatically in the last 20 years, but the HR function in most organizations does not look very different from 10–15 years ago. The period since our last survey in 2007 saw enormous change in the business environment: a global recession, the continuing rise of India and China as global competitors, and tremendous growth in the IT world. Despite the enormous changes which have occurred, our data show that little change from 2007 to 2010 has occurred in how HR is organized and how it operates in large corporations. On the other hand there is widespread agreement concerning how HR needs to change: it needs to be more strategic, more of a business partner, and offer higher-quality HRIS and human capital management systems.

What Has and Hasn't Changed

Our analysis of the results of our 1995, 1998, 2001, 2004, 2007, and 2010 surveys establishes that some significant changes have occurred in how HR functions are organized and how they deliver services. The most significant changes involve the way the HR function is organized, where HR activities and information are located, and HR's role in employee advocacy and shaping a labor market strategy. These changes may well set the stage for a greater HR strategic role, but they are largely focused on how the HR function itself is organized and managed, and how it defines its relationships with its clients. The most important changes are:

- HR is more likely to use service teams to support and service business units.

- HR is more likely to have corporate centers of excellence.

- Companies are more likely to have similar HR practices in different business units.

- HR is paying increased attention to recruitment and selection as well as organization design and development.

- The use of outsourcing for some HR activities has increased.

- More companies have integrated HRISs that can perform a number of HR activities.

- Employees and managers are increasingly making use of HRISs that provide job information and performance management capabilities.

- There is greater satisfaction with the interpersonal dynamics and business understanding skills of HR professionals.

- HR decision support contributions are increasingly associated with HR's strategic role.

- HR is increasingly effective in helping shape a viable employment relationship for the future, providing HR services, operating centers of excellence, and being an employee advocate.

In comparing the 1995 and 1998 results to the 2010 results, it is clear that a number of things have not changed very much, if at all. Many of these elements involve HR's role in shaping strategy and building effective HR skills. Among them are the following:

- The amount of time spent on various human resource activities

- HR executives' belief that HR is spending more time being a strategic partner

- The extent to which HR is a full partner in shaping business strategy

- The failure to rotate individuals into, out of, and within HR

- The desire of HR executives to have HR be a business and strategic partner

- The use of shared services

- The problems that occur with outsourcing

- The use of outsourcing for organization development, employee assistance, and HR planning

- The implementation of HR metrics and analytics systems and their effectiveness

- The effectiveness of HR in adding value through decision support

- The percentage of HR professionals who have the skills they need to be effective

- Most of the business partner skills of HR professionals

- The importance of HR services

- The characteristics of an effective HR function

Impact of Recession

To assess how the HR function has been affected by the recession, we added some items to the 2010 U.S. survey. We asked HR executives and managers how the HR function changed in their organizations as a result of the recession and what steps HR professionals took to deal with the recession (Lawler, Jamrog, and Boudreau 2011).

The results of the survey paint a positive picture of what happened to the HR functions in most organizations. In only a small percentage of companies did the recession result in a decrease in the strategic role, power, and effectiveness of the HR function. In most organizations, the ratings of HR executives and managers indicated they either stayed the same or increased in these areas. As can be seen in Tables 17.1 and 17.2, HR gained power and status, became more strategic, and improved its effectiveness in more than a quarter of the companies surveyed. In short, the data suggest that the HR function was more likely to see an increase than a decrease in power, effectiveness, and strategic role as a result of how HR executives responded to the recession.

To get a sense of what HR did to improve its status and effectiveness, we asked how HR functions changed in response to the recession. Our analysis shows that a number of changes are strongly related to the degree to which HR departments improved their effectiveness during the recession.

Changes in talent management are most strongly related to improving HR effectiveness. HR executives who report that their organizations made stronger commitments to talent management and improving the quality of their talent management decisions showed the most improvement in the effectiveness of their HR functions. This provides one more confirmation that HR executives must be expert talent managers.

The survey results also confirm the importance of performance management. Respondents who reported a greater focus on performance management were likely to see improvements in the status and effectiveness

Table 17.1. Recession impact as reported by HR executives (percentages)			
	Decreased	No Change or Stayed the Same	Increased
Power and status of HR function	14.9	58.2	26.9
Strategic role of HR function	14.0	47.1	38.9
Effectiveness of HR function	8.8	54.9	34.9
Source: Lawler, Jarmog, and Boudreau 2011			

Table 17.2. Recession impact as reported by managers (percentages)			
	Decreased	No Change or Stayed the Same	Increased
Power and status of HR function	7.4	67.6	25.0
Strategic role of HR function	2.9	67.6	29.4
Effectiveness of HR function	14.4	59.4	26.0
Source: Lawler, Jarmog, and Boudreau 2011			

of the HR function. No wonder: times of economic turmoil highlight competitive performance pressures, and often require difficult decisions about what human capital to retain and what to cut. Thus, performance management systems that produce accurate data about the condition of an organization's talent become even more pivotal to making many of the decisions that leaders need to make during economic change and turmoil.

HR executives who emphasized metrics tended to see the biggest gains in the power and effectiveness of their HR functions. These results once again make the point that HR needs data and analytics that show how effectively the HR organization operates and how talent management systems perform.

There were strong relationships between the willingness to change and improvements in the status and effectiveness of the HR function. HR organizations whose executives reported an increased willingness to try innovative HR activities showed large gains in status and effectiveness. These findings represent a confirmation that HR professionals need to be open to new practices, something they are frequently criticized for not being.

Amount and Kind of Change

Our results also indicate the paths that HR executives need to follow to continue to improve the effectiveness of their function. The results strongly suggest that a commitment to talent management, use of analytics and metrics, and the willingness to try new practices should be part of HR functions in the future. The survey showed improvements in some of these areas, but in all cases the improvements were modest and not dramatic.

Overall, our data from 1995, 1998, 2001, 2004, 2007, and 2010 show that more things have stayed the same than have changed. Although many of the changes we found are significant and important, the amount of change is surprisingly small. Frankly, given the tremendous amount of attention that has been given to the importance of HR being a business and strategic partner, and adding value in new ways, we expected much more change. In fact we expected more change than we have seen in every wave of our study since it began. This "stubborn traditionalism" (Boudreau and Ramstad 2007) is also apparent in the continuing flow of articles about frustration among non-HR executives with HR's unrealized potential.

It appears that much about HR has remained the same despite the amount of change that is going on around it. This raises a critical question: are there particular organizational and environmental conditions that are associated with HR being more of a business and strategic partner? The answer may help us understand what it takes to change HR organizations. Next, we highlight some of the findings about change that emerged from our study.

International Differences

There were some interesting differences among the six countries studied, and not surprisingly most of the differences involved China. It is the least developed of the countries studied and the only communist country studied. The key country differences include the following:

- China's HR organizations are lower than other countries on time spent as a strategic business partner.

- China's HR organizations are less involved in helping with succession and compensation issues.

- China's HR organizations are much less involved in business strategy activities including implementation, assessing readiness, and identifying options.

- Chinese HR organizations do not have HR strategies that drive change management and are integrated with the business strategy.

- Chinese HR organizations are low on adding value by improving talent decisions and knowing where human capital makes a difference.

- U.S. HR organizations are the most frequent users of outsourcing and HR service units; Chinese are the least frequent.

- Chinese HR organizations are lowest on using HR metrics and analytics and on doing talent assessments.

- Employee assistance is outsourced most in the U.S., Canada, and Australia; least in China.

- Chinese organizations make the least use of information technology; U.S. makes the most.

- Chinese organizations rate the effectiveness of their metrics and analytics higher than any other country rates theirs.

- Chinese HR executives are the least satisfied with the skills of their HR staffs.

- Chinese HR executives rate the performance of their functions the lowest, and they rate the importance of HR performance the lowest.

Overall, the picture is clear: HR organizations are very similar in the developed countries studied, and they are more strategic than they are in the less developed countries we studied. The similarity among the developed countries is not surprising since most of the organizations studied are large global competitors. Still, there are cultural and legal differences among the countries that might lead to some major differences, but our data indicate they have not. The lower level of strategic activity in China suggests that the level of national economic development is a determinant of HR's role in organizations.

Strategic Focuses

Our study found a strong relationship between what is happening in the HR function and an organization's strategic focuses. In particular, four of the five focuses were strongly related to most of the features of HR organizations. The exception was the growth focus. It was related to HR giving help to the board, but only weakly if at all related to other HR organization features. Generally speaking, it appears that an emphasis on information, knowledge, sustainability, and innovation creates a much more favorable situation for the HR function because it places a premium on acquiring, developing, deploying, and retaining talent.

Overall, our results clearly show that strategy focuses influence the way the HR function operates and its success as a business partner. When there are strong focuses in every area except growth, HR performs more high-valued-added activities and is more strategic, and the HR function is more positively regarded.

These results raise the question of the direction of causality. One possibility is that an organization's strategy causes HR to take on a particular role. The alternative is that a more strategic HR role causes organizations to attempt or adopt strategies that rely more on knowledge and talent quality. Our guess is that the most common causal direction is from strategy to the nature of HR, not the reverse. One implication of this is that how an HR organization operates in a company may be largely determined by the company's business strategy, which in turn is influenced by HR. Perhaps HR is more the victim than the guilty party in cases where it is not a business and/or strategic partner. Certainly, more than one of the senior HR leaders we have worked with have said that it is easier to find an organization that understands and supports strategic HR than to try to change an organization that does not.

Management Approach

We considered five management approaches, and two of them had a strong and consistent positive relationship with the nature of the HR function in organizations. The high-involvement and sustainable approaches were associated with HR being more involved in business strategy activities, employee development and in working with the board, and with advanced levels of decision science, decision support, and HR metrics and analytics. This is not surprising. These approaches, more than the others, require a clear focus on human capital and an organization that understands how talent and organization design decisions affect strategic success.

The bureaucratic and low-cost operator approaches tended to have negative relationships to most of the HR survey items. This is not surprising; these management approaches do not look to talent as a source of competitive advantage, so it is not surprising that they do not invest in building effective HR organizations.

The results for the global competitor approach tend to fall in the middle. It does have a positive relationship to HR being important, but the relationship is not as strong as it is for the high-involvement and sustainable approaches. This may reflect the fact that global competitors focus on many approaches to strategic success, including low cost, and may also use bureaucratic management approaches in order to coordinate global operations. In contrast, the high-involvement approach explicitly focuses on talent involvement as a key to performance, and the sustainable approach specifically emphasizes the quality of the employment relationship as a key performance indicator in and of itself, in addition to its contribution to organization success.

As with the results for strategic focuses, there is the question of what comes first, the management approach or an HR function that is a strong business and strategic partner. As with the strategic focuses, our best guess is that it is more often the high-involvement and the sustainable approaches that lead to the strong HR role, but there are probably organizations where HR has had a major influence on them adopting the high-involvement approach and the sustainable approach.

HR as a Strategic Contributor

The data concerning what determines the strategic role of the HR organization are clearly consistent with the argument that HR can and should be more of a strategic contributor. Yet, the data also show that HR is not a strategic contributor in most organizations. HR appears to have some influence when it comes to how staffing relates to strategy and how organizational structure relates to implementing strategy. But our results suggest that HR plays a less prominent role when it comes to the development of strategy and the consideration of strategic options and other strategy areas, including acquisitions and mergers.

A number of HR practices are significantly associated with a stronger strategic role for HR, including

- Having an HR strategy that is integrated with the business strategy

- The use of information technology

- Focusing on HR talent development

- Using HR service teams that provide expertise and support the business

- Having HR activities that focus on organization design, organization development, change management, employee development, and metrics

- Using computer systems for training and development

- Having an effective HRIS

- Having effective HR metrics and analytics

- Having business leaders who make rigorous, logical human capital decisions

- Having an HR staff with technical, organizational dynamics, business partner, and metrics skills

- Improving talent decisions

- Having an HR function that effectively provides services

Overall, being a strategic contributor demands that high levels of business knowledge and skill be present in HR. It also requires HRISs that have the right metrics and analytics, and organization designs and practices that link HR managers to business units. Last but not to be overlooked is the need for the effective and efficient delivery of HR services.

HR and Organizational Effectiveness

The factors leading to HR effectiveness are a combination of approaches that promote efficiency in routine transactional processing and allow HR professionals to focus on expanding their knowledge base, provide expertise, and partner with others. In Chapter 15 we provided a list of practices that are associated with HR effectiveness; the list provides an actionable agenda for HR functions. It is also marked by another characteristic: most of the practices are not widely used and show little increase in use from 1995 to 2010. This strongly suggests that one of the reasons why HR is not increasing its effectiveness is that it has not done the things that it needs to do in order to be and to be perceived as more effective.

A number of HR practices are significantly related to organizational performance. They are listed at the end of Chapter 16. There are no surprises; the results confirm that HR needs to focus on talent, use metrics and analytics, and develop the skills and knowledge of the individuals who work in HR. What HR needs to do is clear and not surprising. What is surprising is that it has continued to do business as usual in a rapidly changing world.

Obstacles to Change

Why hasn't HR changed more? There are a number of possible explanations. One is that HR executives simply don't feel HR needs to change. Given the results of our surveys and many others, we can say this doesn't seem to be true. In all our surveys, HR executives have said they plan to change and have said that it is important that they act as a business partner. Of course, they may just be saying what is "professionally correct" and giving lip service to the idea of being a business partner, but we do not think this is what is occurring.

A second possible reason for the failure of HR to change is that in most organizations there is no great demand for HR to change. The existing role and activities of HR are well institutionalized and have created a kind of co-dependency relationship. The individuals in the HR function are satisfied with their current role and are comfortable delivering traditional HR services in a traditional mode; at the same time, the recipients of these services are satisfied with HR primarily being an administrative function that does what they see as onerous HR activities for them. This situation leads to an institutionalized devaluation of the HR function because of its low level of contribution to the business, and to an unwillingness to let it change because it serves many organization members well enough as it is. However, our results showing an increase in the use of centralized HR services, HRISs, and the movement of HR activities into the hands of employees and their managers may signal the end of highly attentive and personal HR service.

The managers outside of HR that we surveyed in 2004, 2007, and 2010 acknowledge the importance of HR being a strategic partner, but they also focus on HR contributing to talent management. Ironically, it is possible that their focus on talent may be operating against upgrading the strategic role of HR. It may focus a disproportionate amount of professional HR time on delivering services related to recruiting, orienting, developing, and retaining employees, leaving HR little time and few resources to spend on upgrading the competencies and systems that are needed in order for it to be a contributor to strategy development.

In our book on the 2007 survey, we speculated that HR time and attention might be side-tracked by the war for talented employees and by the need to generate and administer reward systems that are constantly being challenged to provide mass customization for scarce talent. Because of the 2008 recession, the "war for talent" has changed—organizations are in control—but the need to spend time on talent management has not.

Recruiting, developing, and retaining a highly mobile and competitive workforce can often impose very high demands on HR time and energy. It can lock HR professionals into activity patterns that are difficult to change. Certainly, a common refrain from HR leaders is that they rarely have time to think about bigger-picture issues, or to develop in areas beyond their specific functional responsibilities. We found that the attention being paid to almost all HR activities has increased, suggesting that even though there is agreement that some HR activities add greater value than others, HR functions are still required to spend considerable time on activities that they know to be low in strategic value.

The skills of the professionals in the HR function offer an additional reason for the limited change in the HR function. Just how difficult it is to change the HR function becomes apparent when we look at the kinds of skills that members of the HR function must have in order to be rated highly and to perform the strategic and business partner roles.

HR professionals need a broad range of skills, ranging from relatively routine administrative processing skills to organizational dynamics and business skills. Although business and organizational dynamics skills are the most highly related to effectiveness, our results suggest that the HR function cannot be ineffective in core administrative functions if it wants to be respected. Interestingly, HR did not score very highly in administrative skills, especially with respect to managing contractors and managing HRISs.

Business and strategic contributor effectiveness requires knowledge and skills in such areas as change management, strategic planning, and organization design. It also requires a knowledge of decision science for human capital that provides logical and unique strategic insights by using human capital principles. These areas involve complex judgments, and HR professionals have traditionally had little experience with them. Such expertise is both hard to acquire and in short supply. Becoming expert in business partnering demands the acquisition of not only explicit knowledge but also tacit knowledge that comes from experience. Applying this expertise demands the ability to influence line management and to be part of effective teaming relationships with others who have deep business knowledge.

The results of our study show that HR professionals are seen as having increased some of their interpersonal dynamics skills and their business understanding skills since 1995. However, they are still perceived to fall short in most business skills and in metrics and analytical skills as well. HR leaders also often lack cross-functional business experience. Understanding HR strategy is at best a ticket to get a seat at the table. Expertise in business strategy is required to set the table and add value once at the table. Thus, HR is in a bit of a catch-22. It must get to the table and gain experience in order to gain the knowledge and skills it needs to get there!

Conclusion

HR wants to be a strategic partner and the door is opening because of the growing recognition that talent is a key determinant of an organization's effectiveness. But HR cannot seem to get through the door in many organizations, much less get a seat at the table. The good news is that our results consistently identify a pattern of HR activities, skills, and relationships that are associated with HR effectiveness and a stronger strategic role. Difficult as it may be to make them happen, the changes that are required are easy to identify.

CHAPTER 18

What the Future of HR Should Be

What should the future be for the human resources function? What does HR need to do to become a strategic contributor? When we reported on our 1998 results (Lawler and Mohrman 2000), we said, "Change has just begun. The next decade will probably see dramatic change in the human resource function in most companies. The opportunity exists for human resource management to become a true strategic partner, and to help decide how organizations will be managed, what human resource systems will look like, and how human resource services will be created and delivered."

Our 2010 results suggest that many of the changes we predicted have not yet taken place. Yes, there has been some change, but it is not the kind of game-changing change that we thought would happen. Nevertheless, we have not altered our view that transformational change is needed. If anything, we feel more strongly today about the importance of change in HR than we did in 1998. Today, organizations in the United States and the rest of the developed world have an ever higher percentage of their employees doing knowledge work. Human capital has become increasingly important as a source of competitive advantage, as has intellectual capital (Lawler and Worley 2011).

Our results show that when organizations focus on developing their competencies, capabilities, and knowledge assets, especially in combination with a strong focus on the strategy of the firm, HR is a strong strategic and business contributor and the HR function is markedly different. Thus, there is good reason to believe that if organizations increasingly pursue strategic focuses and management approaches that draw on deep and widespread human capital excellence, HR will change.

HR as a High-Value Contributor

We pointed out in Chapter 1 that as a business, HR potentially can have three product lines. The first is to execute the processes and activities required to provide services such as compensation, personnel administration, staffing, development, and deployment.

The second role is to respond to business plans developed by others, helping business units and general managers realize their business plans. In this role, HR provides advice and services concerning how to develop, design, and install HR practices in areas such as employee relations, talent management, organizational development, change management, and connecting HR practices with business operations.

The third role is helping to set and implement the strategic direction of the organization. It requires developing and assessing the organization's human capital and creating the organizational capabilities required to support the strategic direction. It also requires shaping strategy by providing a unique perspective through the lens of the talent market and human behavior. This role requires HR to understand business strategy and how it relates to organizational capabilities and core competencies and how those connect to pivotal talent and organization decisions. In this role, HR leaders need to use their knowledge to help the organization set its strategic direction and develop its business plans in ways that are consistent with a talent decision science.

HR Administration

The HR services that organizations need are increasingly becoming a commodity. Historically, they were delivered by an in-house HR function often in a labor-intensive and costly manner. Three approaches are emerging as ways to acquire and operate the technology and skills needed to deliver HR services.

The first is to use web-based custom systems that are designed and operated by the organization using them. This model is currently being used by information technology companies such as Dell, IBM, Cisco, Hewlett-Packard, and Microsoft. Some of these systems are very impressive and allow individuals, on a self-service basis, to perform a number of important HR tasks and access a great deal of information. However, it is highly unlikely that most companies will ever develop the kind of custom systems that have been developed by large technology companies; doing so is simply too expensive and time consuming.

A second model involves acquiring software and systems from vendors, using one of two approaches. The first is to buy an integrated web-based system from a major ERP vendor (e.g. Oracle, SAP). The second is to acquire individual HR applications for specific tasks like compensation administration, staffing, and training from different software vendors. Some good programs exist and when combined can produce an effective HR system for companies. However, there is a significant disadvantage associated with choosing a set of best-of-breed software applications. Our results suggest there is great value in integration: the best use of HR data often involves integration across multiple HR processes. Software integration is required, and this can be costly and time consuming. This leads some organizations to acquire integrated, total HR systems rather than individual solutions. On the other hand, we may see the evolution of a core set of data standards, against which multiple software vendors can develop their applications.

The third model is to use business process outsourcing. A number of major corporations have signed contracts to outsource all or most of the administrative aspects of their human resource management processes. Case studies of four early adopters show significant cost savings as well as enabling some movement toward HR becoming more of a strategic partner (Lawler, Ulrich, Fitz-enz, and Madden 2004). Recently, more large firms (e.g. Unilever) have adopted this approach. The result of our 2010 survey also suggest that this approach is growing and typically is seen as being effective, although the results do not suggest it is necessarily more effective than the others.

We cannot say from our results which HRIS model will be dominant in the future, but our findings do suggest what the future of HR information systems should be. We found that more HR administration is being done by employees on HRISs. We also found that the effectiveness of HRISs in performing HR processes and enabling employee self-service was positively related to how effective HR is seen to be in providing administrative support. The completeness and integration of these systems also is related to overall HR effectiveness. The most positive outcomes of HRISs to date are the efficiency benefits they produce.

Overall, our results suggest that an investment in a high-quality HRIS should increase the HR function's credibility and perceived value added, while decreasing the time the function spends on administrative tasks. We found some evidence of a substitution effect: providing high-quality systems for administrative processing related not only to perceived administrative effectiveness but to perceived effectiveness in all HR areas. This may occur because a high-quality HRIS allows the function to spend more time on developing valuable new skills and being a business and strategic partner. Furthermore, by offering knowledge and tools to managers and employees, a high-quality HRIS can provide enhanced decision support that increases their effectiveness in HR and talent management.

At this point, HR executives do not perceive HRISs to be particularly effective. They are given relatively high marks by HR executives on improving HR services and speeding up HR processes but are not rated highly in most other areas. Despite this, we believe they can be a key delivery vehicle for HR services and contribute to an enhanced strategic role for HR. In particular, the value of such systems in conveying HR knowledge and decision frameworks to managers and employees represents an untapped opportunity for improving an organization's talent management.

In our book on the 2007 results, we stated that "it is unlikely that any approach to HR administration will be dominant by 2010 when we do our next survey" (Lawler and Boudreau 2009). We were right, and the same is likely to be true in 2013 when we do our next survey. However, we do expect to see that HRISs will have advanced to a point where they are more supportive of HR being a strategic contributor.

Business Partner

But what about the business partner activities of HR? Can and should they be outsourced? Can and should they be put on the web? There is little doubt that some business partner activities can be greatly facilitated by web technology and/or outsourcing.

HRISs can collect, aggregate, and analyze ever increasing amounts of data about the human resources of an organization, at ever lower costs and higher speeds. HR data can enhance change management, business plan implementation, and business operations by making human capital information readily available and by obtaining feedback and suggestions about HR process improvement and effectiveness. It should be pointed out that HRISs are merely enablers; they can enhance but cannot replace human judgment in problem solving and decision making.

As for outsourcing the business partner role, consultants can provide insight about the HR implications of business plans and organizational change. However, our view is that tailoring HR programs and practices to specific strategies and business plans, as well as implementing them, will always need the contributions of some internal, skilled HR professionals to provide the services, information, and knowledge that are necessary for HR to be an effective business partner.

Performing the business partner role entails solving problems and making decisions that are value laden, highly uncertain, and context specific; they require understanding the business, its strategy, the nature of the workforce, and the required competencies. It entails the application of tacit, experience-based knowledge of employee relations as well as knowledge of the HR discipline and the ability to combine HR knowledge with the perspectives of other disciplines, such as business management, marketing, information technology, and product technology.

The key question for us is not whether HR professionals should perform the business partner role, but whether current HR professionals are the ones to do it. The evidence in our study suggests that the comfort level and effectiveness of today's human resource professionals is highest with traditional HR service activities and delivery. It is much lower with respect to business knowledge and HR systems design. Thus, for HR professionals to be effective business partners, they will need to enhance their capabilities in areas such as organization design, vendor management, and decision support.

Strategic Partner

Perhaps the most intriguing results of our study are those that have implications for the strategic partner role. As organizations do more knowledge work, there is an increasing need for HR leaders not only to respond to strategies, but actually to shape them based on talent and organizational competencies and capabilities. In addition, the rapid rate of change, the need to develop new strategies and to quickly translate them into human resource strategies, and the likelihood that the availability of talent will be a key strategic differentiator have greatly increased the importance of HR being a strategic contributor.

The role of strategic partner requires individuals who understand how business strategies and plans connect to talent and organization design and management. They also need to know how to shape business strategies to fit emerging human capital opportunities and threats. Some of this work can be outsourced to HR strategy consultants; however, we believe there needs to be a strong internal presence of individuals who have good HR knowledge, who can manage consultants, and who can be fully engaged when strategies are formulated. HR's strategic role ultimately needs to be led by a senior executive in the organization, not by a consultant.

The importance of the HR strategic role, and the need to fill it with somebody who understands business, may be one reason why almost a quarter of all chief HR executives come from the business rather than from the HR function. In essence, some companies seem to have decided that the HR strategic partner role is too important to be entrusted to someone with an HR background.

The assumption that someone without HR knowledge is the best person to lead HR is flawed. Just as with other functions, such as IT, operations, legal, supply chain, and finance, this role requires not only a strong knowledge of business and strategy; it requires knowledge of the function. In the case of HR it requires the capacity to understand the principles and practices that underlie labor markets and human behavior at work. In the same way, knowledge about portfolio theory or customer behavior is a prerequisite to be the chief financial officer or chief marketing officer (Boudreau and Ramstad 2007). Indeed, effective strategic partnership may require that HR leaders "retool" their current logic frameworks to better apply the principles of disciplines such as marketing, finance, and operations directly to such HR functions as staffing, rewards, and talent management (Boudreau 2010).

Having data available from an effective HRIS is one of several enablers that can strengthen HR's position as strategic contributors. HRISs can, for example, help HR professionals make significant contributions to strategy formulation, by providing both cost and organizational effectiveness data with respect to human resource practices. They can provide information about how to develop key competencies and about the existing levels of organizational effectiveness and organizational capabilities. These are all critical inputs to the strategy planning process. They can codify and teach decision frameworks and principles that enhance strategic decisions. They also can enable HR executives to translate what they know about the existing organization and its capabilities into change programs, thus allowing the organization to develop the necessary capabilities to implement new strategic plans and new directions (Lawler and Worley 2006).

Talent Management

Quite possibly the biggest change that needs to occur in HR has to do with talent management, not elsewhere in organizations but how talent is managed in HR. In many respects talent management in HR is a case of the shoemaker's children lacking shoes. Our results suggest that HR often doesn't have the right talent; and too often it has talent that is inferior to the talent in other key parts of the organization even though HR professionals need to have a comparable set of skills and knowledge.

HR professionals need to understand and be able to formulate a business model for the HR function and to contribute to the firm's business model. They need to understand business operations and be able to craft human resource management approaches that reflect their organization's competitive situation. They need to understand organization and work design and change management principles and approaches, and be able to play a leadership role when these issues are considered. They need to understand different models of staffing, compensation, and other human resources management practices so that they can effectively implement HR systems that support the business plans of the organization. They need to educate and develop business leaders who make human capital decisions that are as logical, rigorous, and strategic as are their decisions about money, technology, and customers. Finally, they need to identify the pivot points in the business that drive strategic and organizational effectiveness, and then connect human capital decisions to those pivot points.

Has the talent level in HR been improving? At least at the senior levels there are some reasons to think it has. More CEOs do recognize the importance of having a talented HR executive and have acted on this recognition. Many highly talented female business leaders have become HR executives because it is their best career opportunity. This has created a gender diversity in HR that offers significant opportunities for the HR profession to provide a unique perspective at the executive and board levels of organizations. Particularly as organizations must consider more diverse employee populations and customers, this is an important change. The downside of it is that many women end up in the HR silo and miss out on opportunities elsewhere in the organization.

The skills and knowledge that HR professionals need are not easily acquired. They are only likely to exist in organizations that take HR talent management seriously and have a very integrated approach to talent management. This has important implications for HR's performance management and staffing practices at all levels.

At the entry level, HR needs to significantly increase the quality of its hires. Today, few of the best students in the leading business schools pursue HR careers, because of low starting salaries and a perception that HR is not a good place to start a career. As a result, there often is a scarcity of highly talented business school students with an academic concentration in HR. Thus, organizations should consider hiring non-HR majors who are very talented and interested in HR. Indeed, the ground may be shifting, as some business school students have been very articulate about the wisdom of their decision to pursue an HR career (Breitfelder and Dowling 2008). However, at least until it does shift, HR needs to hire non-HR majors.

Once hired, it is important that HR professionals spend time working outside HR. Our data suggest that this doesn't happen very often and that most organizations don't plan on increasing it. This is a problem because without experience in non-HR jobs, HR professionals miss important opportunities to understand the business, and they miss the chance to build personal credibility by doing a non-HR job well.

It may be even more important to have non-HR managers and professionals rotate into HR than it is for HR professionals to rotate out. At this point, very few U.S. corporations have CEOs and senior executives other than the head of HR who have worked in HR. Increasing the frequency with which senior managers have HR experience has important benefits. First, it can improve their performance when they make human capital decisions, and when they work with HR. Second, it makes top organizational talent available to the HR function, and brings to HR the perspective of those non-HR executives regarding HR's value proposition. Our results show that business leaders are held to higher standards regarding their capability to use sound principles in areas such as finance and marketing, as compared to human capital and talent management. Considering the acknowledged importance of talent to competitiveness, it would seem prudent to give senior leaders deep experience in HR that builds their understanding of it.

The value of shared and valid principles about human capital and talent also has implications for future HR executives. HR professionals should be trained and should develop and use research-based knowledge about labor markets, human behavior, and organization theory. They need to move beyond just being good to work with and knowledgeable about people and employee relations. They need to know and act on the large amount of research which has been done on talent management, organization design, and a host of other HR issues (Mohrman, Lawler, and associates 2011). Making decisions on instinct or "knowing people" just isn't good enough. Moreover, such evidence needs to be used with a savvy understanding about how to transform organizations through evidence-based change, by using principles such as logic-driven analytics, segmentation, risk-leverage, synergy, and optimization (Boudreau and Jesuthasan 2011).

HR Organization Design

How should HR be managed and structured? Should it be a large function, employing approximately one out of every one hundred employees, and organized primarily upon a service-delivery paradigm focused on activities such as compensation, training, and staffing? There is good reason to believe that it should not. HR needs to utilize a deeper and more fundamental perspective on how it adds value to justify its cost. Strategic influence, business decision support, organizational agility, and sustainability need to define the HR value proposition, which means that providing low-cost, high-quality services is not sufficient.

An increasingly common feature of HR organizations, particularly in companies with multiple business units, is to place HR executives in each business unit. This business-unit role involves HR contributing to business-unit plans and organizational capabilities. It supports some tailoring of human resource practices to the workforce needs of the business unit.

HR executives in the business units are expected to be liaisons to the corporate HR staff on behalf of their business units. This liaison role is likely to be increasingly important in the future. Instead of locating many of the HR services in the business unit, multi-division corporations are creating shared service units and corporate centers of excellence for the business units to draw on. Or they are outsourcing HR transactional services and require business units to use them. In both approaches the role of the business-unit HR executive is to translate business strategies into HR practices as well as coordinate the array of centralized HR services for their business unit.

In this design we are seeing increasing use of "double-hatting" to ensure connections between HR functional expertise and business-unit goals. For example, the head of learning and development may "double-hat" as the business partner for a major organizational division or product line where learning and development are particularly pivotal.

In essence, the HR organization appears to be becoming a type of front-back organization where the business-unit HR leader or "generalist" is the front, customer-focused, part. The back, in this case, is the vendors, shared services units, and centers of excellence that are available to the business units. Our results show that the front-back approach to HR function design has increased in popularity since 1994 and there is reason to believe that it will be the most popular approach in the future, but it is worth considering an alternative organization for the HR function.

Currently HR "houses" three businesses, which are related but require different competencies and capabilities. One comparison here is sales and marketing; another is accounting and finance. They are related, but require different competencies and capabilities; because of this they are split and operate at different levels of the organization's hierarchy. Applying this logic to HR would mean creating an HR function that does administration and business partnering with respect to strategy implementation and HR service delivery to the organization. The other HR business would be called organizational effectiveness (Lawler 2011).

The organizational effectiveness corporate staff function would combine business strategy and planning, human capital management, organization development, and organization design. It would be headed by a chief organization effectiveness officer (COEO), who would have responsibility for strategy formulation, implementation, and talent management.

Having an organizational effectiveness function is a good fit for many of today's knowledge-work organizations because it integrates expertise in business strategy and talent management. It is unlike the typical organization design of most large organizations because it recognizes and creates a function charged with managing the fit between talent and strategy. All too often it is not considered, because no one, except perhaps the CEO, is responsible for the fit.

We are proposing that HR should be the administrative and transactional piece, while the organizational effectiveness unit should be the strategy and design piece. In this design, there would be an HR function responsible for transactional HR and for working with managers on business support issues. It would report to the COEO, as would business strategy, talent management, organization development, and organization design.

Another approach to HR organization design may also accomplish the goal of making HR more effective. HR organizations might centralize operations and infrastructure under a chief operating officer (COO) for HR. His or her function would span both the business partner and the administrative components of the HR function, providing specialized support in areas such as compensation, development, and performance management. This structure frees the chief HR officer (CHRO) of many of the ongoing tasks associated with running the HR department, and allows the CHRO to focus on the strategic role of human capital in the organization, as well as on being a member of the executive team.

Looking Ahead

The opportunity for the human resource function to add value at the strategic level is very great, but at the present time it is more promise than reality. For promise to become reality, HR executives need to develop new skills and knowledge, and HR needs to be able to execute human resource management and administration activities effectively. Doing the basics well is the platform upon which the HR organization needs to build its role as a strategic partner. Doing so is critical, because it demonstrates the capacity of the HR function to operate effectively as a business, and it potentially can provide the information which enables HR to be an effective strategic contributor. But it is not enough; HR must also make strategic contributions.

Indeed, effective HR management increasingly requires spanning boundaries between the HR function, the organization, and the dynamic environment within which the organization operates. As organizations adopt broader definitions of sustainable effectiveness and face the necessity of embracing constant and dynamic change, it will change even today's aspirations for HR as a business partner that contributes to a human capital-based competitive advantage (Lawler and Worley 2011). Consider the following six trends, identified as pivotal to the future of HR (Boudreau and Ziskin 2011):

1. Hero leadership to collective leadership

2. Intellectual property to agile co-creativity

3. Employment value proposition to personal value proposition

4. Sameness to segmentation

5. Fatigue to sustainability

6. Persuasion to education

These trends illustrate the complexity of issues that organizations will face in the future. Where will expertise arise to help organizations craft a point of view and framework for sustainability, co-creation with multiple constituents, mass-customized value proposition and talent segmentation, and the evolution of leadership as vested in a top team to something that pervades the entire organization? These are not "HR issues"; they are strategy and organization design issues that will be central to the success of most organizations, and vital topics for business. They do draw on the disciplines that traditionally underlie HR, including psychology, politics, anthropology, values, culture, and engagement.

Should CEOs expect their chief HR officers to take the lead on these issues? Are HR leaders and their organizations prepared for such leadership? In many cases today, such issues fall outside of the HR function, or fall in the "white spaces" between today's HR job descriptions (Boudreau and Ziskin 2011).

The need for a new business model for HR has been accepted and acknowledged by most HR executives, but the human resource function still appears to be at the very beginning of the changes that are needed in order for it to become a reality. Our study demonstrates that the change process is slower than anticipated, but it identifies a very clear action agenda that can yield an HR function capable of adding more value to the business. We still believe there will be enormous change in the design and operation of human resource functions, but we are not sure when it will occur. We have said it before and we say it again: the HR function needs to look seriously at reinventing itself. The old approaches and models are not good enough.

REFERENCES

Boudreau, J. W. 2010. *Retooling HR*. Boston: Harvard Business School Press.

Boudreau, J. W., and R. Jesuthasan. 2011. *Transformative HR*. New York: Wiley.

Boudreau, J. W., and P. M. Ramstad. 2007. *Beyond HR: The new science of human capital*. Boston: Harvard Butsiness School Press.

Boudreau, J. W., and P. M. Ramstad. 2006. Talentship and human resource management and analysis: From ROI to strategic organizational change. *Human Resource Planning Journal* 29.

Boudreau, J. W., and P. M. Ramstad. 2005a. Talentship and the evolution of human resource management: From "professional practices" to "strategic talent decision science." *Human Resource Planning Journal* 28 (2):17–26.

Boudreau, J. W., and P. M. Ramstad. 2005b. Talentship, talent segmentation, and sustainability: A new HR decision science paradigm for a new strategy definition. In *The future of human resources management*, eds. M. Losey, S. Meisinger, and D. Ulrich. Washington, DC: Society for Human Resource Management.

Boudreau, J. W., and P. M. Ramstad. 2005c. Where is your pivotal talent? *Harvard Business Review* 83 (4):23–24.

Boudreau, J. W., and P. M. Ramstad. 2003. Strategic HRM measurement in the 21st century: From justifying HR to strategic talent leadership. In *HRM in the 21st century*, eds. M. Goldsmith, R. P. Gandossy, and M. S. Efron, pp. 79–90. New York: Wiley.

Boudreau, J. W., and P. M. Ramstad. 1997. Measuring intellectual capital: Learning from financial history. *Human Resource Management* 36 (3):343–356.

Boudreau, J. W., and I. Ziskin. 2011. The future of HR and effective organizations. *Organizational Dynamics* 40 (4):255–266.

Breitfelder, M. D., and D. W. Dowling. 2008. Why did we ever go into HR? *Harvard Business Review* 86 (7–8):39.

Brockbank, W. 1999. If HR were really strategically proactive: Present and future directions in HR's contribution to competitive advantage. *Human Resource Management* 38:337–352.

Bureau of National Affairs. 2001. *Human resource activities, budgets and staffs*. Washington, DC: BNA.

Cascio, W. 2000. *Costing human resources*, 4th ed. Cincinnati: South-Western.

Cascio, W., and J. W. Boudreau. 2011. *Investing in people: Financial impact of human resource initiatives*, 2nd ed. Upper Saddle River, NJ: FT Press.

Csoka, L. S., and B. Hackett. 1998. *Transforming the HR function for global business success*. New York: Conference Board.

Galbraith, J. R. 2002. *Designing organizations*. San Francisco: Jossey-Bass.

Gates, S. 2004. *Measuring more than efficiency*. Research Report R-1356-04-RR. New York: Conference Board.

Gubman, E. 2004. HR strategy and planning: From birth to business results. *Human Resource Planning* 27(1): 13–23.

Huselid, M. A., B. E. Becker, and R. W. Beatty. 2005. *The workforce scorecard*. Boston: Harvard Business School Press.

Lawler, E. E. 2008. *Talent: Making people your competitive advantage*. San Francisco: Jossey-Bass.

Lawler, E. E. 2003. *Treat people right! How organizations and individuals can propel each other into a virtuous spiral of success*. San Francisco: Jossey-Bass.

Lawler, E. E. 1995. Strategic human resources management: An idea whose time has come. In *Managing human resources in the 1990s and beyond: Is the workplace being transformed?* eds. B. Downie and M. L. Coates, pp. 46–70. Kingston, Canada: IRC Press.

Lawler, E. E., and J. W. Boudreau. 2009. *Achieving excellence in human resource management*. Stanford, CA: Stanford University Press.

Lawler, E. E., J. W. Boudreau, and S. A. Mohrman. 2006. *Achieving strategic excellence: An assessment of human resource organizations*. Stanford, CA: Stanford University Press.

Lawler, E. E., J. Jamrog, and J. W. Boudreau. 2011. Shining light on the HR profession. *HR Magazine* 56 (2):38–41.

Lawler, E. E., A. Levenson, and J. W. Boudreau. 2004. HR metrics and analytics—uses and impacts. *Human Resource Planning Journal* 27 (4):27–35.

Lawler, E. E., and S. A. Mohrman. 2003a. *Creating a strategic human resources organization: An assessment of trends and new directions*. Stanford, CA: Stanford University Press.

Lawler, E. E., and S. A. Mohrman. 2003b. HR as a strategic partner: What does it take to make it happen? *Human Resource Planning* 26 (5):15–29.

Lawler, E. E., and S. A. Mohrman. 2000. *Creating a strategic human resources organization.* Los Angeles: Center for Effective Organizations.

Lawler, E. E., S. A. Mohrman, and G. S. Benson. 2001. *Organizing for high performance: The CEO report on employee involvement, TQM, reengineering, and knowledge management in Fortune 1000 companies.* San Francisco: Jossey-Bass.

Lawler, E. E., D. Ulrich, J. Fitz-enz, and J. Madden. 2004. *Human resources business process outsourcing.* San Francisco: Jossey-Bass.

Lawler, E. E., and C. G. Worley. 2011. *Management reset: Organizing for sustainable effectiveness.* San Francisco: Jossey-Bass.

Lawler, E. E., and C. G. Worley. 2006. *Built to change: How to achieve sustained organizational effectiveness.* San Francisco: Jossey-Bass.

Lev, B. 2001. *Intangibles: Management, measurement, and reporting.* Washington, DC: Brookings.

Mohrman, A. M., J. R. Galbraith, E. E. Lawler, and Associates. 1998. *Tomorrow's organization: Crafting winning capabilities in a dynamic world.* San Francisco: Jossey-Bass.

Mohrman, S. A., E. E. Lawler, and associates. 2011. *Useful research: Advancing theory and practice.* San Francisco: Berrett-Koehler.

Mohrman, S. A., E. E. Lawler, and G. C. McMahan. 1996. *New directions for the human resources organization.* Los Angeles: Center for Effective Organizations.

O'Toole, J., and E. E. Lawler. 2006. *The new American workplace.* New York: Palgrave Macmillan.

Society for Human Resource Management. 1998. *Human resources management.* 1998 SHRM/CCH Study. Chicago: CCH.

Ulrich, D. 1997. *Human resources champions.* Boston: Harvard Business School Press.

Ulrich, D., and W. Brockbank. 2005. *The HR value proposition.* Boston: Harvard Business School Press.

Ulrich, D., W. Brockbank, D. Johnson, K. Sandholtz, and J. Younger. 2008. *HR competencies: Mastery at the intersection of people and business.* Alexandria, VA: SHRM.

Ulrich, D., M. R. Losey, and G. Lake, eds. 1997. *Tomorrow's HR management.* New York: Wiley.

APPENDIX A
Research Partners

United States

Conference Board—USA
Russell Morris, Associate Director, U.S. Councils

Executive Network
Barry Leskin, Moderator, Thought Leader Series
Mike Dulworth, President and CEO

Human Resources Planning Society
Walt Cleaver, President and CEO

Institute for Corporate Productivity (i4cp)
Jay Jamrog, SVP of Research
Mindy Meisterlin, Research Coordinator
Jeff Webb, Chief Technology Officer
Mark Vickers
Kevin Oakes

S Benjamins & Company, Inc.
Sherry Benjamins

Australia

Australian Human Resources Institute
Serge Sardo, CEO
Anne-Marie Dolan, Manager—Development & Research
Dana Grgas

Canada

The Conference Board of Canada
Ruth Wright, Associate Director, Leadership and Human Resources Research
Eric St-Jean, CCP Research Associate
Katie O'Brien

China

Institute of Organization and Human Resources, School of Public Administration, Renmin University of China

Chaoping Li, Associate Professor

Europe

Ashridge Business School

Vicki Culpin, Research Director

Corporate Research Foundation

Mike Haffendon, co-founder

Andrew Lambert, co-founder

Baumgartner & Partner

Volker Jacobs, Managing Partner

Sophie Gross

Via Beat Meyer, UBS

India

Society for Human Resource Management India

Singapore

Ministry of Manpower

Alvin Teo, Senior Manager

APPENDIX B

The Future of HR—USA

THIS SECTION ASKS QUESTIONS ABOUT YOUR COMPANY AND THE HR IN YOUR ORGANIZATION.

1. Approximately, how many employees are in your company?_____ **Mean: 29,514.3   SD: 46,051.1**

2. Approximately how many full-time-equivalent employees (FTE's, exempt and non-exempt) are part of the HR function? (This number should include both centralized and decentralized staff. _____ **Mean: 405.9   SD: 1000.2**

3. What is the background of the current head of HR? (Please check one response.)
   77.1% .... 1. Human Resource Management
   22.9% .... 2. Other Function(s), (which one(s)? (_____)

4. How would you gauge your organization's performance relative to its competitors? **Mean: 3.87   SD: 1.01**
   2.4% .... Much below average
   9.4% .... Somewhat below average
   15.0% .... About average
   44.9% .... Somewhat above average
   28.3% .... Much above average

5. To what extent do these describe how your organization operates?	Little or No Extent	Some Extent	Moderate Extent	Great Extent	Very Great Extent	Mean	SD
a. **Bureaucratic** (hierarchical structure, tight job descriptions, top-down decision making)	12.8	29.9	24.6	27.8	4.8	**2.82**	**1.12**
b. **Low-cost operator** (low wages, minimum benefits, focus on cost reduction and controls)	40.0	29.2	21.6	7.6	1.6	**2.02**	**1.03**
c. **High involvement** (flat structure, participative decisions, commitment to employee development and careers)	9.1	25.7	26.2	29.4	9.6	**3.05**	**1.14**
d. **Global competitor** (complex interesting work, hire best talent, low commitment to employee development and careers)	20.4	28.5	23.1	21.0	7.0	**2.66**	**1.22**
e. **Sustainable** (agile design, focus on financial performance and sustainability)	4.8	18.2	27.8	38.0	11.2	**3.33**	**1.05**
6. To what extent is each of the following strategic initiatives present in your organization?	Little or No Extent	Some Extent	Moderate Extent	Great Extent	Very Great Extent	Mean	SD
f. Building a global presence	26.6	12.8	12.2	25.0	23.4	**3.06**	**1.54**
g. Acquisitions	16.5	22.9	23.9	21.3	15.4	**2.96**	**1.31**
h. Customer focus	0.5	4.8	11.2	32.4	51.1	**4.29**	**0.89**
i. Technology leadership	7.0	20.9	27.8	23.5	20.9	**3.30**	**1.21**
j. Talent management	1.1	17.0	33.5	33.5	14.9	**3.44**	**0.98**
k. Knowledge/intellectual capital management	3.2	26.6	32.4	26.1	11.7	**3.16**	**1.05**
l. Sustainability	3.7	9.0	31.9	31.9	23.4	**3.62**	**1.06**
m. Innovation	2.7	19.4	26.9	34.9	16.1	**3.42**	**1.06**

7. For each of the following HR roles, please estimate the percentage of time your HR function spends performing these roles. Percentages should add to 100% for each column.

PERCENTAGES SHOULD ADD TO 100% FOR EACH COLUMN:	CURRENTLY		5-7 YEARS AGO	
	Mean	SD	Mean	SD
a. **Maintaining Records** (Collect, track and maintain data on employees)	13.6%	8.95	23.2%	13.73
b. **Auditing/Controlling** (Ensure compliance with internal operations, regulations, and legal and union requirements)	12.5%	7.86	15.7%	9.63
c. **Providing Human Resource Services** (Assist with implementation and administration of HR practices)	30.4%	15.74	32.8%	15.68
d. **Developing Human Resource Systems and Practices** (Develop new HR systems and practices)	16.7%	8.23	14.4%	9.39
e. **Strategic Business Partnering** (Member of the management team; involved with strategic HR planning, organization design, and strategic change)	26.8%	16.89	13.9%	12.27
TOTAL	100%		100%	

8. Which of the following best describes the relationship between the Human Resource function and the business strategy of your corporation? (Please check one response.)

　4.3% . . . . 1. Human Resource plays no role in business strategy (if checked, go to QUESTION 10).

　17.4% . . . . 2. Human Resource is involved in implementing the business strategy.

　47.3% . . . . 3. Human Resource provides input to the business strategy and helps implement it once it has been developed.

　31.0% . . . . 4. Human Resource is a full partner in developing and implementing the business strategy.

ANSWER QUESTION 9, ONLY IF YOU CHECKED 2, 3, OR 4 FOR QUESTION 8.

Please respond to the following questions by circling one number in each row.

9. With respect to strategy, to what extent does the HR function...?	Little or No Extent	Some Extent	Moderate Extent	Great Extent	Very Great Extent	Mean	SD
a. Help identify or design strategy options	11.4	29.0	31.8	21.6	6.3	**2.82**	**1.09**
b. Help decide among the best strategy options	10.8	27.3	30.7	25.6	5.7	**2.88**	**1.09**
c. Help plan the implementation of strategy	1.1	16.0	26.3	37.7	18.9	**3.57**	**1.01**
d. Help identify new business opportunities	36.4	31.8	25.0	4.5	2.3	**2.05**	**1.00**
e. Assess the organization's readiness to implement strategies	5.7	21.6	26.7	36.4	9.7	**3.23**	**1.07**
f. Help design the organization structure to implement strategy	2.3	15.3	23.3	34.7	24.4	**3.64**	**1.08**
g. Assess possible merger, acquisition or divestiture strategies	20.5	25.0	26.7	18.2	9.7	**2.72**	**1.25**
h. Work with the corporate board on business strategy	23.3	24.4	31.3	15.3	5.7	**2.56**	**1.17**

Your Company's HR Organization 10. To what extent does each of the following describe the way your HR organization currently operates?	Little or No Extent	Some Extent	Moderate Extent	Great Extent	Very Great Extent	Mean	SD
a. Administrative processing is centralized in shared services units	7.6	15.1	24.9	29.2	23.2	**3.45**	**1.22**
b. Transactional HR work is outsourced	33.5	25.9	21.1	14.6	4.9	**2.31**	**1.22**
c. Centers of excellence provide specialized expertise	13.0	14.7	19.0	31.5	21.7	**3.34**	**1.32**
d. Decentralized HR generalists support business units	12.4	10.3	14.6	31.4	31.4	**3.59**	**1.35**
e. People rotate _within_ HR	28.6	24.9	22.7	17.8	5.9	**2.48**	**1.24**
f. People rotate _into_ HR	48.6	31.9	14.1	4.3	1.1	**1.77**	**0.92**
g. People rotate _out of_ HR to other functions	47.3	34.2	13.6	4.3	0.5	**1.77**	**0.88**
h. HR practices vary across business units	27.0	33.0	25.4	12.4	2.2	**2.30**	**1.06**
i. Some transactional activities that used to be done by HR are done by employees on a self-service basis	9.2	29.9	27.7	23.4	9.8	**2.95**	**1.14**
j. HR "advice" is available on-line for managers and employees	24.3	29.2	22.2	14.6	9.7	**2.56**	**1.27**
k. There is a low HR/employee ratio	9.2	26.6	33.2	19.0	12.0	**2.98**	**1.14**
l. There is a data-based talent strategy	17.9	25.5	29.9	20.7	6.0	**2.71**	**1.16**
m. There is a human capital strategy that is integrated with the business strategy	11.4	25.4	25.9	25.4	11.9	**3.01**	**1.20**
n. Provides analytic support for business decision-making	11.4	27.7	32.1	23.4	5.4	**2.84**	**1.08**
o. Provides HR data to support change management	9.2	25.4	28.6	28.6	8.1	**3.01**	**1.11**
p. Drives change management	10.3	15.7	34.1	30.3	9.7	**3.14**	**1.12**
q. Makes rigorous data-based decisions about human capital management	17.8	26.5	29.7	20.5	5.4	**2.69**	**1.15**
r. Uses social networks for recruiting	20.5	30.8	21.6	18.4	8.6	**2.64**	**1.24**

11. A. How has the amount of focus or attention to the following HR activities changed over the past 5–7 years as a proportion of the overall Human Resource activity and emphasis?

   B. Have any of these activities been partially or completely outsourced?

	A. ACTIVITY AND EMPHASIS?							B. OUTSOURCING?				
	Greatly Decreased	Decreased	Stayed the Same	Increased	Greatly Increased	Mean	SD	Not at All	Partially	Completely	Mean	SD
a. Human capital forecasting and planning	0.0	4.9	22.8	57.6	14.7	3.82	0.74	98.3	1.7	0.0	1.02	0.13
b. Compensation	0.5	6.0	37.5	42.9	13.0	3.62	0.81	74.4	25.6	0.0	1.26	0.44
c. Benefits	1.6	6.5	44.6	38.0	9.2	3.47	0.82	27.0	65.7	7.3	1.80	0.55
d. Organization development	2.2	7.1	23.5	51.9	15.3	3.71	0.89	81.5	18.5	0.0	1.18	0.39
e. Organization design	2.2	7.1	33.7	44.0	13.0	3.59	0.88	89.1	10.3	0.6	1.11	0.34
f. Training and education	1.1	14.7	34.8	35.3	14.1	3.47	0.95	39.0	59.9	1.1	1.62	0.51
g. Management development	2.2	9.8	23.9	41.3	22.8	3.73	0.99	56.0	42.3	1.7	1.46	0.53
h. Union relations	10.1	9.5	61.5	15.1	3.9	2.93	0.90	90.8	8.0	1.2	1.10	0.34
i. HR information systems	0.0	4.9	27.2	50.0	17.9	3.81	0.78	54.5	41.5	4.0	1.49	0.58
j. Performance appraisal	0.0	6.0	30.2	49.5	14.3	3.72	0.78	84.2	15.3	0.6	1.16	0.39
k. Recruitment	1.7	8.9	28.3	46.1	15.0	3.64	0.90	48.9	51.1	0.0	1.51	0.50
l. Selection	1.1	6.6	32.6	48.1	11.6	3.62	0.82	78.3	21.7	0.0	1.22	0.41
m. Career planning	1.1	8.8	44.5	37.9	7.7	3.42	0.80	92.0	8.0	0.0	1.08	0.27
n. Legal affairs	0.5	7.1	57.1	29.1	6.0	3.33	0.72	48.6	51.4	0.0	1.51	0.50
o. Employee assistance	1.1	13.7	62.6	20.9	1.6	3.08	0.67	25.8	34.8	39.3	2.13	0.80
p. Competency/Talent assessment	1.1	3.3	26.1	51.1	18.3	3.82	0.81	74.7	24.1	1.1	1.26	0.47
q. HR metrics and analysis	0.5	4.4	25.1	50.3	19.7	3.84	0.81	86.7	13.3	0.0	1.13	0.34
r. Executive compensation	0.0	3.3	38.3	38.3	20.2	3.75	0.81	67.4	31.4	1.1	1.34	0.50

12. a. Do you have a multiple-process HR outsourcing (HRBPO) contract?

   18.9% . . . . Yes

   7.0% . . . . No, but seriously considering (If checked, go to question 13.)

   74.1% . . . . No, not seriously considering (If checked, go to question 13.)

   b. Overall, how satisfied are you with your HRBPO relationship?   **Mean: 4.48   SD: 1.61**

8.0% Very Dissatisfied	8.0% Dissatisfied	8.0% Somewhat Dissatisfied	8.0% Neither Satisfied nor Dissatisfied	44.0% Somewhat Satisfied	20.0% Satisfied	4.0% Very Satisfied

13. In general, how effective do you think the following approaches to HR outsourcing are?	Very Ineffective	Ineffective	Neither	Effective	Very Effective	Mean	SD
a. No outsourcing	26.4	36.8	25.3	10.3	1.1	**2.23**	**0.99**
b. Very limited: only a few transactional services (e.g. payroll)	5.2	23.7	22.5	40.5	8.1	**3.23**	**1.06**
c. Moderate outsourcing to *multiple* vendors	2.9	13.5	34.5	46.8	2.3	**3.32**	**0.84**
d. Moderate outsourcing to a single vendor	2.9	16.4	34.5	40.4	5.8	**3.30**	**0.91**
e. Substantial outsourcing to *multiple* vendors	9.3	33.7	34.3	20.3	2.3	**2.73**	**0.97**
f. Substantial outsourcing to a single vendor	14.0	25.7	33.9	24.0	2.3	**2.75**	**1.05**

14. Please check the one statement that best describes the current state of your HR Information System (HRIS): **Mean: 2.21   SD: 0.76**

16.4% .... 1. Completely Integrated HR Information Technology System.

49.7% .... 2. Most processes are information technology based but not fully integrated.

30.1% .... 3. Some HR processes are information technology based.

3.8% .... 4. There is little information technology present in the HR function.

0.0% .... 5. There is no information technology present. (If checked, skip to Question 16.)

15. To what extent do you consider your HRIS to ...	Little or No Extent	Some Extent	Moderate Extent	Great Extent	Very Great Extent	Mean	SD
g. Be effective	7.7	24.0	38.3	25.7	4.4	**2.95**	**0.99**
h. Satisfy your employees	12.0	27.7	40.2	18.5	1.6	**2.70**	**0.96**
i. Improve HR services	10.4	20.8	36.1	24.6	8.2	**2.99**	**1.10**
j. Reduce HR transaction costs	13.6	21.7	26.6	28.3	9.8	**2.99**	**1.20**
k. Provide new strategic information	23.5	25.7	29.5	16.4	4.9	**2.54**	**1.16**
l. Speed up HR processes	13.6	22.8	27.7	24.5	11.4	**2.97**	**1.22**
m. Reduce the number of employees in HR	27.9	30.1	26.8	10.9	4.4	**2.34**	**1.13**
n. Integrate HR processes (e.g. training, compensation)	25.7	26.8	29.5	14.2	3.8	**2.44**	**1.13**
o. Measure HR's impact on the business	31.0	29.3	25.0	12.0	2.7	**2.26**	**1.11**
p. Improve the human capital decisions of managers outside HR	33.2	26.6	25.0	12.5	2.7	**2.25**	**1.13**
q. Create knowledge networks	48.9	25.8	18.1	5.5	1.6	**1.85**	**1.01**
r. Build social networks that help work get done	60.1	19.7	14.8	3.8	1.6	**1.67**	**0.97**

16. Does your organization currently...	Yes, Have Now	Being Built	Planning For	Not Currently Being Considered	Mean	SD
a. Measure the business impact of HR programs and processes?	27.6	27.6	27.1	17.7	**2.35**	**1.07**
b. Collect metrics that measure the cost of HR programs and processes?	43.3	21.1	25.0	10.6	**2.03**	**1.05**
c. Have the capability to conduct cost-benefit analyses (also called utility analyses) of HR programs?	26.4	22.0	25.3	26.4	**2.52**	**1.15**
d. Use HR dashboards or scorecards?	51.6	22.5	17.0	8.8	**1.83**	**1.01**
e. Measure the financial efficiency of HR operations (e.g. cost-per-hire, time-to-fill, training costs?)	53.8	18.7	15.9	11.5	**1.85**	**1.07**
f. Measure the specific effects of HR programs (such as, learning from training, motivation from rewards, validity of tests, etc.)?	32.4	15.9	28.6	23.1	**2.42**	**1.17**
g. Benchmark analytics and measures against data from outside organizations (e.g. Saratoga, Mercer, Hewitt, etc.)?	54.9	9.9	15.9	19.2	**1.99**	**1.22**
h. Measure the quality of the talent decisions made by non-HR leaders?	18.1	14.3	28.0	39.6	**2.89**	**1.12**
i. Measure the business impact of high versus low performance in jobs?	18.1	11.0	30.8	40.1	**2.93**	**1.11**

17. What describes the way you measure the effectiveness of the following HR programs and activities?	EFFICIENCY	EFFECTIVENESS	IMPACT
(Please check *ALL* that apply) Responses are represented as Percentages (Freq). Cases with missing/zero values across all variables in this section were excluded.	The resources used by the program, such as cost per hire	The changes produced by the program, such as learning from training	The business or strategic value produced by the program
a. Compensation	51.7% (92)	43.3% (77)	47.2% (84)
b. Benefits	63.5% (113)	38.8% (69)	37.1% (66)
c. Organization development	24.2% (43)	51.7% (92)	48.9% (87)
d. Organization design	25.8% (46)	41.6% (74)	38.2% (68)
e. Training/education	39.3% (70)	70.8% (126)	39.9% (71)
f. Leader development and succession	27.0% (48)	57.3% (102)	47.8% (85)
g. HR information systems	68.0% (121)	43.3% (77)	21.9% (39)
h. Performance management	37.1% (66)	55.1% (98)	38.2% (68)
i. Career planning	25.3% (45)	50.6% (90)	22.5% (40)
j. Diversity	30.9% (55)	44.4% (79)	37.6% (67)
k. Employee assistance	51.7% (92)	36.5% (65)	15.2% (27)
l. Staffing	62.9% (112)	53.9% (96)	34.8% (62)
m. Social and knowledge networks	31.5% (56)	37.1% (66)	12.9% (23)

18. How effective are the information, measurement, and analysis systems of your organization when it comes to the following?	Very Ineffective	Ineffective	Somewhat Effective	Effective	Very Effective	Mean	SD
a. Connecting human capital practices to organizational performance	10.7	38.4	36.2	14.1	0.6	**2.55**	**0.88**
b. Identifying where talent has the greatest potential for strategic impact	9.0	27.0	36.5	25.8	1.7	**2.84**	**0.97**
c. Predicting the effects of HR programs before implementation	14.1	31.1	40.7	13.0	1.1	**2.56**	**0.93**
d. Pinpointing HR programs that should be discontinued	14.1	30.5	36.7	17.5	1.1	**2.61**	**0.97**
e. Supporting organizational change efforts	5.6	16.3	41.6	26.4	10.1	**3.19**	**1.01**
f. Assessing and improving the HR department operations	5.1	16.4	44.1	27.7	6.8	**3.15**	**0.95**
g. Contributing to decisions about business strategy and human capital management	7.9	19.2	35.6	31.1	6.2	**3.08**	**1.03**
h. Using logical principles that clearly connect talent to organizational success	8.5	21.5	38.4	26.6	5.1	**2.98**	**1.01**
i. Using advanced data analysis and statistics	14.9	34.3	32.0	13.7	5.1	**2.60**	**1.06**
j. Providing high-quality (complete, timely, accessible) talent measurements	8.5	37.9	32.8	18.6	2.3	**2.68**	**0.95**
k. Motivating users to take appropriate action	9.0	22.6	42.4	22.6	3.4	**2.89**	**0.97**

19. To what extent are these statements true about your organization?	Little or No Extent	Some Extent	Moderate Extent	Great Extent	Very Great Extent	Mean	SD
a. We excel at competing for and with talent where it matters most to our strategic success	6.8	20.9	30.5	34.5	7.3	**3.15**	**1.05**
b. Business leaders' decisions that depend upon or affect human capital (e.g. layoffs, rewards, etc.) are as rigorous, logical and strategically relevant as their decisions about resources such as money, technology, and customers	9.0	24.7	28.7	28.7	9.0	**3.04**	**1.12**
c. HR leaders have a good understanding about where and why human capital makes the biggest difference in their business	4.5	22.5	20.8	41.6	10.7	**3.31**	**1.07**
d. Business leaders have a good understanding about where and why human capital makes the biggest difference in their business	6.2	22.6	28.8	36.2	6.2	**3.14**	**1.04**
e. HR systems educate business leaders about their talent decisions	23.0	28.1	33.7	12.9	2.2	**2.43**	**1.05**
f. HR adds value by insuring compliance with rules, laws, and guidelines	2.8	15.2	28.7	41.0	12.4	**3.45**	**0.99**
g. HR adds value by delivering high-quality professional practices and services	5.1	9.0	25.3	46.6	14.0	**3.56**	**1.01**
h. HR adds value by improving talent decisions inside and outside the HR function	4.6	12.6	25.1	39.4	18.3	**3.54**	**1.07**
i. Business leaders understand and use sound principles when making decisions about:							
1. Motivation	8.0	31.3	36.4	23.9	0.6	**2.78**	**0.92**
2. Development and learning	6.2	27.7	40.1	22.6	3.4	**2.89**	**0.94**
3. Culture	7.4	21.0	32.4	31.8	7.4	**3.11**	**1.06**
4. Organizational design	8.5	27.1	37.9	24.3	2.3	**2.85**	**0.96**
5. Business strategy	2.8	6.2	21.5	44.1	25.4	**3.83**	**0.97**
6. Finance	1.1	5.1	17.5	46.9	29.4	**3.98**	**0.88**
7. Marketing	3.4	15.3	29.4	35.6	16.4	**3.46**	**1.04**

20. How much does your Corporation's Board call on HR for help with the following?	Little or No Extent	Some Extent	Moderate Extent	Great Extent	Very Great Extent	Mean	SD
a. Executive compensation	8.6	8.6	9.2	30.5	43.1	**3.91**	**1.28**
b. Addressing strategic readiness	16.3	19.8	34.3	24.4	5.2	**2.83**	**1.13**
c. Executive succession	6.9	10.3	19.5	35.6	27.6	**3.67**	**1.18**
d. Change consulting	23.3	24.4	24.4	20.3	7.6	**2.65**	**1.25**
e. Developing board effectiveness / corporate governance	38.8	19.4	23.5	16.5	1.8	**2.23**	**1.18**
f. Risk assessment	19.7	32.9	20.2	23.1	4.0	**2.59**	**1.16**
g. Information about the condition or capability of the work force	9.9	16.9	29.7	32.0	11.6	**3.19**	**1.15**
h. Board compensation	31.4	13.6	16.6	24.3	14.2	**2.76**	**1.47**

Regarding the skills and knowledge of your organization's current HR professional/ managerial staff:

21. How *satisfied* are you with current HR professional/managerial staff in each of these areas?	Very Dissatisfied	Dissatisfied	Neutral	Satisfied	Very Satisfied	Mean	SD
a. Team skills	2.2	7.9	25.8	53.9	10.1	3.62	0.86
b. HR technical skills	1.1	9.6	18.6	50.3	20.3	3.79	0.91
c. Business understanding	2.8	13.5	29.8	46.1	7.9	3.43	0.92
d. Interpersonal skills	0.6	6.2	14.7	57.6	20.9	3.92	0.81
e. Cross-functional experience	5.6	27.1	33.9	29.4	4.0	2.99	0.98
f. Consultation skills	3.9	18.0	30.3	38.8	9.0	3.31	1.00
g. Leadership/management	2.8	11.2	26.4	48.3	11.2	3.54	0.93
h. Global understanding	8.0	28.4	37.5	21.0	5.1	2.87	1.00
i. Organization design	5.1	25.8	37.6	28.1	3.4	2.99	0.94
j. Strategic planning	5.6	27.1	33.9	28.8	4.5	2.99	0.99
k. Information technology	6.2	23.7	36.2	28.2	5.6	3.03	1.00
l. Change management	6.2	17.4	30.3	39.3	6.7	3.23	1.02
m. Metrics development	7.9	28.8	32.2	24.3	6.8	2.93	1.06
n. Data analysis and mining	9.6	33.3	29.9	20.9	6.2	2.81	1.07
o. Process execution and analysis	4.0	16.7	31.0	40.2	8.0	3.32	0.98

22. What percentage of your company-wide HR professional/managerial staff possesses the necessary skill set for success in today's business environment? (Circle one response.) **Mean: 4.33   SD: 1.11**

0.0%	6.3%	16.0%	29.7%	35.4%	11.4%	1.1%
None	Almost None	Some	About Half	Most	Almost All	All
0%	1-20%	21-40%	41-60%	61-80%	81-99%	100%

23. Please rate the activities on a scale of 1 to 10 or not applicable. In view of what is needed by your company:

   a. How well is the HR organization meeting needs in each of the areas below?
     (1= Not Meeting Needs, 10 = All Needs Met; NA = Not applicable)

Note: Percentages and mean are computed with N/A (Not Applicable) responses missing.

		Not Meeting Needs	2	3	4	5	6	7	8	9	All Needs Met	NA	Mean	SD
A.	PROVIDING HR SERVICES	0.0	1.1	1.7	0.6	5.1	10.8	17.0	28.4	29.5	5.7	0.0	**7.69**	**1.56**
B.	PROVIDING CHANGE CONSULTING SERVICES	1.7	1.7	7.0	11.6	18.0	14.5	15.7	18.6	8.1	2.9	0.5	**6.11**	**2.02**
C.	BEING A BUSINESS PARTNER	1.7	4.0	2.3	5.1	10.8	13.1	14.2	21.6	21.0	6.3	0.0	**6.93**	**2.15**
D.	IMPROVING DECISIONS ABOUT HUMAN CAPITAL	2.3	2.3	5.1	13.1	11.4	11.4	17.6	18.8	14.8	3.4	0.0	**6.40**	**2.17**
E.	MANAGING OUTSOURCING	3.6	6.7	9.7	6.7	13.3	13.3	18.8	13.9	10.9	3.0	3.2	**5.91**	**2.34**
F.	OPERATING HR CENTERS OF EXCELLENCE	4.9	4.9	4.3	8.0	12.9	9.8	16.0	19.6	14.1	5.5	2.6	**6.34**	**2.42**
G.	OPERATING HR SHARED SERVICE UNITS	1.3	5.3	4.7	8.7	11.3	8.7	20.0	20.7	12.0	7.3	7.4	**6.56**	**2.25**
H.	HELPING TO DEVELOP BUSINESS STRATEGIES	4.1	3.5	9.4	11.7	12.3	17.5	13.5	14.6	10.5	2.9	1.1	**5.88**	**2.27**
I.	BEING AN EMPLOYEE ADVOCATE	0.6	4.0	3.4	4.0	5.7	11.5	19.5	23.6	19.0	8.6	0.5	**7.15**	**2.06**
J.	ANALYZING HR AND BUSINESS METRICS	2.9	5.7	6.3	12.6	14.9	14.3	14.3	16.0	9.7	3.4	0.0	**5.93**	**2.25**
K.	WORKING WITH THE CORPORATE BOARD	3.8	7.0	8.9	7.6	7.0	10.8	17.2	17.8	15.3	4.5	4.2	**6.20**	**2.50**
L.	OVERALL PERFORMANCE	0.6	2.3	1.1	5.1	10.3	17.7	23.4	20.0	16.0	3.4	0.0	**6.89**	**1.78**

   b. How important is it that HR does this well? *(1= Not Important, 10 = Very Important; NA = Not applicable)*

Note: Percentages and mean are computed with N/A (Not Applicable) responses missing.

		Not Impt	2	3	4	5	6	7	8	9	Very Impt	NA	Mean	SD
A.	PROVIDING HR SERVICES	0.6	0.0	0.6	0.6	2.3	5.1	10.8	14.8	28.4	36.9	0.0	**8.65**	**1.54**
B.	PROVIDING CHANGE CONSULTING SERVICES	1.1	1.1	2.3	4.0	3.4	6.3	10.3	27.4	19.4	24.6	0.5	**7.93**	**2.01**
C.	BEING A BUSINESS PARTNER	0.6	1.1	0.6	1.1	4.0	2.3	1.1	14.9	28.2	46.0	0.5	**8.84**	**1.71**
D.	IMPROVING DECISIONS ABOUT HUMAN CAPITAL	0.0	1.1	1.1	1.1	4.0	4.5	3.4	16.9	31.6	36.2	0.0	**8.63**	**1.68**
E.	MANAGING OUTSOURCING	1.8	4.2	6.6	4.8	16.8	13.8	15.6	15.6	12.0	9.0	2.6	**6.47**	**2.28**
F.	OPERATING HR CENTERS OF EXCELLENCE	1.8	0.6	1.8	1.8	4.8	7.2	18.1	21.1	18.1	24.7	2.1	**7.88**	**1.98**
G.	OPERATING HR SHARED SERVICE UNITS	1.3	2.0	1.3	1.3	7.8	11.8	14.4	24.8	20.3	15.0	5.8	**7.56**	**1.96**
H.	HELPING TO DEVELOP BUSINESS STRATEGIES	1.1	1.7	0.6	3.4	6.3	6.8	9.1	21.6	29.0	20.5	0.0	**7.94**	**1.98**
I.	BEING AN EMPLOYEE ADVOCATE	0.0	1.1	3.4	1.7	9.1	6.3	10.2	22.2	22.7	23.3	0.0	**7.89**	**1.97**
J.	ANALYZING HR AND BUSINESS METRICS	0.6	1.1	1.1	1.1	3.4	4.0	13.7	25.7	24.6	24.6	0.0	**8.21**	**1.72**
K.	WORKING WITH THE CORPORATE BOARD	2.5	1.8	3.1	6.7	9.2	7.4	15.3	20.9	14.7	18.4	2.6	**7.23**	**2.31**
L.	OVERALL PERFORMANCE	0.6	1.2	0.6	0.6	1.7	2.9	4.0	14.5	34.1	39.9	0.0	**8.83**	**1.59**

24. How has the recession impacted the following in your organization?	Greatly Decreased	Decreased	No Change	Increased	Greatly Increased	Mean	SD
a. Power and status of HR function	1.7	7.9	57.1	29.4	4.0	3.26	0.73
b. Strategic role of HR function	1.7	9.0	45.2	35.6	8.5	3.40	0.83
c. Commitment to talent development	2.8	13.6	32.2	42.4	9.0	3.41	0.93
d. Focus on performance management	0.0	6.8	27.3	52.8	13.1	3.72	0.78
e. Quality of talent management decisions	0.0	8.5	40.3	42.6	8.5	3.51	0.77
f. Use of contract employees	4.0	22.0	47.5	25.4	1.1	2.98	0.83
g. Use of temporary employees	2.8	23.7	44.1	27.1	2.3	3.02	0.85
h. Use of HR analytics and metrics	1.1	5.7	45.5	39.8	8.0	3.48	0.77
i. Quality of employees in HR function	0.6	4.0	51.7	39.2	4.5	3.43	0.67
j. Attractiveness of your company's brand as an employer	1.7	11.4	34.7	41.5	10.8	3.48	0.89
k. Effectiveness of HR function	0.0	9.6	44.6	42.9	2.8	3.39	0.70
l. Willingness to try innovative HR practices	2.8	12.4	37.3	42.9	4.5	3.34	0.86
m. Use of short term HR system fixes	2.8	11.3	61.6	22.0	2.3	3.10	0.73
n. Commitment to treating people right	1.1	8.6	61.1	22.9	6.3	3.25	0.74
o. Percent of its time HR spends on administration	1.1	24.4	58.0	14.8	1.7	2.91	0.71
p. Focus on HR practices that have shown tangible results	0.6	1.7	54.2	39.0	4.5	3.45	0.64

APPENDIX C

The Future of Human Resources:
A Survey of Executives Not in the HR Function (N=35[1])—USA Only

1. Which of the following best describes the relationship between the Human Resource function and the business strategy of your corporation? (please check one response) MEAN=3.13 SD=0.63

    2.9% .... 1. Human Resource plays no role in business strategy (if checked, go to QUESTION 2).

    2.9% .... 2. Human Resource is involved in implementing the business strategy.

    64.7% .... 3. Human Resource provides input to the business strategy and helps implement it once it has been developed.

    29.4% .... 4. Human Resource is a full partner in developing and implementing the business strategy.

ANSWER QUESTIONS 1a, ONLY IF YOU CHECKED 2, 3, OR 4 FOR QUESTION 1 above.

Please respond to the following questions by circling one number in each row.

1a. With respect to strategy, to what extent does the HR function…?	Little or No Extent	Some Extent	Moderate Extent	Great Extent	Very Great Extent	Mean	SD
a. Help identify or design strategy options	2.9	31.4	42.9	20.0	2.9	**2.79**	**.80**
b. Help decide among the best strategy options	8.6	20.0	48.6	20.0	2.9	**2.79**	**.85**
c. Help plan the implementation of strategy	2.9	2.9	31.4	48.6	14.3	**3.60**	**.86**
d. Help identify new business opportunities	17.1	40.0	40.0	2.9	0	**2.19**	**.74**
e. Assess the organizations readiness to implement strategies	2.9	2.9	31.4	51.4	11.4	**3.56**	**.77**
f. Help design the organization structure to implement strategy	2.9	0	34.3	37.1	25.7	**3.73**	**.90**
g. Assess possible merger, acquisition or divestiture strategies	14.3	25.7	28.6	25.7	5.7	**2.73**	**1.10**
h. Work with the corporate board on business strategy	11.4	25.7	31.4	25.7	5.7	**2.85**	**1.04**

---

[1] Multiple responses per company were aggregated to represent unique company mean scores. There were 83 US Non-HR Executive surveys.

2. Regarding the skills and knowledge of your organization's current HR professional/ managerial staff:

How *satisfied* are you with current HR professional/ managerial staff in each of these areas?	Very Dissatisfied	Dissatisfied	Neutral	Satisfied	Very Satisfied	Mean	SD
i. Team skills	0	0	11.4	62.9	25.7	**4.11**	**.59**
j. HR technical skills	0	0	11.4	42.9	45.7	**4.25**	**.64**
k. Business understanding	0	2.9	20.0	48.6	28.6	**4.01**	**.72**
l. Interpersonal skills	0	0	11.4	51.4	37.1	**4.20**	**.59**
m. Cross-functional experience	0	8.6	37.1	40.0	14.3	**3.57**	**.87**
n. Consultation skills	0	2.9	17.1	54.3	25.7	**3.98**	**.68**
o. Leadership/ management	0	2.9	20.0	40.0	37.1	**4.06**	**.78**
p. Global understanding	0	5.9	26.5	50.0	17.6	**3.72**	**.76**
q. Organization design	0	0	22.9	54.3	22.9	**3.95**	**.62**
r. Strategic planning	0	5.7	34.3	42.9	17.1	**3.64**	**.73**
s. Information technology	0	8.6	42.9	40.0	8.6	**3.39**	**.77**
t. Change management	0	5.7	25.7	54.3	14.3	**3.72**	**.72**
u. Metrics development	0	2.9	40.0	42.9	14.3	**3.63**	**.75**
v. Data analysis and mining	0	14.3	37.1	37.1	11.4	**3.33**	**.88**
w. Process execution and analysis	0	5.7	22.9	54.3	17.1	**3.78**	**.74**

3. What percentage of your company-wide HR professional/ HR managerial staff possesses the necessary skill set for success in today's business environment? (Circle one response.)   **Mean=4.74   SD=1.08**

0%	5.9%	5.9%	20.6%	35.3%	32.4%	0%
None	Almost None	Some	About Half	Most	Almost All	All
0%	1-20%	21-40%	41-60%	61-80%	81-99%	100%

4. To what extent are these statements true about your organization?	Little or No Extent	Some Extent	Moderate Extent	Great Extent	Very Great Extent	Mean	SD
a. We excel at competing for and with talent where it matters most to our strategic success	0	5.9	47.1	38.2	8.8	**3.46**	**.72**
b. Business leaders' decisions that depend upon or affect human capital (e.g. layoffs, rewards, etc.) are as rigorous, logical and strategically relevant as their decisions about resources such as money, technology, and customers	0	2.9	29.4	47.1	20.6	**3.81**	**.74**
c. HR leaders have a good understanding about where and why human capital makes the biggest difference in their business	0	8.8	17.6	52.9	20.6	**3.85**	**.79**
d. Business leaders have a good understanding about where and why human capital makes the biggest difference in their business	0	2.9	20.6	58.8	17.6	**3.79**	**.63**
e. HR systems educate business leaders about their talent decisions	2.9	17.6	47.1	23.5	8.8	**3.11**	**.92**
f. HR adds value by insuring compliance with rules, laws, and guidelines	2.9	2.9	8.8	50.0	35.3	**4.05**	**.89**
g. HR adds value by delivering high quality professional practices and services	0	8.8	26.5	38.2	26.5	**3.74**	**.90**
h. HR adds value by improving talent decisions inside and outside the HR function	0	5.9	26.5	44.1	23.5	**3.81**	**.82**

5. Business leaders understand and use sound principles when making decisions about:

1. Motivation	0	8.7	30.4	52.2	8.7	3.60	.77
2. Development and learning	0	8.7	17.4	56.5	17.4	3.83	.81
3. Culture	4.3	0	30.4	39.1	26.1	3.80	.93
4. Organizational design	4.3	0	39.1	26.1	30.4	3.68	1.01
5. Business strategy	0	8.7	17.4	43.5	30.4	3.85	.91
6. Finance	4.3	13.0	17.4	30.4	34.8	3.73	1.14
7. Marketing	0	17.4	21.7	39.1	21.7	3.60	1.00

6. Please rate the activities on a scale of 1 to 10 or not applicable. In view of what is needed by your company:

a. How well is the HR organization meeting needs in?
   (1= Not Meeting Needs, 10 = All Needs Met; NA = Not Applicable)

Note: Percentages and mean are computed with N/A (Not Applicable) responses missing.

		Not Meeting Needs	2	3	4	5	6	7	8	9	All Needs Met	NA	Mean	SD
A.	PROVIDING HR SERVICES	0	0	0	2.9	0	11.8	26.5	29.4	23.5	5.9	2.9	7.68	1.33
B.	PROVIDING CHANGE CONSULTING SERVICES	0	2.9	2.9	0	20.6	11.8	26.5	23.5	0	11.8	2.9	6.74	1.80
C.	BEING A BUSINESS PARTNER	2.9	0	0	0	8.8	14.7	11.8	26.5	20.6	14.7	2.9	7.50	1.90
D.	IMPROVING DECISIONS ABOUT HUMAN CAPITAL	0	0	2.9	0	11.8	2.9	14.7	26.5	35.3	5.9	2.9	7.68	1.65
E.	MANAGING OUTSOURCING	3.3	0	3.3	3.3	13.3	20.0	23.3	16.7	10.0	6.7	14.3	6.57	2.03
F.	OPERATING HR CENTERS OF EXCELLENCE	0	2.9	0	8.8	8.8	26.5	20.6	17.6	8.8	5.9	2.9	6.61	1.81
G.	OPERATING HR SHARED SERVICE UNITS	0	0	6.3	6.3	0	15.6	31.3	31.3	6.3	3.1	8.6	6.87	1.66
H.	HELPING TO DEVELOP BUSINESS STRATEGIES	0	0	0	18.2	15.2	12.1	18.2	18.2	15.2	3.0	5.7	6.52	1.85
I.	BEING AN EMPLOYEE ADVOCATE	0	0	2.9	2.9	8.8	5.9	17.6	20.6	26.5	14.7	2.9	7.67	1.79
J.	ANALYZING HR AND BUSINESS METRICS	0	0	0	12.1	15.2	3.0	15.2	24.2	18.2	12.1	5.7	7.19	1.93
K.	WORKING WITH THE CORPORATE BOARD	0	3.0	3.0	3.0	6.1	9.1	18.2	18.2	18.2	21.2	5.7	7.50	2.08
L.	OVERALL PERFORMANCE	0	0	2.9	0	8.8	14.7	14.7	23.5	23.5	11.8	2.9	7.53	1.64

b. How important is it that HR does these well? *(1= Not Important, 10 = Very Important)*

		Not Impt	2	3	4	5	6	7	8	9	Very Impt	NA	Mean	SD
A.	PROVIDING HR SERVICES	0	0	0	0	0	0	3.0	21.2	45.5	30.3	5.7	**8.97**	**.84**
B.	PROVIDING CHANGE CONSULTING SERVICES	0	0	3.0	0	6.1	3.0	21.2	33.3	24.2	9.1	5.7	**7.78**	**1.53**
C.	BEING A BUSINESS PARTNER	0	0	0	0	0	6.1	15.2	9.1	30.3	39.4	5.7	**8.75**	**1.32**
D.	IMPROVING DECISIONS ABOUT HUMAN CAPITAL	0	0	0	0	0	3.0	9.1	12.1	42.4	33.3	5.7	**8.85**	**.96**
E.	MANAGING OUTSOURCING	0	0	3.3	3.3	13.3	16.7	23.3	13.3	13.3	13.3	14.3	**7.06**	**1.81**
F.	OPERATING HR CENTERS OF EXCELLENCE	0	0	0	3.0	12.1	12.1	21.2	18.2	6.1	27.3	5.7	**7.59**	**1.85**
G.	OPERATING HR SHARED SERVICE UNITS	3.1	0	0	3.1	9.4	3.1	21.9	28.1	18.8	12.5	8.6	**7.51**	**1.96**
H.	HELPING TO DEVELOP BUSINESS STRATEGIES	0	0	0	0	3.0	15.2	12.1	33.3	27.3	9.1	5.7	**7.90**	**1.31**
I.	BEING AN EMPLOYEE ADVOCATE	0	0	0	0	3.0	0	9.1	33.3	36.4	18.2	5.7	**8.48**	**1.10**
J.	ANALYZING HR AND BUSINESS METRICS	0	0	0	0	0	6.1	12.1	24.2	42.4	15.2	5.7	**8.39**	**1.08**
K.	WORKING WITH THE CORPORATE BOARD	0	6.1	0	0	9.1	12.1	9.1	12.1	18.2	33.3	5.7	**7.80**	**2.25**
L.	OVERALL PERFORMANCE	0	0	0	0	3.0	3.0	6.1	15.2	36.4	36.4	5.7	**8.84**	**1.23**

7 How has the recession impacted the following in your organization?	Greatly Decreased	Decreased	No Change	Increased	Greatly Increased	Mean	SD
a. Power and status of HR function	0	0	48.5	45.5	6.1	**3.54**	**.57**
b. Strategic role of HR function	0	0	27.3	66.7	6.1	**3.69**	**.51**
c. Commitment to talent development	0	0	21.2	60.6	18.2	**3.89**	**.65**
d. Focus on performance management	0	0	33.3	48.5	18.2	**3.82**	**.68**
e. Quality of talent management decisions	0	0	33.3	54.5	12.1	**3.77**	**.60**
f. Use of contract employees	0	12.1	57.6	30.3	0	**3.11**	**.61**
g. Use of temporary employees	0	12.1	57.6	30.3	0	**3.11**	**.59**
h. Use of HR analytics and metrics	0	0	45.5	51.5	3.0	**3.52**	**.46**
i. Quality of employees in HR function	0	0	51.5	45.5	3.0	**3.46**	**.49**
j. Attractiveness of your company's brand as an employer	0	9.1	27.3	57.6	6.1	**3.52**	**.70**
k. Effectiveness of HR function	0	0	48.5	48.5	3.0	**3.50**	**.51**
l. Willingness to try innovative HR practices	0	3.0	36.4	54.5	6.1	**3.60**	**.57**
m. Use of short term HR system fixes	0	3.0	75.8	18.2	3.0	**3.17**	**.51**
n. Commitment to treating people right	0	0	66.7	30.3	3.0	**3.35**	**.50**
o. Percent of its time HR spends on administration	0	6.1	66.7	21.2	6.1	**3.18**	**.61**
p. Focus on HR practices that have shown tangible results	0	3.0	48.5	42.4	6.1	**3.48**	**.62**

8. Where do you currently work (please select one):   **Mean=2.62   SD=1.73**
    39.4% . . . . 1. General Management
    15.2% . . . . 2. Production
    12.1% . . . . 3. Marketing / Sales
    18.2% . . . . 4. Finance / Accounting
     6.1% . . . . 5. Technical / Engineering
     9.1% . . . . 6. Other: _____

THANK YOU FOR YOUR TIME IN COMPLETING OUR SURVEY!